"This is an important and valuable guide to anyone who is serious about people management. Well-rooted in research evidence, it offers a very practical framework for HR leaders and their line colleagues committed to creating and sustaining value through people."

> —Geoff Armstrong, President, World Federation of Personnel Management Associations

"Replete with sound practical insights, examples, and a wealth of references, *The HR Value Proposition* will propel HR into a meaningful role with investors and customers while enhancing its deliverables to its key internal stakeholders. Many thought leaders for the HR community will have to refine and re-interpret their work in the light of these seminal concepts."

> —Visty Banaji, Executive Director, Group Corporate Affairs, Godrej Industries Limited

"Ulrich and Brockbank compellingly demonstrate the need for HR's leadership in creating excellence in the nonfinancial sectors of an organization, and they provide the tools to make that happen and help ensure that all stakeholders achieve success."

> —Judy Bardwick, Clinical Professor of Psychiatry, University of California, San Diego, and author of *In Praise of Good Business*

"Ulrich and Brockbank look at the organization from the outside in—from the customer/consumer back—and provide insight on how HR can add wealth-creating value to a firm. The ideas in this book are brain food for executives. Read it! Better yet, do it!"

> —Richard W. Beatty, Professor of Human Resource Management, Rutgers University, and coauthor of *The Workforce Scorecard*

"Not only does *The HR Value Proposition* provide a useful framework and set of tools for the HR professional on how to add value to an organization, it makes clear that value is determined by the true needs of the key stakeholders of the business (customers, employees, shareholders) and not just what the HR professional believes is important."

> —Ken Carrig, Executive Vice President and Chief Administrative Officer, SYSCO Corporation

"Ulrich and Brockbank push HR professionals out of the 'comfort zone' by inviting HR to become part of business execution. *The HR Value Proposition* takes us from broad concepts to the tactics that will enable HR professionals to deliver greater value to their business."

> —Joan M. Crockett, Senior Vice President, Human Resources, Allstate Insurance Company

"Many of us work on the pieces of the puzzle. Ulrich and Brockbank put the pieces together. And that's what sets this book apart. They've assembled the whole picture, which is nothing short of a comprehensive and doable action plan to transform our field."

 —Lee Dyer, Professor of Human Resource Studies,
  Cornell University

"If you want to be more effective and have a greater impact as an HR professional, this is the book for you. Clear. Complete. Step by step. Research-backed and experience-tested formulas for adding value. It's *HR Champions* and *Results-Based Leadership* together in one great book. You aren't really in the game without what's in this book."

 —Robert W. Eichinger, CEO, Lominger Limited, Inc.

"A practical guide that examines the value HR professionals can add by providing a framework and tools that can demonstrate their effectiveness to the business and shareholders. The focus on external practices and trends, aligning HR strategy and initiatives to those of the business, and being a strategic business partner are behaviors I expect of my team every day. "

 —Ursula Fairbairn, Executive Vice President of HR
  and Quality, American Express

"*The HR Value Proposition* highlights the possibilities for HR to drive critical strategic business initiatives within organizations. Ulrich and Brockbank provide key insights and perspectives that will ensure HR maximizes its potential to become a vital resource to business."

 —Janet Fiola, Senior Vice President, Human Resources,
  Medtronic, Inc.

"Two distinguished HR scholars have given the profession exactly what it has needed—a detailed map for transforming HR from an administration expense center to a value-adding, central business function. It goes beyond why HR needs to move up to how to move it to the strategic level."

 —Jac Fitz-enz, author of *The ROI of Human Capital*

"The authors ask 'what is left after transactional HR has been automated, centralized, eliminated, or outsourced?' Marshaling decades of research and a vast array of experience, Ulrich and Brockbank show that HR can indeed add value in a way that is measurable and linked to the goals of the business. An essential part of the manager's tool kit, *The HR Value Proposition* is destined to become a classic."

 —Lynda Gratton, Associate Professor of Management Practice,
  London Business School, and author of *Living Strategy*

"A must-read for both line management and HR. This book reflects the finest road map for the strategic development of a human capital plan I have ever read. Numerous diagnostic tools and illustrations will assist those who aspire to optimize organizational capabilities. Those who read *The HR Value Proposition* will gain a competitive edge."

—Mike Hager, Senior Vice President, Human Resources, Freddie Mac

"This book not only shows the optimum vision for HR to aspire to but it also gives a road map of how to get there with step-by-step directions. I suggest that all HR practitioners read this book."

—Thomas Hammer, Group Head of Human Resources, UBS

"Exceptionally framed, forward-thinking, and thought-provoking. Any HR professionals reading *The HR Value Proposition*, regardless of industry and geography, will understand how to increase their organizations' competence, connect what they do to what matters most (shareholder value!), and be inspired to turn leading HR concepts into action in their own practices."

—Bob Hargadon, Vice President, U.S. Human Resources,
    Boston Scientific

"Today's environment demands that HR create and deliver value for all of its constituents—shareowners, a company's clients, line leaders, and employees. The authors provide ideas that should be useful to any serious HR professional. Most importantly, they have laid out a blueprint that can (and should) be put into practice."

—Tom Helfrich, Executive Vice President and Chief Human
    Resources Officer, KeyCorp

"*The HR Value Proposition* reminds us of Peter Drucker's sage words that people are a prime resource for organizations. In this action-oriented book, the authors offer the leaders of the future—whether from the public, private, or social sectors—a blueprint for unleashing the economic and intellectual potential of HR professionals."

—Frances Hesselbein, Chairman of the Board of Governors,
    Leader to Leader Institute

"*The HR Value Proposition* identifies critical HR linkages to organizational effectiveness and, with great clarity, provides the HR constructs necessary for organizational success. It successfully captures the elements of HR's influence on value and then offers important and needed perspective on the professional HR competencies necessary to create value."

—R. Kenneth Hutchinson, Vice President of Human Resources,
    University of Missouri System

"Using the methods found in *The HR Value Proposition*, HR professionals at BAE Systems are growing considerably in stature and influence within our business and are recognized to be adding real value in our drive toward a high-performance culture."

> —Alastair Imrie, Group HR Director, BAE Systems plc

"Ulrich and Brockbank's new book, *The HR Value Proposition*, integrates their ideas and knowledge into a blueprint for action that HR professionals as well as line managers should use to create value for their companies."

> —Michael P. Johnson, Senior Vice President and Chief
> Administrative Officer, The Williams Companies, Inc.

"*The HR Value Proposition* is the authoritative statement showing how HR can and must contribute to organizational performance. Based on impeccable evidence, careful analysis, and insights only real pioneers in the field can provide, this book makes the case for HR's real business impact and then shows us how to achieve it."

> —William Joyce, Professor of Strategy and Organizational
> Theory, Dartmouth College, and author of *What Really Works:
> The 4+2 Formula for Sustained Business Success*

"*The HR Value Proposition* provides a conceptual framework and tools for creating value from HR that will be extremely useful for organizations seeking to create value for stakeholders by effectively managing their human capital."

> —K. V. Kamath, Managing Director and CEO, ICICI Bank

"This extensive compendium of proven techniques represents the single most integrated and practical blueprint for adding value to HR professionals at all levels. The authors' passion for and understanding of HR resonates in every chapter."

> —Arnold Kanarick, Chief Human Resources Officer,
> Bear Stearns & Co. Inc.

"Rich in valuable insight, the main strength of *The HR Value Proposition* is that its authors have constantly been 'out there' and have developed, tested, and proved their ideas in some of the most esteemed organizations in the corporate world."

> —Steve Kerr, Chief Learning Officer and Managing Director,
> Goldman Sachs

"Terrific insights, information, what-to-do's, and how-to-do's. A great resource for HR executives!"

> —Ed Lawler, Distinguished Professor of Business, Marshall
> School of Business, University of Southern California

"I am a firm believer that the primary deliverable of the HR function is applying organizational capability to opportunity to create performance. Ulrich and Brockbank give access to the entire logic stream of what HR needs to do and thus make this a must-read for the twenty-first-century HR professional."

—Chris Moorhouse, Vice President for HR, BP

"*The HR Value Proposition* could not arrive at a more opportune time for me and my colleagues at Lafarge North America. I wish we had had your book a few years ago when we began an HR transformation that has been targeted at redefining the HR operating model and its value proposition."

—Jim Nealis, Executive Vice President, Human Resources,
Lafarge North America

"The book is a great value not only for HR but for business heads as well. Its innate simplicity, clarity, and 'easy-to-relate' writing style keeps you hooked. And it not only tells you the 'what', but also shows the 'how-to' in crafting and implementing a HR agenda for sustained success in the marketplace. Immensely useful."

—Rakesh Pandey, CEO, Kaya Skin Care Limited

"Integrating the many complex issues that HR professionals grapple with on a daily basis, this book provides a wealth of practical resources and tools that will help HR leaders raise the level of HR's business impact, no matter what the current level is."

—Denise Peppard, Senior Vice President, HR,
Wyeth Pharmaceuticals

"Packed with frameworks, tools, and approaches of immense practical value. The authors have given the world of business and HR a handle to grab the future and impact the way the people side of the equation can be most powerfully leveraged."

—Satish Pradhan, Executive Vice President, Group HR,
Tata Sons Ltd

"*The HR Value Proposition* demonstrates that a strong HR function can truly add value. Skilled and compassionate HR professionals can and should understand the needs of their business and its various constituencies and contribute unique expertise to achieving results. This book will show them how."

—Fran Rodgers, Chair, WFD, Inc.

"Ulrich and Brockbank once again demonstrate why they are among the clearest thinkers about HR practices today. While many so-called thought leaders keep advocating that HR 'gain a seat at the table,' these two shout 'forget about sitting anywhere; stand up, get out there, and help create real value.' Here they provide a road map for practical, results-based solutions."

—Anthony J. Rucci, Executive Vice President and President
of Strategic Corporate Resources, Cardinal Health

"Ulrich and Brockbank have done it again! Packed with theory and proven practices, *The HR Value Proposition* provides a powerful framework that HR leaders can use to organize the HR function around value-added agendas. They continue to add to the body of knowledge and the tool kits of the HR profession and its leaders."

—Libby Sartain, Senior Vice President, Human Resources, and
Chief People Yahoo at Yahoo!, Inc., and coauthor of *HR from
the Heart*

"This book shows how to unlock the full value of people capability to deliver business results. It provides a rich combination of strategic and operational insights and is energizing in its focus on action, impact, outputs, and practical guidance. A required read for HR professionals worldwide with some particular pointers for HR leaders."

—Valerie Scoular, Group HR Director, Barclays Bank

"Packed with real-world examples and fresh insights, *The HR Value Proposition* offers readers a powerful framework for building a world-class HR organization that creates true and lasting value for stakeholders of all kinds."

—David Shadovitz, Editor, *Human Resource Executive* magazine

"Over the past decade, the evolution of our HR function at Unilever has been much guided by the unique insights developed by Ulrich and Brockbank. This immensely readable book is compulsory reading for anyone who seeks to make a difference through HR."

—André R. van Heemstra, Personnel Director, Unilever

"Ulrich and Brockbank bring together their depth of insight and wealth of experience to provide HR professionals with the tools they need to become strategic players in their organizations."

—Patrick M. Wright, Professor of Human Resource Studies,
Cornell University

The HR Value Proposition

The HR Value Proposition

Dave Ulrich
Wayne Brockbank

Harvard Business School Press
Boston, Massachusetts

978-1-59139-707-6 (ISBN 13)

Library of Congress Cataloging-in-Publication Data

Ulrich, David, 1953-
    The HR value proposition / Dave Ulrich, Wayne Brockbank.
        p. cm.
    Includes bibliographical references and index.
    ISBN 1-59139-707-3
    1. Personnel departments. 2. Personnel management. I. Brockbank, Wayne.
II. Title.
    HF5549.U38 2005
    658.3--dc22

                                                                2005002389

The paper used in this publication meets the minimum requirements of the Ameri-can National Standard for Information Sciences—Permanence of Paper for Printed Library Materials, ANSI Z39.48-1992.

Contents

Preface

WE LIKE HUMAN RESOURCES (HR). We like HR practices that deal with people, performance, information, and work because they create an infrastructure that affects employees, customers, line managers, and investors. When HR practices align with strategies, goals are met and sustained. We like the HR function because it allows functional experts to help sustain organization results. When the HR function operates well, it becomes an exemplar of how to bring specialist expertise to business requirements. We like HR professionals because, for the most part, they value people and they work to create both competitive and compassionate organizations. When HR professionals develop competencies and play appropriate roles, they become partners and players in the business. We like the intellectual challenges of figuring out how HR practices, functions, and professionals add even greater value.

For the last twenty years of our professional lives, we, along with others, have been committed observers of and champions for the HR profession. We have turned our commitment into action through education and practice. We have had the privilege of training thousands of HR professionals at the University of Michigan and elsewhere. We have worked in hundreds of companies to assess and improve their HR effectiveness.

In this process, we have learned a great deal about how to position and focus HR. In the '90s, the book *Human Resource Champions* (by Dave Ulrich) discussed the *deliverables* of HR and identified four roles that HR professionals play: employee champion, administrative expert, change agent, and strategic partner. When HR professionals play these roles, HR focuses more on outcomes than on activities. Employee champions deliver competent and committed employees. Administrative experts deliver efficient HR practices. Change agents deliver capacity for change in individual behavior and organization culture. Strategic partners deliver business results.

In the early 2000s, Dave Ulrich and Norm Smallwood's *Why the Bottom Line Isn't* discussed *intangibles* and suggested that HR investments build organization capabilities. These organization capabilities generate market value through the intangibles they create. Capabilities that lead to intangible market value include talent, speed, collaboration, accountability, shared mindset, learning, and leadership. HR professionals make intangibles tangible by building organization capabilities. Organization capabilities are the deliverables of HR.

Each of us has previously published on the changing role of the HR profession. Wayne Brockbank received the paper-of-the-year award from the *Human Resource Management Journal* for asking what would happen "If HR Were Strategically Proactive?" His paper addresses the future of HR and its role in building competitive advantage.

For over fifteen years, we have conducted ongoing research on HR competencies, most recently synthesizing that work in *Competencies for the New HR* (by Wayne Brockbank and Dave Ulrich) published by the Society for Human Resource Management, the University of Michigan, and Global Consulting Alliance. In this work, we focus on how HR professionals can identify and master crucial competencies for business success. As a result of fifteen years of research, we have accumulated the largest data set in the world on HR competencies that differentiate business performance and define what HR professionals should know and do.

More recently, *Human Resources Business Process Outsourcing,* by Ed Lawler, Dave Ulrich, Jac Fitz-enz, and James Madden, suggests ways to deliver the administrative work of HR through outsourcing. We argue that the field of HR is being split in half. Much of the traditional, administrative, and transactional work of HR—payroll, benefits administration, staffing policies, training logistics, and so forth—must be carried out more efficiently. Most large firms have either built service centers and invested in HR technology or outsourced these transactions. What is left after transactional HR has been automated, centralized, eliminated, or outsourced forms the heart of this book, *The HR Value Proposition*.

As we have attempted to apply the preceding ideas, we continue to be confronted by future-focused questions such as the following:

- Why does HR matter so much more today?

- How do I convince my line manager to pay attention to HR issues?

- What specific things can HR do to connect with customers, investors, employees, and line managers?

- What are emerging HR practices? While deliverables (outcomes, intangibles, or capabilities) are important, what are the investments in HR practices that make these outcomes happen?

- How do we create a powerful line of sight between business strategy and HR?

- How do we organize our HR function? In particular, after we out-source transaction work, how do we organize to deliver more strategic HR work?

- How does HR help to build, not just measure, intangible value creation?

- What are the evolving and emerging roles for HR professionals?

- What knowledge, skill, and ability should HR professionals demonstrate that impact business performance?

- How can we develop more capable HR professionals and departments to do all this?

These are the questions that remain after reengineering, automating, or outsourcing HR. These are the questions we address in this book.

We continue to believe that HR professionals should focus more on deliverables than on doables or activities. We believe that key deliverables are organization capabilities and intangibles that define the organization's identity and personality and that deliver high performance to all stakeholders. We believe that HR leaders can align practices to more effectively execute business strategy. We believe that HR professionals who demonstrate the right competencies and play the right roles will be more effective than those who do not. And we believe that with creative thought and discipline these beliefs will become actions that deliver value. In sum, we believe that this is a great time to be an HR professional.

In this book, we expand on these beliefs and provide empirical and best-practice evidence that shows how to turn these ideas into action.

In writing this book, we made a strategic choice to offer an integrated blueprint for the future rather than to deal with one piece of the overall HR puzzle. Our previous works covered subjects such as HR roles, HR deliverables as intangibles, HR strategy, HR competencies, or HR outsourcing. This book brings all those elements together in an integrated blueprint for the future of HR. As a result, it could be subtitled *HR Not for Dummies*. This is a complex book. It offers more content than cheerleading. It offers a range of ideas on an integrated model of how HR can and should be performed. It is an action book, filled with ideas on how to *do* HR rather than merely advocate positions about what HR can and should become.

The essential message of our work is very simple: HR must deliver value. HR practices must create value in the eyes of investors, customers, line managers, and employees. HR departments must be organized. They must implement strategies that create value by delivering business results in efficient and effective ways. HR professionals deliver value when their personal competencies deliver business results. Value is the foundation and premise of our HR architecture. *The HR Value Proposition* offers an integrated approach to what HR professionals and departments can and should do to create sustained value.

In drafting this book, we chose to present tried and tested work as well as innovative and leading-edge ideas. Often, the tools and cases reflect what we have learned from both successes and failures. By extending what *is*, we hope to be thoughtfully challenging and defining where the HR profession can and should move.

We believe the fourteen criteria for value around which the book is organized apply to large global multinational firms. We offer examples of how firms headquartered in Europe, Asia, and North America create value through investments in HR. But the principles also apply to small firms and public agencies. We share a number of stories of how smaller companies deliver value through HR. In fact, we believe that the HR challenge is greater in firms with only a few HR professionals because those HR professionals must be both generalists and specialists. Also, we believe that as scrutiny of public agencies increases, people will gain an enhanced appreciation of the centrality of HR in building capabilities.

Mostly, we believe the ideas in the book should be actionable. We invariably begin our engagements with the general goals of *think* (outside the box, about how to create value), *behave* (turn ideas into action with honest assessments of what is and tools for what can be), and *have fun* (harder to do in a book, unless the fun is learning and playing with the proposed ideas). Because we have a bias toward action and impact, we generally follow a C-I-A teaching model: *concept* (what theory and extensive empirical research tell us can be done), *illustration* (what is being done by leading companies), and *application* (what the reader can do though assessment and investment). As we wrote each chapter, we asked ourselves, "What would an HR professional charged with this assignment need to know and do?" For example, what would the leader need to know and do to improve the performance management process (chapter 5)? To enhance the flow and utilization of customer information (chapter 6)? To turn business strategy into HR strategy (chapter 7)? Or to develop HR professionals (chapter 11)? So we provide concepts to frame the issue, illustrations of what others have accomplished, and templates with assessments and tools for action that the reader can adapt and apply.

The target audience for this book is HR professionals everywhere in the world. Any HR professional who wants to add value by building a knowledge base concerning external business realities (chapter 2), by specifying the outcomes of HR (chapters 3 and 4), by investing in innovative HR practices (chapters 5 and 6), by upgrading the HR function (chapters 7 and 8), and by improving the professionalism of HR professionals (chapters 9, 10, and 11) should find this book a useful blueprint. But we also believe that line managers who are increasingly worried about intangibles, strategy execution, human capital, and other organization and people issues can use this blueprint to determine what to expect from their HR function. As the HR function begins to be transformed, other staff functions such as marketing, finance, information technology, facilities, and research and development may also choose to adapt these ideas to achieve functional excellence.

We hope the book will generate debate. We know that not all of what we propose will work in every situation. But we hope to provoke thoughts and action that will enable HR to create sustainable value.

While we are responsible for flaws in thinking and writing, we owe a debt of gratitude to many people for their contributions to this book. Most will go unnamed. In thousands of workshops, we have spoken with many thoughtful and dedicated HR professionals about these ideas. We learn from these encounters and are in debt to unnamed professionals who are committed to the HR field, who are dedicated to learning, and who desire to add greater value to business through people. But some colleagues have been particularly instrumental in shaping our thinking and deserve special attention.

Norm Smallwood, a coauthor on other books and partner in RBL, Inc., has a knack for turning ideas into action and for getting quickly to the heart of an issue. He is a great partner, colleague, and friend whose ideas have shaped our thinking. Our faculty colleagues in the HR programs at Michigan and elsewhere have shaped our thinking in ways they probably don't even realize. Dick Beatty, Ron Bendersky, John Boyer, Marshall Goldsmith, Lynda Gratton, Gordon Hewitt, Bill Joyce, Steve Kerr, Dale Lake, C. K. Prahalad, Caren Siehl, and Warren Wilhelm are brilliant presenters and shapers of the HR profession. Our work builds on the legends in HR whose ideas we savor and enjoy. John Boudreau, Ram Charan, Jim Collins, Lee Dyer, Bob Eichinger, Jac Fitz-enz, Fred Foulkes, Jay Galbraith, Gary Hamel, Mark Huselid, Bob Kaplan, Ed Lawler, Mike Losey, Sue Meisinger, Henry Mintzberg, Dave Nadler, Jeff Pfeffer, and Libby Sartain have all influenced the profession of HR by their writing and thinking. We have learned from them. We also have colleagues with whom we have collaborated on numerous projects that have shaped how we perceive HR's place in the business world, including Katy Barclay (GM), Chris Moorhouse (BP Amoco), Tony McCarthy (Royal Mail Group plc), Ralph Christensen (Hallmark Cards, Inc.), Pedro Granadillo (Eli Lilly), Paul McKinnon (Dell Computer Corporation), Tony Rucci (Cardinal Health), Chuck Nielson and Steve Leven (Texas Instruments), Satish Pradhan (Tata Group), Mike Tucker (Baxter Healthcare), Denise Peppard (Wyeth), Michael Johnson (The Williams Companies, Inc.), Glenn Gienko (Motorola), Andre Van Heemstra and Jan Peelen (Unilever Corporation), John Hofmeister (Shell), and Alastair Imrie (BAE Systems).

For this particular work, we owe an unspeakable debt of gratitude to Hilary Powers, a "write knight" who turned our elephant into a jaguar. Marnie Leavitt patiently discovered and edited numerous writing faux pas. We also appreciate the support of Harvard Business School Press, particularly Melinda Merino, who expressed enormous confidence in the project and offered timely suggestions.

We also express our ongoing appreciation to our families: Wendy, Nancy, Carrie, Dave, McKell, Wes, Leah, Monika, Michael, and Brynna. Without them, much of the purpose and joy of all that we do would be lost. With them, life is full of meaning and joy. They are in fact our personal value proposition.

Dave Ulrich
Montreal

Wayne Brockbank
Ann Arbor, Michigan

1

The Premise of HR Value

A WHILE BACK, the vice president of human resources (HR) of a big consumer product company decided to visit with a few key customers and improve his line of sight with his company's marketplace. To avoid wasting his customers' time, he began by reading everything he could—annual reports, 10K reports, product brochures, analysts' reports. His counterpart in sales was leery of the whole idea, but once the HR VP showed how knowledgeable and thoughtful he was, his sales colleague agreed to set up a meeting with the VP of purchasing at one of their main customers. The moment they walked into the office, however, the customer snapped, "I'm busy today. Why should I spend time with you?"

This short story captures the past, present, and future of the field of HR. Twenty years ago, it would have been unthinkable for almost anyone in HR to even consider spending time with external customers. HR professionals built staffing, compensation, training, and other programs and policies that focused on employees and kept companies legally compliant. In the last decade, HR professionals have worked to become business partners and to align their work with business strategies. HR professionals have been coached to spend time with general managers and with their counterparts in sales, marketing, and manufacturing to ensure that HR work helps deliver business results. But this story also suggests what is next for HR: beginning to connect with those outside the firm as well as those inside.

To do so, HR professionals must grasp and master the concept of value. At a basic level, values reflect the standards within a firm. While HR professionals must declare, live, and encourage moral principles, we believe that an HR value proposition goes beyond values. Value also means that someone receives something of worth from a transaction.

1

Value in this light is defined by the receiver more than the giver. HR professionals add value when their work helps someone reach their goals. It is not the design of a program or declaration of policy that matters most, but what recipients gain from these actions. In a world of increasingly scarce resources, activities that fail to add value are not worth pursuing. No matter how interesting or valuable an activity may seem to those doing it, if those who receive the output of that activity don't find it of value to them, continuing the activity cannot be justified. The HR value proposition means that HR practices, departments, and professionals produce positive outcomes for key stakeholders—employees, line managers, customers, and investors.

Value becomes the bellwether for HR. When others receive value from HR work, HR will be credible, respected, and influential. But as the customer in the preceding story points out, HR value for customers will require that HR professionals answer the question "Why should I listen to you?" This is a great question for all HR professionals. How do customers and other key stakeholders—investors, managers, and employees—benefit if they spend time with HR professionals or adapt innovative HR practices? This book offers a blueprint to answer this question and transform how HR work is done.

HR Transformation

Many attempts at HR effectiveness start without defining value. For example, some companies invest in e-HR services such as portals and online employee services and believe that they have transformed HR, but they have not. While e-HR may be a part of an overall transformation, it is merely a way to deliver HR administrative services. HR transformation must change the way to think about HR's role in delivering value to customers, shareholders, managers, and employees and not just about how HR services are delivered and administered.

Moving toward service centers, centers of expertise, or outsourcing does not mean that HR has been transformed. If new delivery mechanisms provide basically the same old HR services, the function has changed but not transformed itself. HR transformation changes both behavior and outputs. The changes must improve life for key stakeholders in ways that they are willing to pay for.

Changing any single HR practice (staffing, training, appraisal, team-work, upward communication) does not create a transformation. Unless the entire array of HR practices collectively adds value for key stake-holders, transformation has not occurred. Transformation requires inte-grating the various HR practices and focusing them jointly on value-added agendas such as intangibles, customer connection, organization capabilities, and individual abilities.

Writing an HR strategy or making a statement about HR roles does not necessarily create a transformation. In presentations on HR strat-egy, we often ask six random participants to complete the following statements as fast as they can:

- Our goal is to be a _____.

- We will do this by leveraging _____.

- And we will ensure that we anticipate _____.

- And we will invest in _____.

- And we will be known for _____.

- And we will work with unyielding _____.

Filling in these six blanks with the first thing that comes to mind and then connecting these statements into a vision generates an amazingly plausible HR strategy statement—but it's a fleeting moment of corporate rhetoric, irrelevant from the get-go. HR transformation must be more than rhetoric; it must shape behavior and create and ensure stakeholder value.

Sending one or two HR professionals to a seminar does not transform an HR department. Often, people return from training with great ideas but little opportunity to apply them. Transformation requires whole new agendas, thoughts, and processes across the entire department, not just on the part of a few individuals.

Finally, gaining credibility and acceptance by management or em-ployees is not transformation. Doing so may be a good stepping-stone to future work, but real transformation must turn relationships into re-sults and also create value for customers, shareholders, managers, and employees.

We believe that a fundamental transformation of HR starts with a definition of HR value—who the receivers are and a clear statement of what they will receive from HR services. It also requires a complete picture of all the elements of HR transformation, so that piecemeal attempts do not become isolated events.

Premise of HR Value

Since value is defined by the receiver, not the giver, any value proposition begins with a focus on receivers, not givers. For HR professionals, the value premise means that rather than imposing their beliefs, goals, and actions on others, they first need to be open to what others want. This fundamental principle is too often overlooked. Often, HR professionals have beliefs, goals, and actions that translate into things that they want to have happen in their organization—so they go straight for their desired results, without paying enough attention to the perspectives of others.

Influence with impact occurs when HR professionals start with the beliefs and goals of the receivers. Who are the key stakeholders I must serve? What are the goals and values of the receiving stakeholders? What is important to them? What do they want? When these requirements are fully understood, then the HR professional can show how an investment in an HR practice will help the stakeholder gain value as defined by that stakeholder.

To an employee worried about getting laid off, HR professionals should demonstrate that being more productive will help the employee stay employed. To a line manager worried about reaching strategic goals, HR professionals need to show how investment in HR work will help deliver business results. With customers, HR professionals need to remember that their interest in customers must create value in the products or services customers receive. For shareholders who are worried about shared returns and growth, HR must create organizations that deliver results today and intangibles that give owners confidence that results will be delivered in the future.

Starting HR transformation with a value proposition has six important implications for HR professionals.

First, human resources work does not begin with HR—it begins with the business. For the last decade, HR professionals have aspired to be more complete players relative to the core issues of the business, as described in a number of phrases: business partners, strategic players, full contributors, players in the business, and so forth. These aspirations are appropriate and desirable, but the fact that HR professionals continue to frame aspirations in these terms communicates a continuing concern. Think, for example, of the key wealth creator in your business. In an investment banking firm, that would probably be an investment banker. In a software company, it could be a systems architect. In the upstream portion of an oil company, it's probably the petroleum geologists who search the world for oil. For none of these three job categories are you likely to find a professional conference titled "Being a Business Partner." All of them would think (assuming they could perceive the issue), "We do not need to aspire to be partners in the business. We are the business."

These key wealth creators can readily show how their activities create substantial value for key stakeholders. Their line of sight runs directly to the best interests of customers, investors, managers, and employees. To be real—not declared—business partners, HR professionals need the same kind of line of sight between their activities and the best interests of key stakeholders. The HR value proposition offers this line of sight.

Second, the ultimate receivers of business reside in marketplaces that companies serve. These markets include customers who buy products and services and shareholders who provide capital. Since HR professionals desire to be business partners and since business begins by meeting market demands, HR must also begin with a line of sight to the marketplace. This places HR professionals in a complex situation. They must create a line of sight to the multiple and frequently conflicting demands of stakeholders ranging from internal clients such as managers and employees to external stakeholders such as customers and investors.

The line of sight of HR professionals to internal customers is important and generally well understood, but the one to external customers and shareholders typically receives less attention. Knowledge of external business issues matters because external realities ultimately determine the relevance and utility of virtually all internal operations. External constituents who compose markets for products, services, and capital ultimately vote with their dollars about virtually everything that occurs in a firm. These realities determine whether HR is successful in creating human abilities and organizational capabilities that generate products, services, and results that customer and capital markets demand. HR professionals must have knowledge of external business realities before they can frame, execute, and create substantive value through even the most basic of HR agendas.

A third implication of the HR value premise is found in framing HR as a source of competitive advantage. Competitive advantage exists when a firm is able to do something unique that competitors cannot easily copy. And what it does better than its competitors must be highly valued by its customers, owners, employees, or managers. The creation of competitive advantage can be simplified as the "wallet test." An internal operation passes the wallet test if it inspires customers or shareholders to take money out of their wallets and put it into the firm's wallet instead of into the wallets of competitors. For example, product development creates competitive advantage when it creates products that customers buy. Marketing creates competitive advantage when it creates advertising programs that inspire customers and shareholders to buy products and stock. If HR is to create competitive advantage, it must create substantial value with similarly concrete results. HR passes the wallet test when it creates human abilities and organizational capabilities that are substantially better than those of the firm's competitors—and thus move customers and shareholders to reach for their wallets.

A fourth implication of the HR value proposition is that HR professionals must align practices with the requirements of internal and external stakeholders. When this is successful, HR creates value as defined by those stakeholders.

For example, an oil field service company (referred to here as OSC, a pseudonym) had dropped from 24 percent to 19 percent in a $15 billion total market.[1] In a senior management team (SMT) meeting, the HR leadership recommended a large-scale customer survey to determine the reasons behind the drop in market share. Marketing was deep into its annual advertising program and, although willing to support the effort, didn't want to take the lead, which defaulted to HR. With the support of the marketing department and working with an outside consulting group, HR and the CEO developed the research questionnaire and determined the sampling logic and process. The question that eventually had the greatest influence focused on the identification of customer buying criteria. The question required respondents to allocate a hundred points over alternative buying criteria including price, service, product quality and availability, sales effort, and ease of distribution. The survey was administered through live interviews with one thousand two hundred of the most influential users of this company's products throughout the world. Before the HR team fed back the results to the SMT, they asked SMT members to give their best estimates of the customers' responses. The logic behind this request was simple: if the HR team had simply given the survey results to the SMT members, their probable response would have been to say, "We already knew that."[2] The SMT response varied dramatically compared with customer responses. The SMT felt customers were much more worried about price than they actually were, while customers were actually much more worried about service than management anticipated.

Management's initial response was to dismiss the data as inaccurate. With this possibility in mind, the HR team had brought all one thousand two hundred surveys to the feedback meeting. Following the review of the numerical results, the SMT demanded an opportunity to review the original customer surveys. After reviewing the records for an hour, the SMT was ready to examine the implications of the management-customer gap. Management had substantially overestimated the importance of price and underestimated the importance of service. Using price as the competitive criterion, the company had been hiring low-cost service personnel and had been providing standardized technical training that included little work on customer relations. Based on the customer data, HR and the SMT agreed to substantially increase hiring criteria and the service training budget.

Over the next two years, a market share that had dropped from 24 to 19 percent now soared to 31 percent—a $1.8 billion increase in top-line growth. Such is the potential influence of HR professionals in creating value when they align their practices with accurate perceptions of the ultimate receivers of the firm's value and collaborate with others inside the firm.

The fifth implication of the HR value premise is that it directs HR professionals to acquire the personal knowledge and skills necessary to link HR activity to stakeholder value. When HR fails to make this linkage, it allows "noise" to occur between HR practices and stakeholder demands. Noise may be a lack of knowledge of external customers and shareholders, business strategy, or new HR processes. The "company party trivia test" exemplifies the importance of blocking out noise: imagine that you're at one of your company's annual parties, and a senior line or staff executive who is known to be critical of HR approaches you. The exuberance of the occasion has worn the usually polite facade away a bit, so this individual feels free to walk up to you, look you in the eye, and say, "I still don't know why we should be giving so much money to you folks in HR. I don't know why we shouldn't simply outsource the whole thing. Why should we continue to invest in you?" (If you haven't experienced this kind of thing face-to-face, do you suspect people are asking such questions behind your back? It's not paranoia . . .). To respond to this challenge effectively, you must show that HR adds value to things that are of value to this individual. This book will help you pass the company party trivia test.

The sixth implication of the HR value premise is that it leads HR professionals to view a company's key stakeholders from a unique and powerful perspective. And the HR perspective must be both. *Unique* implies that other functions or members of the leadership team do not share this same perspective and do not realize they need it. *Powerful* implies that this perspective adds a substantial value in helping the organization succeed.

All departments that matter bring such unique and powerful perspectives of their own. For example, when finance specialists look at product markets, they see margins, profits, cash flow, credit worthiness, risk, return on sales (ROS), economic value added (EVA), and the like. When marketing or sales specialists look at exactly the same product markets, they are more likely to see segments, demographic trends, product or service requirements, sales, buying habits, and so forth. Notice that although the two perspectives are compatible, they have very little overlap. Asking which perspective is more accurate is not useful. Both are unique and powerful.

HR professionals need a perspective that is compatible with and distinct from other business perspectives. That is, they must be able to understand and value the finance and sales perspectives, but they must also add their own point of view. Without such a unique and powerful perspective, they are redundant and fail in their aspirations as full business contributors. For example, an HR perspective that is both unique and powerful is one that establishes the linkages between employee commitment, customer attitudes, and investor returns.[3] This unique view demonstrates a powerful connection between what is carried out by managers and employees inside the firm and what happens with customers and investors on the outside.

With a unique and powerful perspective of their own, HR professionals will see aspects of the business environment that go beyond what other business disciplines bring and that add substantially to business success. Thus when HR professionals view the market environment, they should address the following questions:

- What are the organizational capabilities that my company must have to create products and services that result in our customers' taking money out of their wallets and putting it into ours instead of giving it to our competitors?

- What employee abilities do our people need so that they can understand and respond to short-term and long-term market demands?

- How do we invest in HR practices that deliver business results?

- How do we organize HR activities to deliver maximum value?

- How do we create an HR strategy that sets an agenda for how HR will help our company succeed?

- How do we ensure that HR professionals will know what to do and have the skills to do it?

When HR professionals respond to these questions, they will know why others would benefit by listening to them, because they will be delivering real value—and they will know what that value is. These are the questions we will attempt to answer in this book. When HR professionals begin with the receiver in mind, they can more quickly emerge as full strategic contributors; add greater value for key stakeholders (customers, investors, line managers, and employees); enhance business productivity; achieve measurable and valuable results; create sustainable competitive advantage; and have more fun in their careers.

Five Elements of the HR Value Proposition

The HR value proposition grounds HR and has five elements that form an integrated HR blueprint. Figure 1-1 shows the framework, with each element representing a section of this book: external realities, stakeholders, HR practices, HR resources, and HR professionals. External realities and stakeholder interests determine why HR matters to an organization and why HR needs to focus on what it delivers more than on what it does. HR practices, HR resources, and HR professionals are the elements that encompass the HR function within your organization.

FIGURE 1-1

The HR value proposition

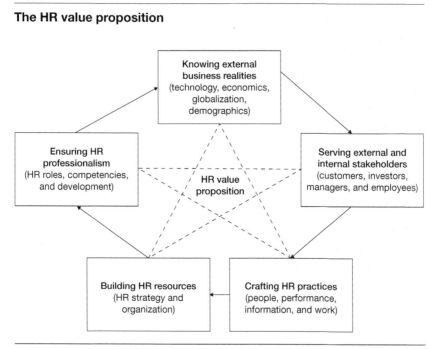

In implementing HR transformation, the ideal logic is to move through these five elements sequentially, following the solid lines in figure 1-1, but sometimes it is useful to follow the dotted lines instead. For example, you might start your transformation of HR with a competency assessment of your staff, but to ensure that this competency assessment leads to an integrated transformation, it must be connected to the other elements of the overall blueprint. Or, you might start by investing in e-HR, then move to the other four boxes to complete the transformation.

From these five elements, we establish fourteen criteria for HR with a value focus.

External Business Realities (Chapter 2)

Every firm operates in the context of external business realities. The external business realities that currently have the greatest influence on external customers and owners are the radical transformation of technology, economic and regulatory environments, and major changes in human demographics, all in a context of increasing globalization. HR actions inside a firm must reflect and influence such business realities outside that firm.

HR professionals should be able to cogently discuss these external realities—the technology, regulatory and economic factors, and demographics of the global business environment—and connect them to their day-to-day work. Knowing business realities makes it possible to put HR practices in context, tie them to competitive challenges, and relate them to concerns facing line managers. These contextual factors offer the rationale for why a transformation should occur. Everyone in your HR function should be conversant with both the realities of the external world and how HR actions will help your firm compete in this changing context. In chapter 2, we review the trends currently influencing key stakeholders for HR. We also provide a sample of the kind of data needed to specify and clarify major external business realities.

- *Criterion 1.* An effective HR function has HR professionals who recognize external business realities and adapt HR practices and allocate HR resources accordingly.

Stakeholders (Chapters 3 and 4)

Value is defined by the receivers of HR work—the investors, customers, line managers, and employees—more than by the givers. HR is successful if and when its stakeholders perceive that it produces value. Delivering what matters most to stakeholders focuses on the deliverables (outcomes of HR) rather than on the doables (activities of HR). We suggest that these realities differ for external and internal stakeholders.

In chapter 3, we examine external stakeholders, focusing on investors who value market capitalization and shareholder return. We then focus on external customers who purchase products and services. Together, shareholders and customers are the ultimate determinants of the relevance of organizational outcomes. With money flowing in the proper wallet-to-wallet direction, firms succeed. This chapter offers specific ideas and tools for how HR can contribute direct and indirect value to customers and investors. We examine powerful research that supports the central role of HR in this area. We also suggest specific ways HR professionals can deliver value to these external stakeholders. We end with an organizational audit that enables HR professionals to assess the alignment between their activities and the demands of investors and customers.

- *Criterion 2.* An effective HR function creates market value for investors by increasing intangibles.

- *Criterion 3.* An effective HR function increases customer share by connecting with target customers.

In chapter 4, we review how HR creates value for internal stakeholders, particularly employees at all levels of a company and line managers who craft and deliver business strategies. This chapter specifies how HR professionals can identify and create organizational capabilities required for line managers to implement strategy. We also identify how HR can add value for employees by encouraging individual knowledge, skills, and abilities that promote productivity and help ensure long-term employability. Again, we review what HR professionals can and should do to exceed manager and employee expectations. We also provide an audit for HR professionals to assess the alignment between their activities and the internal requirements of managers and employees.

- *Criterion 4.* An effective HR function helps line managers deliver strategy by building organization capabilities.

- *Criterion 5.* An effective HR function clarifies and establishes an employee value proposition and enhances individual abilities.

HR Practices (Chapters 5 and 6)

HR practices must be defined and must evolve to deliver what stakeholders expect. In chapters 5 and 6, we offer four domains of HR practice: people, performance management, information, and work. Chapter 5 focuses on the more traditional HR practices of staffing, training, and development, as well as appraisal, rewards, and feedback. We offer a compendium of choices for how these practices can be designed and delivered to add value for each of the key HR stakeholders. This menu of choices allows HR professionals to adapt best practices to their individual situations.

- *Criterion 6.* An effective HR function manages people processes and practices in ways that add value.

- *Criterion 7.* An effective HR function manages performance management processes and practices in ways that add value.

Chapter 6, which follows the same format as chapter 5, introduces best and emerging practices in information and work flows—domains where HR professionals are beginning to have impact. HR professionals tend not to be currently involved in these practice areas to the extent that they will be in the future. These practice areas include the management of internal and external communication and design, who does work, how work is done, and where work is done. We suggest choices for these practices and examine how each of these practice areas can add value for investors, customers, managers, and employees. We end with a menu of choices for each of these emerging HR areas.

- *Criterion 8.* An effective HR function manages information processes and practices in ways that add value.

- *Criterion 9.* An effective HR function manages work flow design and processes in ways that add value.

HR Resources (Chapters 7 and 8)

The HR function must create strategies and organize resources so that individual efforts of HR professionals combine to create value. Chapter 7 integrates the preceding chapters into a proven methodology for designing HR strategy, and it identifies specific steps and actions. We show how Motorola followed these steps in creating a powerful HR strategy. We offer HR leaders a blueprint for building their strategy so as to link and integrate the various stakeholder requirements, business strategies, organizational capabilities, and HR practices. This section of the book gives HR leaders a way to ensure that their function delivers value by setting the way it is governed, measured, and strategically focused.

- *Criterion 10.* An effective HR function has a clear strategic planning process for aligning HR investments with business goals.

Chapter 8 outlines the ways in which the HR function can be organized to deliver work. We suggest that value appears when the HR organization aligns with the business organization. We then discuss how to organize both the transactional work of HR (through service centers, technology, and outsourcing) and the transformational work of HR (through centers of expertise, dedicated HR, and corporate HR). We end by reviewing responsibilities for corporate HR, embedded HR professionals, centers of HR expertise, and line managers in the context of a shared services organization. This chapter can be used by HR executives to assess whether they have organized their function to deliver maximum value.

- *Criterion 11.* An effective HR function aligns its organization with the strategy of the business.

HR Professionalism (Chapters 9 and 10)

HR professionals deliver value through the roles they play and the competencies they demonstrate. Chapter 9 offers specific advice on emerging roles HR professionals play in their organizations. It shows the evolution of HR roles in the last decade and proposes five roles for HR professionals: employee advocate, human capital developer, functional expert, strategic partner, and leader. We suggest frameworks and behaviors for each of these roles and provide examples of HR professionals who play these roles. This chapter describes the full playing field for HR professionals.

- *Criterion 12.* An effective HR function has HR professionals who play clear and appropriate roles.

Chapter 10 summarizes our last fifteen years of research on competencies for the HR professional. Based on data from more than twenty-eight thousand individuals, we show what HR people must know and do to be credible as professionals and to add value to the business. We specifically focus on the 2002 round of our competency study, in which—as mentioned earlier—we asked the following question: "What are the competencies and agendas that distinguish HR professionals in high-performing firms from those in low-performing firms?" This chapter provides HR professionals with a framework for competencies required to be a top HR professional. A key takeaway from this chapter is that the fundamental logic of this book is firmly grounded in the largest global survey ever completed on the competencies of the HR profession.

- *Criterion 13.* An effective HR function builds HR professionals who demonstrate HR competencies.

Developing the HR Department and Profession (Chapters 11 and 12)

In our concluding chapters, we draw implications for both the development of HR professionals and functions. Chapter 11 discusses how to develop yourself as an HR professional and how to build a team or department of more capable HR professionals. It suggests principles of adult learning and applies those principles to HR professional development. We review critical components necessary for training HR professionals and offer specific suggestions on how to develop HR professionals through reading, listening, observing, and doing. This information can be used by those charged with building HR professionalism into their organizations and by any HR professional who wants to improve.

- *Criterion 14.* An effective HR function invests in HR professionals through training and development experiences.

Chapter 12 concludes by integrating the themes of this book into the HR function as a whole (practices, department, and people). It offers HR leaders a comprehensive organizational audit that will enable them to define, assess, and improve their HR organization. We propose fourteen criteria and audit questions as guidelines for establishing a world-class HR function. This HR audit may be used to determine what is and what should be in ensuring HR value.

From Vision to Action: The Fourteen Criteria of the New HR

A summary of the HR value proposition is shown in table 1-1, Blueprint for the future, in three parts. At the simplest level, part 1, your HR transformation is about HR adding value as received by key stakeholders. With this insight, you can do presentations in which you simply talk about why you want to transform HR and how the value you create will relate to the business realities you face. In part 2, you define the elements that create value. These five elements must work together to deliver full value. In part 3, you specify the fourteen criteria for an effective HR function. In part 1, value is the vision; in part 2, the elements are the goals; and in part 3, the criteria suggest the changes that you must implement to make your HR transformation complete.

In discussions with your HR colleagues, line managers, and employees throughout your organization, you may ground your transformation logic in terms of vision, goals, and actions. Ideally, every HR professional will be able to recite why value matters, what HR value means, and how HR value is created.

With the HR value proposition defined, you may assess where you are now and where you need to focus to get better. Through an assessment, you can determine which elements of the HR value framework are in place in your organization and which are not.

Assessments, like audits, rely on assembling data, a task that involves two issues: content and process. Content deals with what information you collect, process with how you collect it. The blueprint for content in table 1-1 suggests a framework for assessing your overall HR function. Based on the fourteen criteria, you can create an interview protocol like the HR value assessment in assessment 1-1 (for more information, see http://www.rbl.net). Responses to these questions provide an assessment

TABLE 1-1

Blueprint for the future: the fourteen criteria of the new HR

Part 1: Vision *Premise of the HR value proposition*	Part 2: Goals *Elements of the HR value proposition*	Part 3: Actions *Criteria for the new HR (An effective HR function . . .)*
HR succeeds when it creates value.	Knowing external business realities	1. Recognizes external business realities and adapts its practices and allocates resources accordingly
	Serving external and internal stakeholders	2. Creates market value for investors by increasing intangibles 3. Increases customer share by connecting with target customers 4. Helps line managers deliver strategy by building organization capabilities 5. Clarifies and establishes an employee value proposition and ensures that employees have abilities to do their work
	Crafting HR practices	6. Manages people processes in ways that add value 7. Manages performance management processes and practices in ways that add value 8. Manages information processes and practices in ways that add value 9. Manages work flow processes and practices in ways that add value
	Building HR resources	10. Has a clear strategic planning process for aligning HR investments with business goals 11. Aligns its organization to the strategy of the business
	Ensuring HR professionalism	12. Has staff who play clear and appropriate roles 13. Builds staff ability to demonstrate HR competencies 14. Invests in HR professionals through training and development experiences

ASSESSMENT 1-1

Your HR value proposition

	Score (low=1 high=5)	If you score less than 4, go to chapter
1. To what extent do the HR professionals in my department understand how external realities of technology, economics, and demographics in the global context affect our industry and business?		2
2. To what extent does our HR work link to the intangibles that investors value?		3
3. To what extent do we use HR practices to build long-term connections with target customers?		3
4. To what extent do we audit and create organization capabilities that will turn strategy into action?		4
5. To what extent do we have a clear employee value proposition that lays out what is expected of employees and what they get in return?		4
6. To what extent do our HR practices that focus on people (staff, training, development) add value?		5
7. To what extent do our HR practices that focus on performance (setting standards, allocating rewards, providing feedback) add value?		5
8. To what extent do our HR practices that focus on information (outside-in and inside-out) add value?		6
9. To what extent do our HR practices that focus on work flow (who does the work, how is the work done, and where is the work done) add value?		6
10. To what extent does our HR strategy process turn business goals into HR priorities?		7
11. To what extent is our HR organization (e-HR, service centers, centers of expertise, embedded HR, and outsourcing contracts) aligned with the business strategy?		8
12. To what extent do our HR professionals play employee advocate, human capital developer, functional expert, strategic partner, and leadership roles?		9
13. To what extent do our HR professionals demonstrate competence in strategic contribution, HR delivery, business knowledge, personal credibility, and HR technology?		10
14. To what extent do we invest in our HR professionals through training and development?		11

Total

Interpretation:
63+:	*Do not read this book; write your own.*
50–62:	*You are in good shape; the goal is to keep fit.*
37–49:	*Close, but focus on the areas you need to upgrade.*
24–36:	*You've got a long way to go. Get started.*
Less than 24:	*A long way to go. Find one area to excel in and get going now.*

about the strengths and weaknesses of your HR function and will help you focus on which sections of this book deserve the most attention. Check out your scores on this assessment. For those criteria that scored highest, you may want to skim those sections of the book. For those criteria that scored lowest, you may want to read and work through the tools in those sections of the book.

Blueprint for the Future

The universal value premise is that value is defined by the receiver more than by the giver. This premise mandates that HR professionals begin with the end in mind by ensuring a line of sight to their key stakeholders. It requires that HR professionals focus less on what they do and more on what they deliver. The value focus we suggest shapes conversations between HR professionals and their constituents.

Conversations with investors will focus on how investors gain market value from HR services. Conversations with key customers (as in the beginning of this chapter) will focus on how the customer receives unique products and services because of HR investments. Conversations with business leaders will focus on accomplishing their business strategy through the creation of organizational capabilities. Conversations with employees will focus on making sure that employees have the abilities they need to do what is expected of them.

These conversations begin when HR professionals master the knowledge of the external realities of today's business environments. They must be fully literate in knowing how HR can add value for investors, customers, managers, and employees. With an understanding of these issues, HR professionals can become active players and partners with business leaders, and they can begin to develop human abilities and organizational capabilities that enable a company to compete now and in the future. With this understanding, HR professionals will be proactive rather than reactive, control their destiny, and add sustainable value. Ultimately, with this understanding, HR professionals will be able to engage in conversations with all company stakeholders and bring substantial value to the table.

We are advocating for a dramatic refocusing of HR: from what is done to what is delivered; from building HR functions for efficiency to building them for stakeholder value; and from implementing best HR practices to delivering value-added HR practices. HR professionals anywhere in the organization should have a clear line of sight from HR agendas, practices, and skills to the ultimate receivers of those agendas, practices, and skills; from HR practices to the outcomes they create for key stakeholders; and from HR function and organization to the results of investments in HR.

2

External Business Realities

*To what extent do the HR professionals in my department understand
how external realities of technology, economics, and demographics
in the global context affect our industry and business?*

H R PROFESSIONALS and their stakeholders have too frequently
operated in separate worlds. However, to create value, you have
to know what value is—and value is defined more by the receiver than
the giver. That means HR professionals must learn to help their stakeholders address the issues that matter most to them. They must, therefore, understand the fundamental external business realities that shape
industries and companies. The realities that influence business may be
grouped under three headings:

- Technology

- Economic and regulatory issues

- Workforce demographics

A fourth factor, globalization, cuts across and influences the other
three.

To maintain their credibility, HR professionals must know the trends
in each of these areas, the facts behind the trends, and where these facts
may be accessed. Assembling this pool of information requires constant
awareness of the world. Knowledge of external realities isn't something to
be accomplished once and ticked off on a to-do list. Instead, it's essential
to ask—and keep asking—four questions: What are the important trends

for each of these realities? What are the key data points that illustrate these trends? What do I need to know about these trends in order to contribute to management team discussions? Where can I find this information?

In this chapter, we synthesize the key trends in each area with a brief sample of the logic and supporting data and information on how to access the data. We also provide a self-test that you can use to assess your knowledge. Our experience is that HR professionals must understand the basic trends. To have credibility at the strategy table, you must also be able to support your statements with empirical data about business trends, lest you be seen as ill prepared or superficial. This chapter does not attempt to review all categories of external business realities, but it does give a broad indication of the kind of information that HR professionals will increasingly be expected to master as management team members.

Technology

Technology—the application of knowledge to the transformation of things into other things—drives almost every aspect of the changing business environment. As applied to organizational processes, technology may be used to automate transactions in HR, finance, sales, legal, operations, and purchasing. Technology enhances engineering and design processes, and moves goods efficiently and accurately through the manufacturing process. It can also be applied to the design of new products or services.

HR professionals cannot ignore technology either in their own operations or in those that affect the organizations they serve. Depending on the industry in which they work, they must be able to understand how people create new technologies that keep their firms ahead of the competition. They may also need to understand how to apply existing technology to new applications.

They need to help their organizations and people adapt to the pace of transformation spawned by emerging technologies. They need to understand and create cooperative and synergistic cultures in which people can freely and accurately communicate across departmental and national boundaries. They also need to know how to create and sustain the new forms of organization—flatter, virtual, and horizontal—that are made possible and mandated by emerging information, process, and product technologies.

The major trends in technology fall into four dimensions:

- *Speed.* Things are moving faster and faster. "Moore's Law," the 1965 projection that microprocessor speed would double roughly every eighteen months, has held true to this day. In the last forty years, the speed of microprocessors has increased 4.5 million percent. Prototypes exist to maintain Moore's Law through 2011.[1] In many ways, the whole world seems to be following suit.

- *Efficiency.* Per-unit costs are dropping as speed increases. For example, in chip manufacturing, the cost per transistor unit has dropped from a dollar to a millionth of a cent in the past thirty years.[2] By continually applying technology to enable business process improvement, Dell has created impressive manufacturing results. Its manufacturing workstations are 400 percent more productive than industry standards. In its new facilities, production output is up 40 percent as it produces a customized computer every four seconds.

- *Connectivity.* Up and down the supply chain, stakeholders are being tied more and more closely together as technology brings "Reed's Law" to life.[3] Reed's Law suggests that the number of possible connections in a network rises exponentially compared to the number of nodes. The world is rapidly reaching a point where every human being can be a node in a network that includes every other. Large and powerful human networks are created through technology on a massive scale in unforeseen and radical ways.

- *Customization.* Technology allows companies to identify customer requirements more quickly and more accurately and to translate requirements into customized products and services. BMW customers electronically feed their new-car specifications directly to thousands of suppliers and factories. Based on supplier parts availability, distribution information, and Original Equipment Manufacturers (OEM) production schedules, the delivery date of the customized vehicle is calculated and communicated to the customer in five seconds. Eighty percent of BMW sales in Europe are now customized in this manner.

All these changes will have an impact on the work of HR over the next few years; any of them will likely have an impact on your work *tomorrow*. It's that close. Since any of these changes could be—and many already are—the subject of whole books, we will explore just one major trend here.

Smart Mobs

The spiraling growth in connectivity has profound implications for organizations and for HR. Technology enables "people to act together in new ways in situations where collective action was not possible before."[4] New blocks of customers, suppliers, employees, and owners can form overnight. Called *smart mobs*, these groups can mobilize themselves to undercut pricing, raise product and service standards, communicate satisfaction or dissatisfaction, and impose substantial pressures on their target organizations. Examples range from the company-sponsored to the upstart. People with major complaints about products and services, companies, and politicians create Web sites that allow them to access large-scale audiences, thereby mobilizing collective action that otherwise would not have been possible. Based on their personal interests, people then vote with their time and energy for the espoused cause. For example, SaveDisney.com was established by dissident shareholders to voice their dissatisfaction with the Disney executive leadership in hopes of ousting that leadership and reorienting the strategic direction of the company and its values. EBay has turned into one of the great success stories of the Internet, with a transaction volume larger than half of the world's economies.[5] More cars are sold on eBay than in the largest dealership in North America. At the same time, among its 12 million daily listings are toothbrushes and dental floss. It is estimated that more than one hundred fifty thousand cyber-entrepreneurs earn their full-time living selling merchandise through eBay. What makes eBay work? At its heart, eBay facilitates a forum for the swarming of groups around specific personal interests that have economic value. Buyers and sellers conduct transactions and regulate cheaters on a global scale without face-to-face interaction. EBay provides the technological context for the nearly instantaneous creation and execution of frictionless markets within a self-regulating global democracy.

But technology-enabled connectivity has a dark side as well: online gambling and pornography can expand unabated without the social moorings of family and community restraint. International terrorists, pedophiles, and emerging slave traders find one another online. To counter these unsavory forces, legal and commercial online surveillance mechanisms are being developed that may compromise individual privacy. Grappling with the dark side of technology has obvious strategic and policy implications for organizations and their HR departments.

Globalization and Technology

Globalization occurs when goods and services, capital, information, and people move across national borders. Such movement is intensified and accelerated by technology. For example, global trade has been substantially enabled in recent years through massive reductions in transportation, freight, and communications costs. During the last half of the twentieth century, air transportation costs dropped by about 60 percent, sea freight costs by 20 percent, and both digitized voice and data communications by more than 99 percent.[6]

Meanwhile, through more sophisticated job design, companies are able to split up the value chain and allocate work on a global scale to locations anywhere in the world where work can be done at the highest quality-to-cost ratio. This trend is a key feature of contemporary trade. It occurs under a variety of different vernaculars, including outsourcing, vertical trade, multinationalization of production, slicing up the value chain, and disintegration of production. Eli Lilly allows hobbyists to swarm over its most difficult technical issues. At Lilly's InnoCentive.com Web site, the company describes thorny problems in some detail. Anyone with an Internet connection anywhere in the world can read about a problem, take it to a garage workshop or basement hobby room, develop a solution, and submit it back to Lilly—receiving a financial reward for success ranging from $5,000 to $100,000. Through this means, Lilly is able to access intellectual capital that was heretofore not only inaccessible but unknown.

The globalization of information likewise is occurring on an unprecedented scale. Information is instantaneously available around the world. Furthermore, repeat visits to Web sites create a market for accuracy and credibility—and can at the same time also reinforce misperceptions and feed fanaticism on a global scale.

What HR Professionals Need to Know About Technology

To contribute to management team discussions about technology, HR professionals need a knowledge base about the current technological possibilities and a general vision about the future role that technology might play in their firms. With this knowledge, they will be able to add value to strategic discussions that involve technology, understand the dynamics that influence their key constituents, and align strategies and practices to these constituents' needs in a timely and accurate manner.

ASSESSMENT 2-1

Knowledge of technology

	To what extent do I have this knowledge?
	Low High
1. What applications of technology can enhance the design and production of our products or services?	1 2 3 4 5
2. How is technology influencing the ability of our customers to act as a "smart mob" in evaluating and buying our products or services?	1 2 3 4 5
3. How fast are the technologies that have direct impact on my business changing?	1 2 3 4 5
4. How can technology be used more effectively on a global scale to drive down costs per unit of products or services?	1 2 3 4 5
5. How do we direct the flow of information through technology so that the organizational whole is greater than the sum of the parts?	1 2 3 4 5
6. How do we employ technology to access sources of intellectual capital that we might otherwise overlook?	1 2 3 4 5
7. What is the next generation of technology that might put us ahead of or behind our competitors?	1 2 3 4 5

Total

Total your scores and compare to the following interpretation scale.

30–35: Impressive. You are at the top. Write a case study.
25–29: You know a lot and add value in business discussions.
20–24: You have opportunities to add greater value through greater knowledge.
15–19: Read more to stay current.
Less than 15: A long way to go to add the value that you should.

The questions in assessment 2-1, Knowledge of technology, can help HR professionals determine what they already know and what they might need to know about technology.

Resources Regarding Technological Trends

A major purpose of this chapter is not only to review current trends and data relative to technology, economy, and demographics but also to provide an overview of sources to which you may turn in order to stay current in these topics over time. Many magazines, newspapers, and journals are dedicated to presenting, analyzing, and projecting trends in current and emerging technologies. The basic business magazines regularly review technological trends: *Business 2.0, Business Today, Business-Week,* the *Economist, Far Eastern Economic Review, Fast Company, Forbes,* and *Fortune.* The major business newspapers in Europe and the United States likewise carry informative articles: *Financial Times, Handelsblatt,* and the *Wall Street Journal.* For greater detail, several magazines and journals specialize in various aspects of technology: *Invention & Technology, Technology Review, Scientific American, Science, American Scientist,* the *New Atlantis, International Journal of Technology Management, Technology and Culture, TechComm,* the *Journal of Technology Transfer,* and *Journal of Information Technology.* Several online sources are also useful for staying current with economic trends: CNN.com, MSN.com, News.BBC.co.uk, FoxNews.com, MagPortal.com, SciTechResources.gov, InfoTech-Trends.com, CDT.org, and www.Publications.parliament.uk. You might access this information by selecting key information sources and regularly following them, by assigning someone to synthesize key technology advances and share this with you and others, or by inviting technology experts to periodically update HR professionals.

Economic and Regulatory Issues

Economic and regulatory environments provide the context for business operations. They are frequently the precursors to changes in the expectations of customers, shareholders, managers, and employees. If HR professionals are to contribute to business decisions, they must know where to go to learn the basic trends in these areas. They must have data about these factors; and they must be able to use this knowledge in providing intellectual richness to strategic business discussions.

Economic Factors

Even in the context of an economic downturn of the early years of the twenty-first century, the overall U.S. economy has been growing at a healthy pace. However, many economists project that the world economy will continue to grow but will become more volatile in coming years, with periods of rapid improvement followed by periods of rapid decline. Several trends predict prospects for sustainable global economic growth:

- *Workforce quality.* The collective knowledge and skill level of workers continues to increase on a global scale. The population of highly

skilled workers in countries such as China and India is high and
rising.

- *Workforce flexibility.* The flexibility of the U.S. workforce is one of
  the primary strengths of the U.S. economy, especially when compared to the relative workforce immobility of Japan, Germany,
  France, and Italy. The movement of people from one industrial
  sector to another encourages growth where growth is possible and
  greater productivity where demand is diminishing. While workforce
  flexibility creates substantial turmoil and pain in the lives of many,
  the long-term total economic benefits are clear.

- *Investment.* Although investments in new products, services, technologies, processes, and equipment may be erratic in specific industry sectors, the overall trend is toward continued and substantive
  investment. Likewise, investment in merger and acquisition (M&A)
  activity is anticipated to continue in upwardly spiraling waves that
  roughly track upward fluctuations in stock price.

- *Health.* The world is generally becoming a healthier place. However, the cost of maintaining human health is an issue of concern for
  the countries as a whole as well as for individual companies. U.S.
  HR professionals face three challenges: keeping the workforce
  healthy at a low cost, reducing the total costs of health care insurance, and contributing to the national debate on health care.

- *Increasing wage disparity.* Over the past three decades, the number of
  people with poverty-level incomes has continued to sharply decline.
  However, real wages for the top income brackets continue to
  sharply increase at 1.5 percent per year. Meanwhile, average real
  wages of those in the lower bracket continue to decline.[7]

- *Productivity improvement and long-term economic optimism.* Most
  developing countries are experiencing strong growth in labor productivity, with the United States surging ahead at a remarkable 2.8
  percent annual increase.[8] This improvement matches the post–
  World War II productivity surge of 1948 to 1973 and is almost
  double the productivity figure of 1.4 percent from 1973 to 1995.
  The implications of such statistics are dramatic. At an annual productivity increase of 1.4 percent, real national income doubles in
  fifty years. At an annual productivity increase of 2.4 percent, real

national income doubles in approximately twenty-six years. The implications for the economic well-being of a country are obvious; productivity is a major driver of the economic growth.

Workforce Productivity

The importance of productivity as driver of economic well-being warrants some additional discussion. Productivity per worker continues to improve across many segments of the economy. In recent years, productivity in the U.S. manufacturing sector has increased at twice the rate of the overall nonfarm economy. As a result, gains in manufacturing productivity now contribute more to gross domestic product (GDP) growth than the gains of software and retail combined.[9]

The U.S. steel industry serves as an example. During the last two decades, production in the U.S. steel industry increased 35 percent. At the same time, the number of workers in the steel industry decreased 76 percent. Those workers who remain earn on average from $18 to $21 per hour.[10]

While manufacturing jobs decline, the number of jobs that require analysis and intellectual judgment—such as systems designers, product engineers, financial analysts, and marketing specialists—is growing. In the service sector, jobs are also on the rise in both the low- and high-end pay categories. Relatively low-paying McJobs at fast-food restaurants, hotels, and convenience stores are increasing, as are service jobs that pay well, such as nursing, computer consulting, and after-sales service.

Some people believe that technology-driven productivity is an enemy. They reason as follows: technology increases labor productivity. This means, by definition, that fewer people produce each unit of output. This causes unemployment, which reduces consumer spending, which in turn reduces demand. Thus, the economy should go into decline. This logic makes sense, especially in the short run and in times of recession. Over the long run, however, empirical evidence simply does not support it.

Over the past fifty years, real wages grew fastest and unemployment was at its lowest during periods of greatest productivity. As productivity gains spread broadly over the economy, the result is higher income per person, cheaper products, and greater competitiveness for the companies that produce them. These outcomes increase demand for products and services, and increased demand produces new jobs. This is sometimes referred to as the "virtuous cycle of productivity." The good news is that this cycle is anticipated to continue for at least much of the decade. And the cycle will be experienced not only by high-tech firms such as Intel and Dell but also by low-tech firms such as Wal-Mart as they apply technology to their operations.

A Big Question

Totaling $44 trillion, the U.S. federal deficit is at an all-time high by a substantial margin.[11] And the intensity of the problem appears on the upswing, as the impending retirement of baby boomers places additional burdens on Social Security, Medicare, and Medicaid. The diversion of resources from corporate investments toward paying the deficit is likely to make the United States less and less attractive to foreign capital. The implications of this challenge have yet to be defined, but we are safe in assuming that the business implications will be nontrivial.

Globalization and Economics

Global trade now approximates more than a quarter of total Gross Domestic Product (GDP).[12] Since the years immediately following World War II, imports have risen from $60 billion to $6.5 trillion, and exports from $58 billion to $6.3 trillion. Over the past two decades, global merchandise trade expanded 300 percent to a total of $6.4 trillion. Trade in services increased by 400 percent to a total of $1.5 trillion. The service sector represents a small proportion of the total, but it is growing more quickly than the merchandise sector. Both are growing at a much faster rate than the globally aggregated domestic GDPs. While more pronounced in high-income countries, trade growth is also increasing in middle- and low-income countries at 19 percent and 8 percent, respectively. Furthermore, these trends are likely to continue. For example, it is estimated that the annual U.S. trade rate will increase by approximately 7.9 percent.[13]

As might be expected, the flow of capital across international borders correlates closely with the flow of goods and services. Capital flow across borders occurs in two different ways.[14]

First, nondomestic companies invest in operations in other countries or purchase equity in other countries. This is referred to as foreign direct investment, or FDI. Such FDI is an important element of the U.S. economy. In recent years, non-U.S. firms operating in the United States accounted for 16 percent of the employment and 18 percent of the sales in the U.S. manufacturing sector, and they tended to pay salaries at parity with their domestic counterparts.

Second, nondomestic companies invest in the purchase of bonds, equity, and other financial instruments. For example, non-U.S. firms or individuals may seek to maximize their long-term returns by investing in relatively stable but low-return U.S. financial instruments, or they may invest in the relatively unstable but potentially high-return China markets. In this way, global capital flow can be healthy for both the investor and the investee. In a potentially unsettling trend, however, countries are beginning to acquire so much capital that they could potentially influence the foreign policy of the debtor countries. Such debt disequilibriums are beginning to occur as China and Japan control a substantially disproportionate percentage of the U.S. debt.

However, globalization will continue to be limited by local political and social dynamics. Many countries experience both positive and negative effects on national sovereignty from international governing bodies such as the World Trade Organization and the United Nations. Regional trade agreements such as the North American Free Trade Agreement (NAFTA) have proliferated and are hotly debated for both their positive and negative outcomes. In many countries, free access to nontraditional information and social norms interrupts and threatens traditional sources of information and norms such as religion and family. Knowledge and special interest bonds through the Internet, the media, or direct contact frequently increase conflicts with family relationships and ethnic ties. These dynamics may place pressures on the free flow of trade. However, individuals, communities, industries, and companies that are prone to limited foreign trade and allow protectionist trade barriers will do well to remember that national regulatory protectionism was a major contributor to the intensity of the global financial crash of 1929.

Globalization will continue to diminish the influence of organized labor. Four factors contribute to the decline of unions in an ever-increasing global business environment:[15]

- The large multinational corporations that drive much of economic globalization have jobs and work that tend to be geographically mobile.

- Global population growth in low-income countries provides greater labor supply on a global scale while at the same time technology-driven productivity improvements have reduced labor demand in high-income countries.

- Especially in developed countries, there has been a shift away from the relatively more organized manufacturing sector to the less organized service sector.

- Most low-income countries that are moving onto the global playing field tend to have weak traditions of unionized workforces.

In the short run, there are clearly winners and losers in the dynamics of global trade, among individuals, job categories, industry sectors, and countries. Developed countries are currently experiencing a loss of jobs to countries that are able to process digital information or transact administrative tasks at equal or higher skill levels and at lower cost. However, other sectors benefit from job creation that occurs through foreign trade (for example, the U.S. agriculture and entertainment industries). The net good news is the general consensus among economists that the world is generally better off with global trade than without it.

Regulatory Factors

Ask any group of line or HR managers if they believe the world is becoming more or less regulated, and the response will probably be that the world is becoming more regulated. It certainly feels that way—especially in light of legislation about the environment, discrimination, harassment, privacy, board composition, whistle blowing, and so on and on.

Yet the last two decades have seen deregulation on a scale unprecedented in human history. HR professionals need to bear in mind that since the mid- to late-1980s, trillions of dollars of economic activity has been deregulated. This deregulation has been most intense in the easing of trade restrictions with the former U.S.S.R, China, and India as well as deregulations in many domestic industries (such as utilities, interstate banking, and transportation). Deregulation has also contributed to a substantial reduction of tariffs that has enabled the steady and profound increase in global trade.[16] Throughout this century, tariffs have been erratic in the short run, but steadily declining in the long run. This trend is expected to continue.

HR professionals must understand this massive worldwide trend toward deregulation and the implications of this trend in order to add value at the strategy table. Otherwise, they may be tempted to overemphasize regulatory matters.

HR departments have traditionally been among the most regulated; they are heavily involved in dozens of major legal issues that must be addressed if the company is to focus on issues more germane to its competitiveness. Despite unprecedented deregulation, important regulatory forces are still active. HR professionals, as contributing members of the strategy team, must be aware of these forces—the Sarbanes-Oxley Act, for example, as well as efforts to rein in the mutual fund industry to ensure ethical practices. In addition to these large-scale business-focused regulatory matters, HR professionals will continue to remain the caretakers of more traditional HR-related legal issues:

- Legal requirements for collective bargaining. How do you optimally work with the National Labor Relations Board (NLRB)? How do you make your case to the union leadership and to union members? How do you effectively work within the provisions of the labor contract?

- Legal rights of individuals to work free from discrimination based on gender, race, color, religion, sexual orientation, ethnicity, age, or disability.

- Legal protections that allow people to work in a safe environment, free from physical threat or forms of psychological harassment.

- Legal rights of employees relative to testing, evaluation, discipline, compensation, severance, and privacy.

- The implication of legislation concerning maternity and paternity leave, medical care, insurance, and white-collar collective bargaining.

In recent years, the highest-profile discussions in the area of regulation affecting HR and companies in general have revolved around the question of ethics. The Enron debacle became a lighting rod for society's discomfort with conflict of interest, misuse of positional influence, greed without constraint, and complex financial deception. Public demand for reform intensified with revelations of malfeasance from WorldCom, Global Crossing Ltd., Tyco International Ltd., and Arthur Andersen. The involvement of HR professionals relative to ethical issues is substantially increasing. For example, almost every provision of the Sarbanes-Oxley Act has implications for HR professionals and the discussions they may have with their counterparts in other departments.

What HR Professionals Need to Know About Economic and Regulatory Issues

To contribute to management team discussions about economic and regulatory issues, HR professionals need to be aware of the basic trends relative to these issues and know where to find them. However, they also need to be able to back up generalizations about basic trends with specific data. With this knowledge, they may then

- Add value to strategic discussions about economic and regulatory issues.

- Understand the economic and regulatory dynamics that influence their respective firms directly as well as those that influence their firms indirectly through customers, shareholders, managers, and employees.

- Align their HR strategies and practices to HR's key constituents in a timely and accurate manner.

The self-assessment in assessment 2-2 gives HR professionals an idea of what they already know about economic and regulatory issues and what they might need to know for the future.

Resources Regarding Economic and Regulatory Trends

Potential sources for information about economic and regulatory trends are plentiful and easily accessible. The major business magazines and newspapers provide reasonable, and usually credible, summaries of economic and regulatory matters that have implications for business organizations: *Business Today, BusinessWeek, Dun's,* the *Economist, Far Eastern Economic Review, Forbes, Fortune, Inc., Financial Times, Handelsblatt, Investor's Business Daily,* and the *Wall Street Journal.* Many publications are available that specialize in economics and regulatory matters and are generally user-friendly: the *Columbia Journal of World Business, Comparative Strategy, Economic Policy, Economic Policy Review, Encyclopedia of American Industries,* the *EU Economy Review, Foreign Policy, Handbook of North American Industry, Harvard Business Review,* the *Journal of Comparative Economics, Journal of Economic Literature, Journal of Economic Perspectives, Journal of Public Policy, Journal of World Trade, Standard & Poor's Industry Surveys, US Industry & Trade Outlook,* the *World Bank Economic Review,* the *World Bank Research Observer,* and the *World Economy.* Web

ASSESSMENT 2-2

Knowledge of economic and regulatory issues

	To what extent do I have this knowledge? Low / High
1. What are the past and current trends in the economy, and how will those trends influence my industry and my company?	1 2 3 4 5
2. From an economic standpoint, how is the next decade likely to differ from the last?	1 2 3 4 5
3. How does productivity in my company compare to productivity trends in my industry and my country?	1 2 3 4 5
4. What are the present and current trends relative to mergers and acquisitions in my industry?	1 2 3 4 5
5. Is my industry moving toward greater regulation or toward greater domestic and global competition?	1 2 3 4 5
6. How does my firm seize market opportunities being created by global deregulation?	1 2 3 4 5
7. What pending legislation is likely to have a major impact on my company? How do I influence this legislation and how do I prepare for it?	1 2 3 4 5

Total

Total your scores and compare to the following interpretation scale.

30–35: Impressive. You are at the top. Write a case study.
25–29: You know a lot and add value in business discussions.
20–24: You have opportunities to add greater value through greater knowledge.
15–19: Read more to stay current.
Less than 15: A way to go to add the value that you should.

sites that contain useful information about economic and regulatory issues include Business.com, bized.ac.uk, IndustryLink.com, www.Census.gov, Europa.eu.int, Ita.doc.gov, and Stu.findlaw.com.

Workforce Demographics

Workforce demographics that influence the pool of labor available to conceive, develop, produce, distribute, and sell products and services are changing in turbulent ways. Demographics likewise directly influence the demand for types and volumes of products and services. HR professionals need a grasp of basic global and domestic demographic trends—and, at the strategy table, they also need to have specific data to back up their assertions regarding these trends.

Five categories of demographic trends—declining workforce growth, increasing age of the workforce, changing gender balance, increasing ethnic diversity, and deteriorating family economic health—are most relevant for business discussions.

Declining Workforce Growth

Over the last twenty years, labor-force growth rates have been declining, and this decline is expected to continue for the next twenty years, into the 2020s.[17] This trend will have a substantial impact on the demand for goods and services as well as on the ability of society to supply those goods and services, and it will eventually put the brakes on economic growth.

Increasing Age of the Workforce

Over the next two decades, the U.S. population aged 55 and older will increase 73 percent, while the number of younger workers will grow by only 5 percent. As a result, the proportion of working-age people to retired people will be about half what it was in 1950. The resulting stress on social systems will be partially counterbalanced by a tendency for people to stay active in the workforce into their later years—partly in response to economic necessity, partly as a result of the more widespread health and vigor in older folks that are permitted by medical developments.

There is substantial economic need for people to stay active in the workforce: (1) to support the health and welfare programs they will require as they age, (2) to continue their contributions to national productivity, and (3) to drive demand for consumables. Because of the economic mandate for older people to work more in their later years than they have in the past, a number of provisions have been implemented to encourage them to remain active in the workforce, such as raising the retirement age for full Social Security benefits from 65 to 70. The general shift from defined benefit pension plans to defined contribution plans also reduces the incentives for early retirement. During the last decade, 90 percent of defined benefit plans specified that employees retire at 62 or earlier.[18] That percentage is beginning to decrease.

In addition to overall economic requirements and financial incentives, other factors are enabling older people to remain active workforce participants. As we move into the twenty-first century, older individuals are physically and psychologically healthier than they were a few years ago. The percentage of people over 65 with one or more chronic disabilities declined 5 percent over the past twenty years or so.[19] Meanwhile, employers are recognizing the desirability of older workers, who tend to be more flexible than workers with young families in terms of work schedules and work requirements. They represent an enormous volume of proven knowledge and skills, and can serve as effective developers and mentors of future talent as they transfer their skills to the next generation.

As a result of these inducements and incentives, we can expect an increase in workforce participation among the elderly. During the next decade, the percentage of individuals 65 to 74 years old that are active in the workforce is projected to increase from 14.8 percent to 17.3 percent.[20]

However, older workers also present a unique set of challenges to their employers. Older workers tend not to be as technologically current as their younger counterparts. They may be less flexible in their thought and behavior patterns. And they tend to be relatively more expensive. To address these obstacles, companies will need to make investments in updating the general as well as technical skills of older workers. They will also need to think through alternative job-sharing and job-transfer policies that will provide on-the-job skill development.

Many developed countries besides the United States are aging at a considerably faster rate due to the double impact of increased longevity and reduced birth rates. In Europe, for example, the overall birth rate has declined more than 50 percent to a low of 1.4 children per person. This results in a dramatic shift in the ratio of elderly to working-age adults. During the next fifty years, the ratio will more than double (from 21.7 to 51.4). In Japan, the ratio will almost triple (from 25.2 to 71.3). This translates into only 1.4 working adults for every elderly person. The number of elderly people per 100 working-age adults in developing countries will increase dramatically. In China the ratio will almost quadruple, from a relatively low 10 to a high of more than 37 older people for every 100 workers.

Europe is now beginning to take steps to encourage older workers to remain active in the workforce. These steps are politically unpopular, but they are occurring nonetheless. In 2003, Austria raised its retirement age for men from 61.5 to 65 years and for women from 56.5 to 60 years. In Germany, the effective retirement age has increased from 63 to 65 years.

Changing Gender Balance

Since 1950, men's workforce participation rates have declined steadily, while women's rates have increased. The decline is especially notable for older men. In 1948, 90 percent of men aged 55 to 65 were work-ing.[21] By the turn of the century, the proportion of working males in this age group had declined to 67 percent. Meanwhile, during this same time period, women from age 16 to 64 increased their workforce partic-ipation from 34 percent to 60 percent.

As women make up a greater proportion of the total workforce, their influence at all organizational levels is being felt. In 1995, 8.7 percent of *Fortune* 500 corporate officers were women. Currently, that number has risen approximately 64 percent. The U.S. Labor Department has reported that women hold 45 percent of managerial positions.[22] Yet women occupy only 5 percent of the CEO positions in U.S. public companies with net sales over $5 billion. This has at least four possible explanations. First, it may be that male-dominated boards continue to harbor the unverified view that women are unable to handle the intellectual and emotional demands of the top jobs. Second, the top jobs in most companies place extraordinary demands on the time and psychological reserves of their incumbents. It may be that women are more evenly balanced in their approaches to work, life, and family. For example, in business positions, females tend to work shorter work hours than males.[23] (It has been argued that this indicates that women require fewer hours per week to complete their work. Other explanations are also possible.) Third, women are disproportionately represented in staff positions such as HR, finance, and marketing. These positions do not provide the general management experiences necessary for senior line positions. Fourth, men may be more overtly aggressive in business settings. For example, Linda Babcock of Carnegie Mellon University found that male graduates with a master's degree earn 7.6 percent more than their female counterparts. Most of this difference can be attributed to the fact that only 7 percent of the women negotiated for pay greater than the initial offer, whereas 57 percent of the men did so.[24]

If performance in academic and extracurricular leadership experi-ences is indicative of future success, then women are likely to continue to achieve and prosper in senior management jobs. Women achieve 33 percent more bachelor's degrees than men, and 38 percent more master's degrees.[25] These numbers are expected to increase for at least the next decade. In both primary and secondary schools, girls tend to receive higher grades. Boys tend to score better on the SAT. However, much of the difference in SAT scores is accounted for by the fact that 10 percent fewer boys take the SAT, and those 10 percent tend to be boys who would have had lower scores on the SAT.[26] Currently, slightly more girls than boys are enrolling in high-level math and science courses. More boys are suspended from school. Seventy-three percent of children diagnosed with learning disabilities are male, and boys are 400 percent more likely to be on Ritalin or similar drugs.

The irony of these statistics is that the fear that prevailed in the mid-1990s—that girls were falling behind in academic achievement—turns out to be questionable. During those years, public school researchers, administrators, and teachers allocated considerable money, time, and attention to elevating girls to greater scholastic success. The data may indicate the need to allocate similar resources to help the boys. It is not a win-lose situation. Both boys and girls are the foundation of the economic future.

Increasing Ethnic Diversity

Whites will continue through the first half of the twenty-first century to be the largest segment of the U.S. population. However, that situation will change dramatically toward the middle of the century. By the year 2020, their numbers will have fallen to 63.3 percent, and by 2050 to 50.1 percent.[27] Hispanics will almost triple their proportion, from 6.4 percent of the population to 17 percent, as will Asia/Pacific Islanders (from 1.6 percent to 5.7 percent). The Asian population in the United States will more than double, to a total of 33 million. The African American population will pick up one percentage point, from 12 percent to 13 percent. Native Americans, who form the smallest segment of the population, will grow from 0.6 percent in 1980 to 0.8 percent in 2020.

It is clear that the social and economic influence of Hispanics will increase significantly.[28] Hispanics now make up 12 percent of the U.S. workforce. In two generations, that 12 percent will more than double to 25 percent. The family income for Hispanics averages around $33,000. This is well below the U.S. average of $42,000. However, over the past decade, Hispanic disposable income in the United States has increased approximately 46 percent. This rate of increase is double the pace of the rest of the U.S. population.

Deteriorating Family Economic Health

During the second half of the twentieth century, households inhabited by married couples slipped from 80 percent to 50.7 percent.[29] Thus, unmarried or single households are on the verge of defining the new majority. The traditional family structure is not only under social pressure; it is under economic pressure as well.[30] In the last quarter of the twentieth century, family bankruptcies increased 400 percent. Much of this was due to the loss of the cushion provided by normally unemployed mothers and wives, who could often find at least some income if the main breadwinner became unemployed. With mothers working full-time, the traditional economic buffer of middle-income families is now gone.

The Influence of Globalization

The world's labor forces are becoming more global in two ways.

Through Migration of People, Countries Are Becoming More Global

As people migrate across national boundaries, the demographic makeup of countries becomes more global. Cross-border movement of labor tends to be from south to north, from poor to wealthy, and from less stable to more stable. In recent years, 175 million people, or 3 percent of the global population, lived in countries different from the ones where they were born. One out of ten people in developed countries and one out of seventy people in developing countries are immigrants. And the percentages are increasing.

Through the Migration of Work, Companies Are Becoming More Global

The dominant globalization of labor is not through the migration of people but through the migration of work from one country to another, either from the organizing of work on a global scale or from the outsourcing of work to nondomestic locations. Organizing in-house work on a global scale allows companies to increase their speed, quality, and efficiency and to implement 24/7 work processes. Work that is started in the United States is passed to Europe, on to Asia, and then back again—sequentially and continually. Companies are also increasingly moving work to offshore subcontractors, wholly owned foreign subsidiaries, or large-scale offshore suppliers. This has become one of the dominant trends in business in the first decade of the twenty-first century. However, it is useful to remember that there have been at least four waves of labor offshoring since World War II:

- *1960–1975.* Exodus of low-skill jobs such as the production of toys, inexpensive electronics, and leather goods

- *1975–1990.* Exodus of simple service work such as the writing of software and the processing of credit card receipts

- *1990–2000.* Movement of knowledge work to anywhere on earth where people are intellectually capable and where cost advantage exists

- *1995–today.* Movement of any work that can be digitized to any countries that have skill, knowledge, and an Internet connection

Industrialized countries have adjusted their labor markets to be consistent with these trends in the past. The adjustments have not been without substantial pain for those who had to move their jobs or change their careers, but over time the industrialized nations have been economically better off for having done so. Nations that have resisted such labor market flexibility have not thrived.

Estimating the numbers of outsourced jobs requires a bit of guesswork. Most informed estimates are that 100,000 U.S. service jobs went offshore in 2000. That number will increase to 1.6 million by 2012, and to 3.3 million by 2015.[31] Jobs to be outsourced run the full gamut of service vocations, including financial analysis, office and technical support, sales, middle management, architecture, legal services, art and design, life sciences, and general business. Especially hard hit will be IT jobs such as software development, reengineering, maintenance, documentation, telephone support, remote network monitoring, systems management, and administration and operations.

Currently, 5 percent of U.S. firms with sales above $100 million were engaged in offshoring or had immediate plans for doing so. That number is expected to grow dramatically. Some examples:

- Fluor Corporation employs 1,200 engineers and draftsmen in the Philippines to turn layouts of large-scale industrial facilities into detailed specs and blueprints.

- Procter & Gamble (P&G) employs 650 people in Manila to assist in the processing of its tax returns from around the world.

- Bank of America has moved 3,700 of its 25,000 technical support and head office jobs to India, where the wages are $20/hour instead of the $100/hour they would cost in the United States.

Educational Advantage

Productivity and innovation are critical sources of comparative advantage for U.S. companies, and both are directly linked to the educational level of its workforce. A 10 percent increase in the average education of workers is associated with an 8.6 percent increase in productivity.[32] But the advantage that the United States has had in education over other countries is shrinking.

In spite of robust U.S. educational college and high school completion rates and a high proportion of GDP expenditures on education, the country falls in the middle of the G-8 members relative to performance on standardized achievement tests in reading, mathematics, and science. Obviously, how long a person goes to school is irrelevant when compared to what a person has learned during the years in school. One likely explanation for this problem is the fact that the United States has the greatest average spread on achievement tests of G-8 countries. The ninety-fifth percentile of U.S. students represents the highest standardized test achievement of equivalent percentile students among G-8 countries, but the fifth percentile of U.S. students represents the lowest.

The United States is generally acknowledged as having the highest-quality colleges and universities in the world.[33] Increasingly, the proportion of nonnative graduate students in U.S. universities is increasing. One important boon to the U.S. economy is the fact that 70 percent of foreign-born individuals who receive their PhD's in U.S. universities remain in the country for long-term employment.[34]

What HR Professionals Need to Know About Workforce Demographics

To contribute to management team discussions about the human component of work, HR professionals need to know the basic trends relative to these issues and where they can find current information. They need to back up generalizations about basic trends with specific data. With this knowledge, they may then

- Add value to strategic discussions about workforce planning.

- Understand the demographic forces that influence their firms directly as well as those that influence them indirectly through customers, shareholders, management, and employees.

- Align their HR strategies and practices to HR's key constituents in a timely and accurate manner.

Assessment 2-3 contains a self-evaluation of the knowledge that an HR professional might need to have about workforce demographics.

ASSESSMENT 2-3

Knowledge of workforce demographics

| | To what extent do I have this knowledge? | | | | |
	Low				*High*
1. What demographic trends influence the labor supply for my industry?	1	2	3	4	5
2. How can we better hire and use women leaders?	1	2	3	4	5
3. How do we identify and accommodate key contributors who are immigrants educated in the United States?	1	2	3	4	5
4. How can we maintain the experience and knowledge of retired workers?	1	2	3	4	5
5. How does the reduction in numbers of traditional families influence my industry?	1	2	3	4	5
6. What training do our immigrant and aging workers need to be more able contributors?	1	2	3	4	5
7. How do we create an inclusive environment for the nontraditional workforce?	1	2	3	4	5

Total

Total your scores and compare to the following interpretation scale.

30–35: Impressive. You are at the top. Write a case study.
25–29: You know a lot and add value in business discussions.
20–24: You have opportunities to add greater value through greater knowledge.
15–19: Read more to stay current.
Less than 15: A way to go to add the value that you should.

Resources Regarding Workforce Demographics

With some degree of regularity, many popular business publications provide overview articles pertaining to workforce demographics and other labor trends: *BusinessWeek*, the *Economist*, *Forbes*, *Fortune*, *Inc.*, *Financial Times*, *Handelsblatt*, and the *Wall Street Journal*. Many journals and popular magazines abound from every global region: *Ageing and Society*, *American Demographics*, *Demography*, *Demographic Research*, *Profiles in Diversity Journal*, *Gender and Society*, *Human Resource Management Journal*, *International Journal of Diversity in Organisations*, *Communities and Nations*, *International Migration Review*, *International Migration*, *Journal of Cultural Diversity*, *Journal of Ethnic & Cultural Diversity in Social Work*, *Journal of Labor Research*, *Journal of Population Economics*, *Journal of Population Research*, *Monthly Labor Review*, *Population and Development Review*, *Review of Population Reviews*, *Society*, and *Women and Work*. Ample Web sites on various aspects of demographics contain statistics, statistical summaries and conceptual reviews: CensusScope.org. (census data), www.clusterbigip1.claritas.com (segmented population data), fedstats. gov (statistics from the U.S. government), prb.org (summary population data), BLS.gov (Bureau of Labor Statistics), Demography.anu.edu.au (demographics and population studies), gksoft.com/govt (government studies), esa.un.org (United Nations population studies), Libr.org/wss/ WSSLinks (gender studies), and Sciencedirect.com (general portal for scientific research).

Business Realities and HR Responses

In today's fast-changing world, it is imperative that HR professionals be "at the table." This requires more than simple familiarity with HR issues or internal operations; it requires knowledge about the driving forces that shape the fundamental nature of business. For credibility, HR professionals must not only understand the logic of the external trends, they must also have data to back up their positions and must know where to find such data. The key areas that frame much of today's business realities include technology, economic trends, demographics, and the global environment in which each of these exist. With this knowledge foundation, HR professionals are prepared to begin the discussions about customers, shareholders, management, and employees.

3

External Stakeholders

Investors and Customers

To what extent does our HR work link to the
intangibles that investors value?

To what extent do we use HR practices to build long-term
connections with target customers?

I MAGINE THIS: Dan Bennett returns from an HR conference full of ideas for a new initiative (in performance management, say), assembles a task force, and implements the program companywide. After some initial resistance, the ideas take hold, and the program becomes part of the way HR does its work. Dan declares victory, and the design team delightedly moves on to the next new thing. Sounds ideal, doesn't it?

When we tell this kind of tale, people tend to snort and say, "Nothing ever goes that smoothly." True, we say, but even if it did, would it be a success story? And the answer we get is generally *yes*.

We disagree. Dan's adventure is an ideal case of a false positive, something that sounds successful but is at best incomplete. The success of an HR initiative should be measured not by how well its design and implementation go but by what the initiative does for the organization's key stakeholders. HR actions create value only when they create a sustainable competitive advantage.

As discussed in chapter 1, competitive advantage comes from the marketplace. Sales or research and development (R&D) creates competitive

45

advantage when customers buy your product. Improvements in logistics or technology become a competitive advantage when customers notice benefits in cost and service—and buy your product. And you have proof of competitive advantage when increased revenue translates to increased share price.

In a boundaryless and borderless world, what happens inside an organization—HR included—must connect with what goes on outside. Changes in HR can help create employee commitment, which in turn creates customer commitment, which in turn boosts financial results. This finding has been replicated in many companies and industries (Sears, GTE, Cardinal Health, IBM). Internal focus may lead to efficiency but not effectiveness. McDonald's may continuously improve its production of hamburgers and french fries, but all the efficiency in the world will not create competitive advantage for hamburgers and french fries if consumers are shifting toward healthier food.

HR work should likewise be judged, in part at least, by the outcomes it creates for external stakeholders. By creating a line of sight from its practices to external stakeholders, HR makes itself more relevant. HR professionals who look outside first can then tailor their actions to results that matter to two primary external stakeholders: investors and customers.

Investors and HR

Investors ultimately care about total shareholder return or market value. For publicly traded firms, the stock price represents how investors value both current and future earnings. For public agencies, privately held firms, and nonprofits, external value is harder to specify but still measurable via bond ratings, donation levels, and political goodwill. We focus on publicly traded firms in showing how HR should add value for investors, but similar arguments could be made for any organization. HR professionals can take six actions to link their work to stakeholder value:

1. Become investor literate.

2. Understand the importance of intangibles.

3. Create HR practices that increase intangible value.

4. Highlight the importance of intangible value to total shareholder return.

5. Design and deliver intangibles audits.

6. Align HR practices and investors' requirements.

In taking these six actions, HR professionals move out of their comfort zones and partner with other staff experts. For example, in linking organization actions to investor results, HR teams up with those in investor relations to prepare materials for the investor community. When they invite investors to participate in HR practices, they need to understand investor expectations and show that investor understanding of HR practices will help investors make more informed investment decisions. Weaving HR into investor relations starts with becoming "investor literate," so that those in investor relations trust the HR professional to engage appropriately with investors.

Investor Literacy

For HR professionals to deliver value to investors, they must first learn who is investing in their organization—and why. Consider this investor literacy test:

- Who are your five major shareholders and what percentage does each of them own?

- Why do they own your stock? What are their investing criteria (i.e., dividends, growth, and so on)?

- What is your tangible value? And your intangible value?

- What is your price/earnings (P/E) ratio for the last decade, and how does it compare to your industry average and to the firm with the highest P/E ratio in your industry?

- Who are the top analysts who follow your industry? How do they view your company compared to your competition?

Few senior HR executives can answer all these questions—and we've asked them many times. Yet these questions form the base of knowledge that will enable HR professionals to link their work to investor value.

Investor literacy also includes attention to corporate governance. With corporate malfeasance increasingly drawing media and legislative attention—and investor ire—HR professionals should be aware of governance processes within the firm. This includes knowledge of legislation like Sarbanes-Oxley, which prescribes board and leadership behavior, and assessments like that from Institutional Shareholder Services, which rates corporate governance. But it also includes focusing on how well your board governs itself on processes essential for good board governance, such as managing dissent, reaching consensus, and focusing on the right issues.

The Importance of Intangibles

Firms with higher earnings ought to have higher stock prices. This intuitively sensible proposition has led to rigorous standards in codifying and comparing earnings (as in the policies of the Financial Accounting Standards Board and the U.S. Securities and Exchange Commission). But the situation is changing. Accounting professors Baruch Lev and Paul Zarowin at New York University report that the regression between earnings and shareholder value was between 75 percent and 90 percent from 1960 through 1990.[1] That is, 75–90 percent of a firm's market value (stock price times shares outstanding) could be predicted by its financial performance. Since 1990, however, this figure has dropped to about 50 percent in both up and down markets—meaning that half the market value of a firm is not directly tied to present earnings. Instead, it is tied to what the financial community calls *intangibles*. Intangibles represent value derived from choices about what happens inside the firm and from how investors value those decisions, rather than from its physical assets.

Intangibles can be observed outside business. Successful sports teams have them: the quality of coaching, the ability to win, and the like. Restaurants have the setting, reputation, and atmosphere of committed service. Government agencies have political goodwill and access to political support and budget allocations. For any organization, intangibles are the perceived outcomes of specific actions.

It is all too easy to focus intangible value on what is easy to measure—investments in R&D, technology, or brand—but that leaves crucial intangibles, involving investments in organization and people, under the radar. Organizations and people become intangible assets when they give investors confidence in future, tangible earnings, and this is an area where HR can make a major contribution.

Support for Practices That Build Value

With the intent of making intangibles tangible, we have proposed a pattern of techniques that increase organizational intangibles, beginning

TABLE 3-1

Architecture for intangibles

Level	Area of focus	Action potential
1	Keep your promises.	Build and defend a reputation among external and internal stakeholders for doing what you say you will do.
2	Imagine the future while investing in the present.	Define growth strategy and manage trade-offs in customer intimacy, product innovation, and geographic expansion to achieve growth.
3	Put your money where your strategy is.	Provide concrete support for intangibles by building core competencies in R&D, sales and marketing, manufacturing, and the like.
4	Build value through organization and people.	Develop capabilities of shared mindset, talent, speed, collaboration, leadership, accountability, learning, and the like throughout the organization.

with the basic essentials at level 1 and proceeding to more complex concepts. We call this the *architecture for intangibles*, as illustrated in table 3-1.[2]

This architecture is progressive and sequential. And at every level, HR practices can be integral to success—helping leaders behave in ways that engender trust and promote learning and communication among internal stakeholders, making them more likely to behave in ways that engage and delight external stakeholders.

But HR really adds value at level 4 by defining and creating capabilities as intangibles. This shifts HR from a focus on just people to organizations where people work. Traditionally, organizations have been characterized by their visible hierarchy and structure or by their work processes. Recently, however, the study of organizations has shifted focus from structure and processes to capabilities.[3] *Organization capabilities* represent the capacity of an organization to use resources, get things done, and behave in ways that accomplish goals. They characterize how people think and behave in the context of the organization. They form the organization's identity or personality. Capabilities define what the organization does well and, in the end, what it is.

Organizations can be viewed as bundles of capabilities—and not just by researchers. External stakeholders and even casual observers see the same things. When we ask people to identify firms they admire, we often hear names such as Microsoft, Nordstrom, or GE. We then ask how many layers of management each firm has—and (unsurprisingly) no one knows or cares. But when we ask the reasons for their admiration, people quickly pinpoint capabilities such as the ability to innovate or to deliver high-quality customer experiences. These responses capture the transition from the age-old adage "structure follows strategy" to "capabilities follow strategy." With this logic, an effective organization is defined less by structure than by the capabilities that enable it to respond to business demands.

An organization's capabilities are the deliverables from HR efforts. These capabilities enhance (or reduce) investor confidence in future earnings and increase (or decrease) market capitalization. HR professionals who link their work to capabilities and who then find ways to communicate those capabilities to investors deliver shareholder value. Mark Huselid, Brian Becker, and Richard Beatty found that firms with speed, talent, learning, shared mindset, innovation, and accountability capabilities significantly outperformed lower-capability firms in productivity, profitability, and shareholder value.[4]

Firms differ so much that no one can produce a magic list of universally desirable or ideal capabilities. However, table 3-2 captures a subset of capabilities that do seem to be inherent in well-managed firms.[5]

Clearly, qualities such as efficiency, collaboration, talent, and speed are not the only capabilities an organization may require, but they illustrate the types of capabilities that make intangibles tangible. They delight customers; they engage employees; they establish reputations among investors; and they provide long-term sustainable value. HR professionals should be architects and thought leaders in defining and creating each of these capabilities.

Education in the Value of Intangibles

Intangibles need to be presented in the financial terms that leaders understand. Here are three visual exercises that highlight the importance of intangibles and spotlight HR's impact on shareholder value.

Earnings and Shareholder Value

To put the whole question of intangibles in context, go through the last ten or fifteen years of your firm's results and plot (1) earnings and (2) stock price (or total market capitalization) by quarter. This chart will show whether market value is above or below the earnings line—that is, whether the firm has a net positive or negative intangible reputation.

TABLE 3-2

Capabilities of exemplar companies

Capability	Definition	Exemplar company
Talent	We are good at attracting, motivating, and retaining competent and committed people.	Hitachi McKinsey Microsoft
Speed	We are good at making important changes happen fast.	Dell Samsung Toshiba
Shared mindset	We are good at ensuring that customers and employees have positive images of and experiences with our organization.	Harley-Davidson Nordstrom UBS
Accountability	We are good at the disciplines that result in high performance.	Continental Airlines Honeywell Total
Collaboration	We are good at working across boundaries to ensure both efficiency and leverage.	BP Ericsson Time Warner
Learning	We are good at generating and generalizing ideas with impact.	BAE Toyota Unilever
Leadership	We are good at embedding leaders throughout the organization who deliver the right results in the right way—who carry our leadership brand.	Cathay Pacific General Electric Hewlett-Packard
Customer connection	We are good at building enduring relationships of trust with targeted customers.	Harrah's Marriott Nippon Telegraph & Telephone
Innovation	We are good at doing something new in both content and process.	3M Herman Miller Intel
Strategic unity	We are good at articulating and sharing a strategic point of view.	Hallmark ICICI Bank
Efficiency	We are good at managing costs of operation.	SKF Southwest Airlines Wal-Mart

Price/Earnings Ratio Race

How do your firm's intangibles compare to those of your competition? For ten or fifteen years' worth of results, plot your firm's quarterly P/E ratio against that of your most successful competitor. This trend line offers an overall report card on how investors perceive your firm and its leading competitor. Once when we tried this, we found that a firm had a P/E ratio consistently 20 percent below that of its largest competitor. Investors were less confident in the firm's management team than in the competitors', and the gap persisted over time. This firm's market value was about $20 billion at the time, implying that reputation had cost the firm about $4 billion. The management team did not like the insight, but they could not run away from it.

Management View of Impact of Organization and People

Sometimes, making leaders' assumptions explicit helps frame a dialogue on HR and shareholder value. Give each member of the top management team a blank graph showing shareholder value on one axis and quality of organization and people (HR) on the other. Ask each member of the management team to plot their assumptions. Share the responses and talk about the implications of the slopes of the lines. Some will have a flat line (regardless of HR quality, shareholder value does not go up), but more often we generally find ratios in the 3:2 or 2:1 range (every three points of organization results in two points in shareholder value). With this data, you can lead a discussion about how much HR issues matter in leaders' perceptions of shareholder value. Without having to "prove the case," leaders implicitly believe that increasing the quality of people and organization will lead to shareholder value.

Intangibles Audits

An *intangibles audit* assesses what is necessary to deliver investor value given an organization unit's history and strategy, measures how well intangibles are being delivered, and leads to an action plan for improvement. Assessment 3-1 shows a sample template for an intangibles audit (for more information, go to http://www.rbl.net/Survey/intangibles.html). This self-assessment tool helps HR leaders evaluate their organizations on four core dimensions: (1) keeping promises, (2) growth strategy, (3) core competence, and (4) organization capabilities covering eleven possible strengths. Many organizations have adapted this template with productive results. HR professionals can be the prime mover for these audits as they collaborate with other staff experts and prepare information for business leaders.

ASSESSMENT 3-1

Intangibles audit

Directions: Select an organization unit (plant, division, region, zone, business, company) and answer the following questions.

Intangible	Questions	Assessment Low High
Level 1: keeping promises	To what extent do we keep promises to investors by delivering consistent and predictable earnings?	1 2 3 4 5
	To what extent do we keep promises to customers with our products and services?	1 2 3 4 5
	To what extent do we keep promises to employees with opportunities and expectations?	1 2 3 4 5
Level 2: growth strategy	To what extent have we articulated a primary growth strategy (customer intimacy, product or service innovation, or geographic expansion)?	1 2 3 4 5
	To what extent do our decisions align with this primary growth strategy?	1 2 3 4 5
	To what extent do stakeholders (investors, customers, employees) understand our primary growth strategy?	1 2 3 4 5
Level 3: core competence	To what extent do we have the right core competencies to deliver our strategy?	1 2 3 4 5
	To what extent do we invest in the core competencies most relevant to our growth strategy?	1 2 3 4 5
	To what extent do our leaders demonstrate support of our investments in building companywide technical core competencies rather than optimizing their own area?	1 2 3 4 5
Level 4: organization capabilities	Given the firm's strategy and core competencies, assess your current performance for each organization capability; then rank the eleven according to which needs most improvement.	

		Rank	*Assessment*
1. Talent	To what extent do employees in the organization have the competencies required to deliver the strategy and to what extent are they committed to it?	____	1 2 3 4 5
2. Speed	To what extent are we able to move quickly to make important things happen fast?	____	1 2 3 4 5

continued

Intangibles audit *(continued)*

		Rank	Assessment
3. Shared mindset	To what extent does our organization have a culture or identity that reflects what we stand for and how we work that is shared by both customers and employees?	___	1 2 3 4 5
4. Accountability	To what extent are we able to ensure execution though a mindset that high performance matters here?	___	1 2 3 4 5
5. Collaboration	To what extent is our organization able to collaborate in ways that gain both efficiency and leverage?	___	1 2 3 4 5
6. Learning	To what extent are we able to generate new ideas with impact and generalize those ideas across boundaries?	___	1 2 3 4 5
7. Leadership	To what extent do we have a brand for leadership that directs leaders on what results to deliver and how to deliver them?	___	1 2 3 4 5
8. Customer connection	To what extent do we build enduring relationships of trust with key customers?	___	1 2 3 4 5
9. Innovation	To what extent do we innovate in content (product, strategy) and process (administrative work)?	___	1 2 3 4 5
10. Strategic unity	To what extent do we have a clear strategic point of view?	___	1 2 3 4 5
11. Efficiency	To what extent do we manage costs of operation?	___	1 2 3 4 5

Total Score

Interpretation:

Overall:

80+: You have fantastic intangibles and simply need to keep it up.
65-79: Doing well, but should be careful.
50-64: Need some work; might look for areas of weakness.
35-49: In some trouble and your stock is probably undervalued.
Under 34: Good news is you have a lot of upside and can start almost anywhere; bad news is you have to.
Specific—Levels of intangibles:
Examine the scores in each of the four levels and see which level is strongest and weakest. Generally, improvement is cumulative, beginning with level 1 and working through level 4.

Specific—Level 4:
Look at the rank order of your intangibles and see which ones are in best and worst shape. This will give you a sense of where to start with your capabilities and HR deliverables.

Interpretation and Use

To perform an intangibles audit, go through the following five steps:

1. Decide whether the audit should occur in the entire organization, a business unit, region, or plant. Remember that although HR can architect the audit, the unit leadership must own and sponsor it. For example, if you want to audit the entire company, you need the board of directors or senior executives to sponsor the effort. HR would seldom do an intangibles audit without support from business leaders and collaboration of other staff experts.

2. Create the content of the audit (i.e., the dimensions to be audited). Assessment 3-1 lists generic questions that describe each of the four levels of intangible value. Recast these questions into words and phrases that will make sense to people in the organization. Involve those from other staff functions like finance to help you tailor the questions to your organization.

3. Collect data on the current and desired status of the intangibles being assessed. This information may be collected by degrees:

   • *90 degree.* Collect data from the leadership team of the unit being audited. This gets quick results but is often deceptive; the leadership team's self-report may be biased.

   • *360 degree.* Collect data from many groups within the company. Such assessments can tell very different stories, depending on how each group sees the information.

   • *720 degree.* Collect information not only from inside the company but from outsiders: investors, customers, suppliers, or regulators. These external groups matter because they are the groups who ultimately determine if the organization has intangible value.

4. Synthesize the data to identify the intangibles requiring managerial attention. Create a summary score by averaging the items for each of the four levels to determine your performance at each level. Scores 4–5 suggest that you are doing a good job and need to be sustained; 3 means that you have areas to work on; and 2 or below indicates that your intangibles are detracting

value. Look for patterns in the data: for example, do all rating groups consistently rate you low in one area? Pick action items that require leadership attention to deliver strategy goals. Identify which intangibles will have the most impact and be easiest to implement.

5. Share the results with investors. The report will give investors confidence not only in past and present earnings and in the firm's ability to produce future earnings, but also in the firm's ability to be self aware. HR professionals who design and deliver these intangibles audits add value for the investment community. Initially, peers in other departments may be hesitant or resistant, but when they see that this information helps create investor confidence, their concerns will turn to support.

Alignment Between HR and Investor Requirements

Traditionally, HR practices focus on dynamics inside the organization. When HR professionals take investors' desires into account, their practices can develop a more value-focused meaning. In the next few sections, we suggest ways that HR practice might align with investors. Selecting one or two ideas from the following illustrations might become a starting point in building investor-focused HR practices. Again, these practices would be crafted by partnering with staff experts who know and understand investor expectations and behaviors.

Investors and Staffing

What if the investors could vote on individuals hired or promoted in the firm? In some limited cases, investors do so through the surrogate voice of the board. But what if some of the large institutional investors actually participated in interviews for senior officers? What questions would they ask? What leadership and management qualities would they look for? What types of individuals would convince them that the management team was able to make correct decisions? Or, alternatively, what if institutional investors reviewed competence models used as candidate screens in the hiring process? Would an institutional investor focus on the same attributes as the traditional hiring manager? Or would the interview questions be different?

HR professionals should seek ways to engage targeted investors in hiring and promotion decisions. Using investor criteria and participation in the staffing process brings a rigor and discipline that is often overlooked. In addition, if investors participate in the selection of the management team, they may be more committed to this team's decisions and choices.

Investors and Training and Development

Assume someone representing your largest single investor sat through the last five-day leadership program your firm offered. What would be their investment response (buy, hold, sell) at the end of the week?

This question imposes a new filter on what is taught, how it is taught, and what participants in training leave with at the end of the week. We predict that most investors would be more positive if participants focused on real business issues within their firm rather than case studies of other firms; faced competitive realities in candid conversation; and, as a result of the training experience, left with a vision of clear and specific actions to take. That sort of training would show investors that the leadership team knows what needs to be done, understands strategic choices, and is willing to make and implement bold decisions. In addition, we predict that investors would relish candid dialogue and disagreement before reaching consensus on what to do. Many of the training dollars currently spent would not lead to "buy" recommendations, because the link between training activities and business results is obscure at best.

Investors and Appraisal and Rewards

Many firms already tie management behaviors to investor-focused rewards. Putting a larger percentage of total compensation into stock-based incentives (grants, options, and the like) links management actions to investors. Many claim that CEO pay relative to average employee pay is excessive. Such arguments are less tenable when CEO pay is linked to long-term stock price. The boundary between managers and investors is removed when managers become investors through stock ownership programs. In addition, the wider and deeper the investment mindset throughout a firm, the more managers act and think like investors.

We had a chance to work with a firm going through a leveraged buyout. To keep their jobs, managers were required to invest from $100,000 to $5 million cash in the new firm. The changes in mindset and action patterns were dramatic. The new owner-managers stopped flying three people to visit a customer when one would do. Instead of holding conferences at five-star hotels, they used company facilities. Instead of making visits to plan visits, they used phones and faxes for preliminary work. Literally thousands of decisions were made differently under the new regime. When managers act as both owners and agents, they respond differently.

Institutional investors might examine the firm's compensation philosophy and practices. In theory, board members act on behalf of the owners, but institutional investors might become more active by reviewing standards set in performance appraisals, compensation practices used to change behavior, and feedback mechanisms used to share information.

Investors and Governance and Communication

Investors in publicly traded firms have traditionally been hands-off. They do not participate in teams, help develop processes, or set and accomplish strategies. However, when investors realize that the intangibles predict as much of the shareholder value as financial performance does, their interests may change. They will start looking at how well the organization makes decisions, allocates responsibilities, and meets commitments. Peter Lynch, the savvy and well-known investor, has suggested smart investors recognize firms that provide customers what they want (such as Toys "R" Us).

As these and other HR practices are applied through an investor filter, investors gain confidence in the organization's ability to deliver future earnings.

Customers and HR

Keeping a customer is more profitable than attracting a new one.[6] With ever-expanding global competition, however, today's customers tend to be both demanding and exacting, so keeping them requires ongoing, across-the-board attention.

Long-term customer loyalty to a product or service develops as people have consistently positive experiences with the firm and as the firm meets their expectations. If their expectations are not met, continued loyalty depends on whether problems are resolved quickly.[7] The customer experience is often based on perceptions of *reliability* (dependability and accuracy), *responsiveness* (promptness of service), *assurance* (trust and confidence), *empathy* (personal care and attention), and *presentation* (appearance of facilities and personnel).[8] All these perceptions derive from employee behavior, and that means that all are opportunities for

HR to contribute to the bottom line. We suggest five specific things HR professionals know and do to improve customer experiences:

1. Develop customer literacy.

2. Think and act like a customer.

3. Measure and track the firm's share of targeted customers and the customer value proposition.

4. Align HR practices to the customer value proposition.

5. Engage target customers in HR practices.

In connecting with customers, HR does not replace marketing and sales, but collaborates with them. HR translates customer expectations into employee behavior, which helps meet and exceed those expectations. As such, marketing research is not just about the nature of the market, but about how to respond to the market. When HR knows customers, they can help with that response.

Develop Customer Literacy

Some customers—to echo Orwell's telling phrase—are more equal than others. This is obvious, but few HR professionals can identify which customers matter most to their employers. Customer literacy begins with knowing the customers and their buying criteria. Which customers represent 80 percent of your firm's revenues and profits? These are the target customers who should be the focal point of your firm's activities. They are the customers whose loyalty and intimacy you want. They should be uppermost on the mind of every employee.

Once the target customers are known, it is critical to determine their buying criteria. Why do they purchase from you as opposed to your competitors? What is unique about your offering that consistently attracts target customers? What combination of service, value, reputation, product features, innovation, or quality keeps them coming back? HR professionals are ideally placed to find and present this information, along with equally interesting information about what employees in various departments *think* customers want.

This kind of information allows a firm to turn customer buying criteria into visible actions that customers will experience. Once employees know what customers value, they can concentrate on those values, which, in turn, makes customers more likely to have a positive experience. At Burger King, for example, HR identified purchase criteria, then turned these ideas into specific behaviors that customer contact employees should master. Employees show customer friendliness by smiling, maintaining eye contact, and saying thank you. They anticipate customer needs by providing extras before being requested, by taking corrective action on the spot, and by running the express line at busy times. They monitor quality of service by filling each order in less than three minutes. Customer criteria become employee behaviors.

HR professionals should be able to pass a customer literacy test with questions such as:

- Who are the five major buyers in the markets you serve?

- Who are your firm's five major customers?

- If the market includes major potential customers who do not buy from you, why not? What is the customer value proposition of your competitor that attracts and keeps these customers?

- Why do your target customers buy from you? What are their buying criteria?

- What do your potential target customers like better about your competitors than about you?

- How do you ensure that your target customers have a positive customer experience?

- What do you do to build connectivity or intimacy with your target customers?

Knowing this information allows you to collaborate with customer contact personnel.

Think and Act Like a Customer

Customer literacy defines who the customers are and why they are buying from you. A positive customer experience ensures that they will continue to buy from you. For HR professionals to fully appreciate customer experience, they must learn to think and act like customers. Ask yourself, If I were a customer of this business, would I like being treated the way we treat our customers? If I were anticipating a purchase and could choose among several vendors, would I pick my firm?

Now think like a competitor—what are the weak links of this firm's offering that a rival would go after? By asking what-if questions, an HR professional can begin to imagine the firm through the eyes of a customer. This will lead to better customer experiences and increase the likelihood that they will continue to buy from you.

To fully see the firm through the eyes of customers, it is important to put yourself in the customers' shoes. Buy your own firm's products without telling anyone where you work. Attend trade shows where you can talk with customers or go where customers buy products and watch them in action. Use competing products to see how customers fare with them. Join sales reps for their calls on key accounts. Activities like these probably aren't in your job description or within your expectations, but they will help you see what your firm's customers really care about. They will also bond you with customer contact people who may be hesitant to involve HR in customer relations.

Measure and Track Customer Results

Customer share—the proportion of the target customer population buying from your firm and not from your competitors—is replacing market share as the key measure of success. It provides a direct indicator of your firm's reputation among its best customers—and it doesn't just happen. Instead, it is driven by relationship management with targeted customers. And HR professionals have the ideal skills, background, and position to assist in developing these relationships. By encouraging organized steps designed to ensure that target customers have a positive experience with the firm and then tracking and reporting the results, HR professionals can have a direct positive impact on customer share and ultimately, on the bottom line.

Up-Selling and Cross-Selling

Gaining customer share means selling additional products and services to existing customers within the domain of the firm. For example, Disney cross-sells products in its theme parks and stores—that is, employees in the theme parks recommend Disney products, and employees in Disney stores recommend Disney theme parks. HR professionals charged with orientation and training can help employees know and discuss the array of products offered by a firm and help them understand how to sell its full range of products or services.

Constant Customer Feedback

To please customers, employees need to know how customers react to their experience with your firm. HR can step in and work with marketing specialists to help develop ways to identify, gather, and distribute concrete customer data. At one retail chain, for example, HR was part of the team that designed a system to track customer experience by asking purchasers these questions:

- Overall, how satisfied were you with your shopping experience?

- How reliable was the employee who helped you?

- How responsive was the employee who helped you?

- How much empathy did the employee who helped you demonstrate?

These items then formed an index of overall customer satisfaction. In addition, each sales receipt identified the employee who worked with the customer, and the retailer prepared a monthly customer experience score for each employee. Despite occasional efforts to bias the results (by urging customers to give positive answers), the index provided useful information on employee performance. For the first six months of the system's operation, the data was simply shared with employees each month; then it became part of the formal performance review system.

Another firm asks executives to work a couple of hours a month at the 1-800 service call center. Participating executives not only see summaries of call data but actually answer calls, giving them a firsthand sense of the patterns of customer responses. Other mechanisms for creating a constant flow of customer feedback include mystery shoppers in retail, customer follow-up surveys or phone calls, and customer focus groups.

HR professionals can participate in the design teams for all these types of customer feedback efforts. In the process, they should pay particular attention to how the customer data translates into changes in employee behavior patterns and corporate policies.

Tailored Customer Value Proposition

Mass customization gives each customer a personal value proposition. For example, by combining size and style variants, Levi Strauss has about 1.5 million options for a pair of pants. The company makes it possible for customers to order based on their own measurements and style choices rather than choosing from the necessarily limited selection of ready-made product, boosting their chance of having pants that fit and look the way they want. As a result, they are more likely to buy most of their current and future pants from Levi Strauss.

HR professionals can help create a mass customization mindset through communication programs about the importance of tailored customer service; by monitoring customer data and making sure it translates into employee behavior; and by designing customization into performance management programs.

Employee Accountability for Customer Share

When each employee feels responsible for customer share, customer share goes up. HR programs should include the satisfaction of target customers as one of the indicators of employee performance. In addition, they should offer rewards and recognition for outstanding employee service. The more effective these measures are in getting the message across, the more powerfully they will instill accountability for customer share.

Align HR Practices to the Customer Value Proposition

The best HR practices are the ones designed to meet the needs of customers and ensure that they have a positive experience. That is, HR needs to make sure that the firm's employee selection, development, reward, and communication programs all work to encourage the skills needed for customer satisfaction. Such HR practices will build customer loyalty over time (see chapters 5 and 6 for details of these HR practices).

Staffing and the Customer Value Proposition

We once asked a senior executive team, "If the customers could hire twenty officers to run the firm, would they be willing to hire the twenty of you?"

Someone answered, "How could they do that? They don't know who we are."

We suggested they think about this comment, pointing out what was going on inside the firm might not be well enough connected to what was going on outside it. Customer values, after all, should permeate all phases of talent flow, beginning with the criteria for hiring and promotion. What would a customer want to see more of or less of in behaviors of employees in the firm? What skills, values, and norms would customers want key employees to have? If the criteria that brought the executive group to their current positions included the things that target customers value, then, yes, they could all be reasonably sure that the customers would find them acceptable.

Training and the Customer Value Proposition

If customers attended a training event, how would they feel about the content being taught? Would they say that the training event helped employees gain value-adding skills? Would they be willing to pay for the event? In essence, customers do pay for training, albeit indirectly. Yet too often, training and development experiences are created without careful consideration of customer criteria.

Measures and Rewards and the Customer Value Proposition

Standards for what employees should be, know, do, and deliver need to reflect customer expectations and enhance customer experiences. Too often, however, standards are focused inside and not outside the organization. If customers were to review one of your firm's performance appraisal forms, how would they react? Would meeting the explicit standards and measures mean that employees will have provided good customer experiences?

Rewards can also be aligned to customer expectations. Employee bonuses, for example, may be tied to customer experience ratings (loyalty, satisfaction, customer share). And don't limit the process to financial rewards; nonfinancial rewards may well have more lasting impact. For example, consider allowing customers to honor exceptional employee service—as defined by the customer.

Communication and Governance and the Customer Value Proposition

The best brand is the one that works both inside and outside the company, sending consistent messages about what the company stands for. One high-tech firm went so far as to encourage employees to share its core values with target customers—integrity, respect for individuals, teamwork, innovation, and contribution to customers and the community. That may sound somewhat generic, but the firm also encouraged employees to ask customers to define what employees should do to embody these ideals—and to bring the replies back so that procedures could be designed to accommodate them. The quality of employee and customer communications may be measured by the percentage of both employees and customers who feel that the company hears and responds to their needs.

Governance (i.e., how the organization is organized, allocates resources, and makes decisions) should also be tailored to customer requirements. Some customers want a single contact point; others prefer being able to work with each subunit of the firm separately. Likewise, some customers will want (and pay for) personal contact; others will be more comfortable with an online interface. Ideally, a firm should be responsive to differences in individual customer preferences.

And in each of these cases, HR practices should reflect and reinforce target customer value propositions. As the keeper of the system, HR is ideally placed to institutionalize customer value into the organization.

Engage Target Customers in HR Practices

Commitment often follows action. By including targeted customers in HR practices, HR professionals can increase customer commitment to the firm. This effect is so powerful that it hardly matters what the content of the performance appraisal is as long as customers are involved in designing and administering it. Likewise, the content of training pales in importance beside the response if customers are doing the teaching or are in the room when training occurs. Many HR professionals are finding creative ways to include customers in HR practices.

Customer Involvement and Staffing

An airline attempting to make flying more fun screens flight attendant résumés, then invites job finalists to audition interviewees in front of a panel of frequent fliers. A restaurant selecting a chef invites target customers to taste the selections of the finalists and to offer their vote on which chef they would prefer. A hospital invites physicians, third-party payers, and investors to interview potential administrators.

Customer participation in staffing can increase the quality of decision making. Observing teachers teach and soliciting data from students in the class helps boost the quality of teachers hired. Asking customers to define competencies of first-line supervisors creates a dialogue about what matters most to customers and how that translates to internal managerial behaviors. In addition, customer participation in staffing tends to increase customer commitment to the person hired as well as to the business.

Of course, hiring is traditionally the most closely held of organizational prerogatives, and many executives—inside and outside HR—may worry about letting the fox guard the henhouse. However, it isn't necessary to let go entirely—giving customers *a* voice is enough. They don't need or want the *only* voice.

Customer involvement can include sharing talent. For example, a utility firm that wanted marketing experience for one of its executives arranged a three-month exchange with a major customer, who was equally interested in quality control experience for a similar rising talent. The two participants learned more than concepts as they worked on projects for their loaner management; they also forged relationships across boundaries.

Customer Involvement in Training and Development

GE's Crotonville training center opens many of its programs to customers, particularly in emerging markets. By including key customers and thus educating the value chain in its language, management philosophy, and decision processes, GE finds it can shape how customers think and act—thereby redefining the rules of engagement and succeeding quickly in new markets.

Few companies take full advantage of the opportunities their own training programs offer. Most internal courses draw students only from within the company, even though the payback may be often huge and the incremental costs of adding a few outside participants are diminishingly small. Consider the advantages of identifying customers who would be well served by the content of a course, inviting them to attend, and building relationships with them during the program. One company now requires 10 percent of the seats in all its courses to be open to customers and encourages sales and marketing to promote the benefits of course attendance as part of the sales package—a special offer that valued customers welcome.

It can also be valuable to offer programs designed primarily for customers. In one case, a firm that repaired railroad cars cut its in-process time from twenty days to ten, but rather than reacting with the expected delight, customers yawned. The repair people met with customers to explore this disappointment, and learned that they'd barely dented the total downtime, because the cars were also out of commission about ten days on either side of the repair itself. They held a customer productivity workshop, sharing the technology and processes they'd used internally. By focusing on the total time a car was unavailable, they were able to reduce the original forty days to about fifteen.

Another useful move is to enlist customers as presenters—and not just on technical topics. Customers are often willing to share candid observations about why they do or do not purchase. For example, an electronics company invited three customers who had recently gone with a competitor to attend an officer meeting and talk about their decision processes. Collectively, these three lost customers represented a major account erosion, and officers at the seminar not only listened but committed to act upon what they learned. The customers were, at the very least, disposed to see if management succeeded, and the insights the company gained helped reduce further erosion.

Customer Involvement in Appraisal and Rewards

Customers in the appraisal process? Some companies are giving customers a voice in allocating rewards based on quality of employee service. This yields a double benefit: customers grow more committed to employees, and employees to customers.

For example, one airline sends its best customers this annual letter: "We know you are one of our most frequent fliers. We are committed to excellent customer service. Because you travel our airline so often, we assume you know how to define customer service. Enclosed with this letter are ten coupons, each worth $50. When you experience exceptional service from an airline employee, ask for the employee's name, sign the coupon, send it to the company, and we will pay the employee $50." This program uses part of the regular bonus pool to create a clear line of sight between customers and employees.

Customer Involvement in Governance and Communication

The task forces most organizations use to design and deliver systems and services usually consist only of employees—and even gathering members from multiple functions often seems like a stretch. But as the railroad car repair company found, enlarging the task force to include more of the supply chain invariably improves its results.

And task forces are only the beginning. Both public communications (i.e., newsletters, videos, and the like) and personal contact can help transfer knowledge. The benefits can be emotional, as when Medtronic invites recipients of its implants to talk to employees about what the company's product means to their lives. Or the benefits can be directly tied to day-to-day production, as when Wal-Mart connects its electronic system to its supplier network to provide immediate information about what is selling and what is not selling so suppliers can adjust their production accordingly.

Customer Summary

What employees do inside the organization affects customers outside the organization. When HR professionals define target customers, make the customer value proposition explicit, align HR practices to customer values, and involve customers, they create customer experiences that build loyalty and add value.

The Value Proposition as Defined by Investors and Customers

Remember Dan Bennett and the innovative HR program that opened this chapter? Despite its smooth implementation, the program couldn't be counted a success based on the information we provided. But now we can add that Dan's task force designed and delivered the program not only with customers in mind but also with customers fully involved. They carefully linked it to organization capabilities that built intangibles important to investors and also supported a customer value proposition. This is not a "false positive." It's a genuine success. HR professionals can and should blur boundaries by integrating what happens in the organization with what customers and investors experience outside it.

4

Internal Stakeholders
Line Managers and Employees

*To what extent do we audit and create organization
capabilities that will turn strategy into action?*

*To what extent do we have a clear employee value
proposition that lays out what is expected of employees
and what they get in return?*

H R EARNS ITS PLACE by providing deliverables, not just doables.
That's a major reversal for most firms, where HR requirements
tend to look like chores to the rest of the organization rather than
things that add value. Measuring activities (doables) is often easier than
measuring outcomes (deliverables). It is easier to measure the percentage of managers who received forty hours of training than to track the
impact of the training on managerial performance. But outcomes are
what ultimately determine value, and they can become as tangible—and
as measurable—as the activities.

Internal stakeholder outcomes take the form of organization capability and individual ability. *Capability* represents the identity and reputation of the organization; *ability* the competence, skill, and know-how of

employees. Employees focus most of their attention on enhancing their personal abilities, but still need to use and help build organization capabilities. Senior managers, in contrast, must build organizational capabilities but must also cultivate personal abilities. HR investments produce deliverables when they develop both capability and ability. This chapter prescribes what you can do to help your line managers create capability and all employees develop their abilities.

HR Helps Line Managers Build Organization Capability

HR professionals and line managers have always talked together, but their topics have shifted dramatically over the last seventy years. When HR functions began in the 1930s, conversations focused on terms and conditions of employee contracts. Industrial relations professionals would talk to line managers about policies governing employee behavior and strategies for implementing these policies with unions. As the HR field evolved, personnel specialists began talking with line managers about how to design and deliver HR practices like staffing, training, appraisal, and compensation. Lately, HR partners have begun to engage line managers in aligning HR practices with business strategies and goals—moving from the practices themselves to ways to help the managers reach business goals.

This evolution is far from linear; many of the original conversations continue. For example, employees still have terms and conditions of work, now often cloaked in what we call the "employee value proposition," and employees are still rated and paid according to a process now often called "performance management."

But more and more, conversations with your line manager will be on how business leaders can reach their goals. Armed with the kinds of knowledge of external business realities, investors, and customers outlined in chapters 2 and 3, you will engage in conversations that add value for line managers in four primary ways.

1. Resolve misconceptions of HR.

2. Build relationships of trust.

3. Focus on deliverables, not doables.

4. Prioritize capabilities and create an action plan for delivering them.

Resolve Common Misconceptions

Although some line managers already recognize HR as central to their goals, many regard it as irrelevant or something someone else should do. You can resolve these misunderstandings by introducing the following ideas:

- Competitiveness does not equal strategy but strategy × organization.

- Organization is not structure but capability.

- Ultimately, HR work is carried out not by HR but by line managers.

- HR is based not on simple common sense but on a body of knowledge.

- HR work is not a collection of activities but an integrated set of outcomes.

- HR work is not an isolated event but an ongoing process.

- HR should focus not on what has been but on what will be.

Competitiveness Equals Strategy × Organization

To win in the marketplace, leaders craft strategies that allocate resources and set direction. Too often, once they have a set of strategies, they believe the game is over—when, in fact, it is only beginning. True competitiveness requires strategy execution, and designing an organization that can deliver strategy is as important as developing the strategies themselves. The equation is a multiplier because failing in strategy or organization will cause you to lose competitiveness. You need to sensitize line managers to the importance of organization as an essential part of any competitiveness equation.

Structure Versus Capability

Once leaders have accepted that organization matters, they need to define what it is. Too many organizations are defined by morphology—number of layers, processes, the roles people play. Important as they are, these structural elements do not represent the identity of the organization, the capabilities it can exercise. It is more productive to rewire line managers' concepts of organization away from structural solutions (downsizing, removing layers, reengineering) to capability-based solutions (talent management, collaboration, learning, speed of change, and so forth).

Line Managers' Role and Responsibility for HR

HR professionals are staff. They architect, facilitate, recommend an HR agenda, and coach line managers, but line managers have ultimate responsibility for approving and executing HR—just as they have ultimate responsibility for approving and executing finance, marketing, and R&D. The misfocused tendency to delegate HR to HR allows a line manager to avoid responsibility and gives an HR professional a false sense of being solely responsible. This is an illusion you need to avoid. To make HR practices work, line managers must model what they want others to accomplish—and HR leaders need to ensure that line managers stay aware of and accountable for HR work.

HR as a Body of Knowledge

Line managers often attribute HR recommendations to common sense—which is not the good thing it may seem, even when it promotes easy agreement. Rather than relying on the appeal of maxims like "If you involve people, they will be more committed," it is more effective to master theory and present evidence showing how HR insights change real-life behavior: "Here are the five best ways to involve people, and three ways to measure the resulting commitment," for example. The problem with common sense is that everyone has it—or at least claims to have it—so it doesn't merit anyone a place at the table.

Focus on Outcomes

Beware the lure of the "Do something, anything, just do it" mentality. Even to skeptical line managers, new HR programs may sound interesting, promise much, and engender hope. It's easy to fall prey to the pleasure of talking about activities and forget about the outcomes of those activities. HR professionals sometimes spend more time deciding who will speak on the third morning of a five-day executive program than on the results that program or module should deliver. Avoid getting so lost in details that you lose sight of what your practices are creating for investors and customers as well as for the organization and its employees.

The Long Haul

It is gratifying to cross things off your to-do list and move on—"We did HR work in February when we ran our training program, or in April when we did the all-employee meeting, or in December when we handed out the bonus." Unfortunately, most HR practices that add long-term value are not so easily accomplished. Events are important for symbolic value and rallying resources, but they do not create sustained change. You might help managers plan and deliver events, but stay focused on the longer-term process and patterns they create.

Sunk Costs

People find it hard to change what they have created. Often, line managers are pleased with the HR system that led to their promotion—unsurprisingly, since they have been well served by it. Nonetheless, it's important to look forward rather than backward. It is important to focus equally on what will be while learning from what has been. The goal is to build on a strategy for the future rather than rely on a strategy that worked in the past.

Build Relationships of Trust

"I don't care how much you know until I know how much you care." This thought, whether explicit or not, is at the center of any human relationship, and especially any working relationship. People build trust based on shared interests and caring. The same is true as you work with your line managers and peers.

Listen and Learn

Listen to the line managers you work with. Understand and adopt the logic, language, and concepts they use to think about business. Be able to express their thoughts in their words. Recognize their personal styles—via Myers-Briggs or simple observation—so you know who works better in person, by phone, or by e-mail; prefers to hear bad news as problems or solutions; or would rather make decisions quickly or slowly. Rather than trying to change someone's style, learn to work with it. In addition, learn about their backgrounds: where they went to school, what they enjoy as hobbies, what they did in previous jobs, and so forth. Be interested in them as individuals, not just in their managerial roles. When appropriate, share some of your own experiences. Mutual disclosure builds trust. Make sure that your recommendations align with their goals, not just yours. Delight in their success.

Resolve Concerns

Inevitably, differing points of view arise in any relationship. Trust grows when concerns are resolved openly and honestly. Model ways to resolve concerns and bring unity to decision making with some of the following suggestions:

- Be open and candid in your comments while expressing support and concern.

- Clarify specific issues and points of view as you explore options.

- Identify common threads, and set criteria for selecting among options.

- Figure out what additional information is required to make a decision.

- Discover a way to make a decision while ensuring that all parties feel heard.

- Focus on implementation and the future.

Generally, the biggest barrier to resolving concerns is a reluctance to air differences. When you practice openness, you generally have a chance of finding a way to work things out.

Demonstrate "-Ability"

Trust comes from -*ability*: adaptability, affability, availability, credibility, dependability, indispensability, predictability, reliability, sociability, stability, workability. With this spectrum of attitudes in place, the parties have a good start on developing confidence in each another. You earn trust by doing small and simple things rather than one big thing. Trust is a cumulative process of learning from shared experiences that build on one another, and it is the foundation for conversations that add value all around.

Focus on Deliverables, Not Doables

The unique value you contribute stems from offering rigorous and useful ways to deliver line managers' strategy and help them reach their goals. This requires that you build both organizational capabilities and individual abilities that deliver value.

To assess the difference between organizational capability and individual ability, it helps to set up a grid like the one in table 4-1. At the individual-technical intersection (cell 1), people possess functional abilities and competencies (for example, technical expertise in marketing or manufacturing). The individual-social intersection (cell 2) shows that

TABLE 4-1

Individual ability and organizational capability

	Individual	Organization
Technical	1. An individual's functional competence or ability	3. An organization's core competence
Social	2. An individual's social competence or ability	4. An organization's capabilities

individuals also have a set of social abilities often defined as "leadership competencies" (the ability to set direction, learn, and build relationships). Cell 3, the organizational-technical intersection, represents the business capabilities or core competencies of a firm (things such as risk management or R&D that the firm must know how to do). Cell 4 represents organizational capabilities, the underlying DNA, culture, and personality of the firm.

Organization capabilities amplify individual abilities. A team made up of all-stars who don't play well together would probably lose to a team of competent individuals who play well together. When players meld their individual abilities into organization capabilities, their collective strength is magnified.

Capabilities help line managers deliver strategies, investors receive intangible value, customers maintain connectivity, and employees stay engaged. Capabilities are the deliverables or outcomes of HR investments. They are stable over time and are harder for competitors to copy than strategies or physical assets. HR professionals working with line managers can identify the capabilities required to accomplish business strategies.

The ideal capabilities differ depending on a firm's strategy. However, building on the intangibles identified in table 3-2, capabilities of exemplar companies, HR professionals can help line managers define capabilities that suit their own circumstances, review how to build them, and suggest ways to measure them.

Talent

Developing talent means going beyond platitudes like "People are our most important asset" to investing time and hard resources in making sure that employees are both competent and committed. Competent employees have the skills they need for today and tomorrow. Committed employees deploy those skills regularly and predictably. Ensuring employee competence is possible when HR helps leaders buy (bring in new talent), build (develop existing talent), borrow (access thought leaders through alliances or partnerships), bounce (remove poor talent), bind (retain the best talent), and boost (promote the right talent). (See chapter 5.)

Employee competence can be tracked by a number of measures:

- Percentage of employees with the skills to do their job today and in the future

- Percentage of employees targeted by search firms

- Output per unit of employee input (a productivity measure)

- Investor or customer ratings of employee service

Sustaining commitment is possible when a firm builds an employee value proposition that rewards outstanding workers with what matters to them most. HR can track commitment by measures such as

- Retention of top employees.

- Response to employee attitude surveys.

- Direct observation.

Building a foundation of competent and committed employees can ensure a flow of talent that will help the organization perform well over time.

Speed

An organization with speed identifies and moves quickly into new markets, new products, new employee contracts, and new business processes. You can help leaders develop this capability by focusing on rigorous decision making, by implementing organizationwide change processes, by breaking down bureaucratic barriers, and by eliminating change viruses. Stepping up the capacity to change helps even large firms—like GM with CEO Rick Wagoner's "changefast" program—act like small, nimble firms.

Speed may be tracked by the time expended between

- Concept to commercialization of an idea.

- Changeover of an assembly line to new product output.

- Collecting customer data to changes in customer relations.

- Proposing an administrative change to fully implementing it.

Measures like these operate like inventory turnovers, tracking efficient use of time and labor instead of tracking physical assets. They lead to increased labor productivity as well as increased enthusiasm and responsiveness to opportunities.

Shared Mindset

Many firms have moved from individual product brands to firm brands, reflecting a shared mindset among their people inside and customers outside. The Marriott name on a hotel, for example, adds value because it gives travelers confidence in the product. The more real that identity is to both customers and employees, the more it will benefit the firm.

Shared mindset can be measured with a simple exercise: ask senior management, "What are the top three things we want to be known for by our best customers in the future?" Collect the responses and measure the degree of consensus as the percentage of responses that fall into the three most common categories. We have conducted this exercise hundreds of times and often find a shared mindset around 50 to 60 percent—but leading firms tend to score around 80 to 90 percent. The next step in the exercise is to invite key customers to determine their top three priorities. It is then possible to monitor the extent to which the internal and external mindsets are shared and to shape the ultimate value of the culture.

Accountability

For firms with the habit of accountability, it is simply unacceptable to miss goals and delivery deadlines. Their strategies translate into measurable standards of performance, rewards are linked to those standards, and employees recognize that they must meet their targets. Both financial and nonfinancial rewards reinforce these efforts and provide definitive feedback on personal performance.

Accountability is simple to monitor when HR practices support it. By looking at a performance appraisal form, you should be able to identify the strategy of the business, as well as the employee's own goals and strategies for achieving them. Does the appraisal reflect the business strategy? What percentage of employees receive an appraisal each year? How much does compensation vary based on performance? Some firms claim a pay-for-performance philosophy, but their annual increases range only from 3.5 to 4.5 percent—proving the claim false. Finally, what percentage of employees feel they have received a helpful feedback session in the past year?

Collaboration

Collaboration encourages efficiencies of operation through shared services, technology, and economies of scale as well as leverage from learning and sharing ideas across boundaries, allocating resources as needed, and merging strategies for cross-selling and customer service. It permits an organization to be much more than the sum of its parts. HR professionals can help build collaboration by promoting and highlighting both efficiency and leverage throughout the organization.

HR can track collaboration, monitoring the flow of talent and ideas across boundaries within an organization. Are people moving from one area to another? Are ideas or practices in one part of the firm being replicated elsewhere? Collaboration can also be measured by tracking administrative costs, as shared services have been found to produce a 15–25 percent cost savings. For example, the average large firm spends about $1,600 per employee per year in administration, making it a simple matter to calculate the probable cost savings of shared services.

Learning

Learning means generating and generalizing ideas with impact. New ideas may be generated from four activities:[1]

- Benchmarking (seeing what others have done and adapting it)

- Experimentation (trying new things to see if and how they work)

- Acquisition (hiring or developing people with new skills and ideas)

- Continuous improvement (via suggestion systems and process analysis)

For maximum usefulness, ideas also need to be *generalized*—that is, to move across a boundary of time (from one leader to the next), space (from one geography to another), or division (from one business unit to another). This can be accomplished by creating communities of practice, by moving people, and by encouraging individual and team learning. As HR leaders, you can play a major role in selecting the technology and establishing the practices that make it possible. You can also establish baselines and track results on questions of knowledge turnover, such as "What is the half-life of knowledge in your current job? When will 50 percent of what you know be out-of-date?" By emphasizing the need to generate and generalize new ideas, you can help make learning part of the organizational improvement effort.

Leadership

Organizations that produce leaders generally have a leadership brand—a clear statement of what leaders should know, be, do, and deliver. HR professionals are uniquely well placed to help current leadership produce the next generation of leaders by establishing the leadership brand, assessing the gaps in the present leadership against this brand, and investing in future leaders.

You can track the leadership brand by monitoring the pool of future leaders. How many backups are in place for the top one hundred leaders? In the middle of an aggressive downsizing initiative, one company discovered that it had dropped from 3 to 0.7 qualified backups for each of the top one hundred workers—seriously impairing its leadership bench strength.

Customer Connection

Often, the target customers mentioned in chapter 3—the ones responsible for 80 percent of the business—amount to no more than 20 percent of the customer population. HR practices can help link those customers more closely to the firm by including them in staffing, training, compensation, and communications. HR can also promote procedures that give employees meaningful exposure to or interaction with external customers. All these efforts produce an information and mindset convergence between employees and customers.

You could encourage the firm to track customer connectivity through share of targeted customers and through regular customer service scores. They can use the resulting numbers to assess the effectiveness of HR practices designed to promote employee attitudes and abilities that generate strong customer connections.

Innovation

Innovation focuses on share of opportunity by creating future success rather than relying on past successes. Innovation matters because it fosters growth. It excites employees, it anticipates customer requests and delights customers by providing pleasures they did not expect, and it builds confidence among investors.

You can encourage top management to track innovation through a vitality index such as revenues (or profits) from products or services created in the last three years. Innovation can also be monitored by tracking the introduction and deployment of new processes in the organization.

Strategic Unity

A firm with strategic unity makes sure that all employees share an understanding of what its strategy is and why it is important. It presents its strategy through simple messages repeated constantly, and it seeks to ensure that the strategy actually shapes how employees behave. It also aligns processes (budgeting, hiring, decision making, and the like) with strategy. HR leaders can advise and assist every step of the way, shaping messages and encouraging procedures by asking employees what they will do given the strategy rather than by simply telling them what to do. When employees define their behaviors relative to the strategy, they are more likely to become committed to it.

Strategic unity can be tracked by measuring the extent to which employees' answers match when you ask, "What strategy sets this business apart from competitors and helps us win with customers?" You can track the behavioral agenda for strategic unity by asking employees what percentage of their time directly contributes to the business strategy, and whether their suggestions for improvement are heard and acted upon.

Efficiency

In competitive markets, efficiently managing the costs of processes, people, and projects increases flexibility. Of course, a strategy of managing costs and ignoring growth will fail, because no business can save its way to prosperity. However, firms that avoid cost and efficiency improvements will generally not have the opportunity to grow the top line. Tracking efficiency may be the easiest of all. Costs of goods sold, inventories, direct and indirect labor, and capital employed can be measured by the balance sheet and income statement.

Prioritize and Deliver Capabilities

To add value for line managers, it is necessary to identify and implement only the most critical capabilities. Many HR professionals fall prey to an

"I can do it, so it must be worth doing" mentality. They offer line managers expertise and advice on talent because this is what they know how to do rather than help managers define which capabilities (for example, collaboration, learning, efficiency, or customer connection) they require to meet business goals. HR leaders also need to prioritize capabilities since not all can or should be delivered at once.

Level 4 of the intangibles audit in assessment 3-1 offers a template for identifying and prioritizing key capabilities. Once the critical capabilities have been identified, you can work with other staff experts and line managers to design a consistent process for delivering each capability. This can be accomplished by assigning teams to deliver critical capabilities and by putting together a focused and timely action plan with steps to take and measures to monitor.

While capabilities emerge over time, we have found that the best capability plans have a ninety-day window. That is, the plans identify specific actions and results that occur within ninety days to demonstrate that capability development is under way. These are rapid-cycle actions that will make immediate progress. To have ninety-day results, it is often useful to bring the senior team together for a half-day meeting to cover the following points:

- *Goals of capability.* What do we want to accomplish by having a key capability such as speed, talent, or collaboration?

- *Decisions that promote capability.* What decisions can we make immediately to foster this capability?

- *Actions that deliver capability.* What can we, as leaders, do in the short term to invest in this capability?

- *Indicators that track capability.* What will we measure to monitor our progress on this capability?

The goals statement should include a clear outcome that can be measured and tracked, and the decisions should involve adopting the goals and promoting the actions. Actions will vary depending on where the firm is in the process, but any or all of the following might be warranted: education or training events, staffing and assigning key people to a project or task force, setting performance standards for those responsible for the capability, creating task forces or other units to house those doing the capability work, sharing information across boundaries, and investing in technology to sustain the capability. HR professionals can be involved in all these actions, either directly or in an advisory capacity.

HR Helps Employees Build Personal Ability

"Human resources" begins with *human*, yet too many HR professionals forgo the human touch so central to their role. No matter how wide they cast their nets to help build intangibles, bind customers, and support line managers, they must remain sensitive to the human needs of employees. Over and above the personal satisfaction employee care provides, employee advocacy and human capital development are key roles (chapter 9) because they help HR link employee behavior to investor, customer, and line-manager results. Employees receive value from the work of HR professionals, and HR professionals represent the soul of the enterprise, when HR practices accomplish the following:

1. Create an employee value proposition that lets employees know they are valued and are allowed to add value.

2. Represent employee interests to line managers so that employees are heard.

3. Deliver administrative support that genuinely serves and cares for employees.

4. Ensure that employees have abilities to deliver organizational capabilities.

Create an Employee Value Proposition

Whether or not they're in a union, employees have a contract—written or psychological, or both, with the latter often the more important—that engages them with the firm and specifies what they give and what they get.

Employees can be asked to contribute in meaningful ways and to represent the values of the firm. More specifically, the firm's expectations can be woven into appraisal systems by way of standards and performance requirements. These requirements focus on behavior (what the employee should know and do) and results (what the employee should produce). With clear standards, employees know what commitment they are expected to make. In return, the employee value proposition (EVP) specifies what employees will get from the firm when they meet expectations. We have found that the most satisfactory EVP provides the following:

- *Vision.* The firm has a clear sense of the future that engages hearts and minds and creates pride among employees.

- *Opportunity.* The work provides a chance to grow both personally and professionally, and to develop skills and knowledge that promote present and future employability.

- *Incentive.* The compensation package is fair and equitable, including base salary, bonus, and other financial incentives.

- *Impact.* The work itself makes a difference or creates meaning, particularly as it connects the employee with a customer who uses the employee's work.

- *Community.* The social environment includes being part of a team (when appropriate) and working with coworkers who care.

- *Communication.* The flow of information is two-way, so employees are informed about what is going on.

- *Experimentation.* Working hours, dress, and other policies are flexible and designed to adapt to the needs of both the firm and the employee.

We call these inducements VOI^2C^2E. Employees differ regarding which of these seven elements they want most. An effective EVP will personalize the agreement so that employees who meet standards will be rewarded with VOI^2C^2E elements most important to them. Such EVPs build commitment to the firm. By stating what workers can expect if they fulfill their part of the contract, the EVP makes it clear that employees who give value to the firm will receive the kind of value that matters most to them in return.

The EVP also helps communicate the firm brand to the world at large. It answers potential employees' basic question "Why should I work for you?" It helps the firm become the employer of choice in its field or location, supporting efforts to attract top talent. As Wharton professor Peter Cappelli points out, recruiting has become more like marketing: "What if you had to sell your jobs in a competitive marketplace? What would you say about what it's like to work at your company?" He notes that IBM's ads don't mention products; they project an image of the company's culture and values. He estimates that one in five job applicants is responding to the tone of general advertising.[2]

HR professionals play a key role in drafting, declaring, and demonstrating the EVP.[3] They work to articulate what employees should both get and give in ways that add value to all stakeholders. They may use EVP discussions to clarify a philosophy toward people and to turn this philosophy into action. Demonstrating or delivering on the EVP can also be part of HR practice. HR professionals are in a position to ensure that all HR practices are designed with the EVP in mind. They can advocate for fair treatment of employees, and they can work to resolve employee differences.

Exhibit 4-1 shows one fully developed employee value proposition. Crafted by HR professionals at CIGNA, it is shared with current or prospective employees to illustrate the firm's expectations and promises.

EXHIBIT 4-1

Cigna employee value proposition

Our Employee Value Proposition is this:

CIGNA is a leading employee-benefits provider to employers and employees in the U.S. and selected international markets. We succeed through our commitment to serving our customers, the strength of our people and our drive for superior financial results.

We recognize the value of a passionately committed, energized and *diverse* workforce. We reward excellence, promote development, expect high standards and encourage work/life balance.

Our employees come to work every day looking for better ways to improve our customers' quality of life. They're on the front lines answering the phones, behind the scenes developing new products, or in a country far from home providing service to our international community of members and subscribers. They're the reason we're an industry leader. They're our competitive edge and we know it.

That's why we developed a People Strategy: to take care of the people who power our success.

People Strategy

We refer to our determination to attract, develop, motivate and retain the best people as "the CIGNA People Strategy."

What sets us apart from other employers? We believe it's the strategy and resources we created and implemented to challenge, develop and reward our employees.

All necessary resources, such as training, coaching and mentoring, are provided. Expectations are clearly defined. Performance is quantitatively measured. Challenges are identified; achievements are rewarded.

Some employees choose to grow and develop in their current position. Others prefer to take on increasingly responsible positions. Either way, the People Strategy makes it easy for employees—and their managers—to map a course to suit each employee's individual career goals. As we want our employees to succeed because . . .

Employee success fuels company success. It's simple.

Represent Employee Interests

It's part of your HR job to make sure that employees' wants and needs are heard and understood by line management, both in the face of specific events and as a general practice. Your goal is to form a bridge between management and employees so that mutual understanding makes the best of whatever the company faces.

One Event

When a manufacturing firm decided it had to close down a plant, the HR professional on the management team explained how many employees would be affected, their demographics (age, years' service, positions, skills), and their likelihood of finding other employment readily. He also presented options for how to communicate the plant closing and how to move employees to jobs inside or outside the firm. Finally, he presented a specific plan for how to help people work through the grieving process of losing their jobs.

By being visible and active in the management meetings, the HR professional became simultaneously the voice of the employees and the mind of the managers. While the financial status of the facility required that it be closed, the dual role enabled the HR professional to manage this transition with dignity and tact. Here are some specific strategies he sponsored or facilitated.

EARN THE TRUST OF EMPLOYEES BY BEING VISIBLE AND ACCESSIBLE

The HR professional convinced the entire eight-person management team to spend several days at the plant. On the first half day, management shared data with all employees: the erosion of customers, the competitive landscape, the financial performance of the plant, the condition of the plant, and all the other factors that went into the decision to close. Then, for a day and a half, the top team members made themselves available to talk to any employee. The last half day, the management team brought all employees together to explain again why the plant would be closing and what the next steps would be. At the end of this meeting, although unhappy about losing their jobs, the employees gave the management team a standing ovation. They respected the team's courage in visiting the plant and being available to respond to questions and concerns.

Pay Attention to Fair Treatment and Equity of All Employees

Each employee who was being let go had the opportunity for an individual conference and assistance in developing a personal action plan. In this case, fair treatment did not mean that employees got their way (some who wanted to move to other sites were not qualified to do so), but each person was treated with dignity. HR professionals can be the grantors and guarantors of equity (not equality).

Use Symbolic Events

The on-site visit was supported by policies that turned events into patterns (for example, who would get a chance to relocate in the company and who would not). These policies communicated fairness and equity to employees, and the symbolic events communicated care and concern.

Move Quickly with Difficult Decisions

The time between the date for closing the plant and the management visit was about two weeks. This speed avoided the paralysis another company faced when it announced in early February that on June 30, 7 percent of the employees would be let go. About half the employees thought they might be the ones to go, so they were too worried about protecting themselves to get their work done. Once a decision is made to close a plant or let people go, HR professionals should make sure that it is executed swiftly—within legal bounds, of course.

React Strongly to Ensure Fairness

The HR professional stayed at the plant to respond to grievances. Employees were able to express their concerns and personal desires, and even those disappointed in the results knew they'd been heard and treated fairly.

Ongoing Interactions

In addition to listening to employee views and voices in demanding situations, HR leaders add value when they set up regular opportunities for workers' thoughts and feelings to be heard. You can encourage employee feedback in many ways and can take the lead in design, administration, and follow-up for each one—ensuring that the offering is tailored to the organization, that it is efficient and easy to use, and that the results are not only obtained but applied.

Surveys

Regular employee surveys—now often conducted online—are an increasingly common way to assess employee attitudes and measure managerial effectiveness.[4] Shorter surveys as pulse checks allow employees to participate quickly and often. The trend is away from satisfaction questions ("Do you like your pay?") and toward questions about commitment ("Does your pay induce you to contribute in meaningful ways?").

Suggestion Systems

Suggestion systems range from formal (with standardized idea forms and payout schedules) to informal (where employees share ideas on a continuing basis). The Toyota suggestion system has generated more than 20 million suggestions over forty years, or about one per employee per week. Much of the credit for Toyota's commitment to continuous improvement comes from employees' willingness to offer suggestions and management's to receive them.[5]

Town Hall Meetings

Town hall meetings originated in civic affairs, allowing political leaders to speak directly with constituents. These meetings have been adapted to many business settings, where leaders interact with employees on issues of interest to both parties.[6]

Chat Rooms

Internet technology allows managers to engage with employees online. Company chat rooms make it easy for leaders and employees to communicate at mutually convenient times.

Ombudsmen

HR professionals can make themselves available to employees to mediate concerns and problems. Maricopa County, Arizona, for example, has formalized the role of an employee ombudsman who "investigates grievances on behalf of the County Administrative Officer, facilitates solutions to workplace conflicts and complaints, provides information, and gives a personal and confidential hearing to employees involved in a dispute."[7] Managed through the HR function, this role enables all county employees to resolve disputes fairly and openly.

Deliver Administrative Support

The administrative infrastructure of an organization—all the procedures and forms for hiring, processing benefits, getting paid, relocating, planning for retirement, and so forth—can often seem burdensome, but it is necessary. Rather like the infrastructure of a house (plumbing, heating, electricity), it is generally taken for granted until something breaks; then there's a crisis until it's fixed.

HR professionals can add value by ensuring constant and equitable administrative support. Increasingly, excellence in administration means meeting the following criteria.

Personalization

Personalized administrative support promotes flexibility, which helps engage employees. It is the equivalent of mass customization—but for an internal audience, permitting the EVP to be tailored to the specific needs of each employee. Traditional HR systems categorized employees into groups that received similar services, but these days, each employee can be addressed as an individual. For example, a compensation package includes the types of financial rewards (cash today, deferred cash, stock, benefits, services); the way the rewards are delivered (by check mailed home, check delivered in the office, direct deposit to a chosen bank); and how often the rewards are paid (from weekly to annually). Instead of making the selections, the company can let employees choose what best matches their lifestyle and needs. HR professionals are the ones who create systems to offer and respond to those choices.

Rapid Response

In a world of instant news, employees' expectations of timing for administrative support have increased. No longer will people wait weeks to receive reimbursement for travel expenses, for example. HR needs to build rapid-response systems that grant employee requests on demand.

Ease of Use

Traditional paper forms are cumbersome and often difficult to use. Increasingly, administrative support takes place online, where employees can quickly and easily exchange required information. Online support gives employees nearly unlimited access to important personal information such as retirement portfolios and development opportunities. And the new technical complexity can generate administrative ease, as in one company where the online system applies updates across a range of databases. For example, when an employee transfer is reported, changes cascade across the employee's workstation, supervisor, job description, insurance coverage, and so forth.

Flawless Execution

Accuracy inspires confidence in the systems and underpins the integrity of the HR function. By contrast, errors rapidly turn into problems, as when a new payroll system overpaid a group of employees for a few weeks. Even though people were well aware that the overpayment was an error, the company's attempt to recover the money became an issue in the next round of contract negotiations and led to ongoing discontent among the workforce.

Responsiveness

When employees have questions about administrative matters, what they want most are *timely* answers. This implies a single point of contact so that employees don't have to seek out the specific HR professional who may be able to answer their questions. HR systems should be designed accordingly.

Ensure Employees Have Abilities

Just as you help line managers create organizational capability, you also need to help employees acquire work-related abilities. The eleven organizational capabilities discussed earlier all have personal counterparts. Once organizational capabilities are defined, individual abilities must be demonstrated to deliver the desired capabilities. It may be useful to have conversations with employees about the skills they need to demonstrate.

These conversations are part educational, as you teach the employee how organizational capabilities translate into employee abilities. They are part coaching, as you help employees turn ideas into action; part managerial, as you create specific plans that can be implemented to help employees have the ability to do the right work; and part personal, as you help individual employees understand strategic priorities and develop the skills to achieve their personal aspirations.

Keeping in mind the top two or three capabilities most salient to delivering strategy (using assessment 3-1, Intangibles audit), you could initiate an "ability" conversation with employees by following the script in the next several sections. These conversations form the basis of the employee value proposition. Each conversation begins with a statement of why organization capabilities help the organization compete. This is followed by a list of corresponding skills that employees must demonstrate, as well as suggestions for acquiring those abilities.

Talent

We (our firm) are in a war for talent. We compete by having the most talented employees who are both competent (able to do the job) and committed (willing to do what they say they will do). Customers in our industry pay for the output of our talented employees.

Having talented employees occurs when each employee knows what is required for both current and future work and is able to identify specific knowledge, skills, and behaviors required to meet customer demands. When you have instituted a regular and disciplined process of evaluation, you will know what is expected of you and where you stand. You will also be able to inventory your strengths and weaknesses, and craft a plan to guide your ongoing development. Let me help you become an all-star player on an all-star team.

Speed

We compete by being fast, which means first to market and fast to innovate. To be fast, we need each employee to change, experiment, and try new things more quickly than our competitors.

Employees who master the challenges of rapid change let go of outdated knowledge and activities, and discover and develop the knowledge and skills needed for the future. When you try new ventures and accept 80 percent solutions and realize that you don't have to be perfect in all things, you will learn faster and savor the process of continuous personal improvement. As you develop resilience, you will be able to bounce back from failure, stick with change, and accomplish difficult things quickly. Your confidence will enable you to face an uncertain future while responding positively today. Let me help make you a change master.

Shared Mindset

Our company competes by having an exceptional reputation and brand. Customers go out of their way to buy from us. Each of our employees needs to develop a personal identity consistent with our corporate identity. Employees need to understand how others see them, and compare it to what our organization wants to be known for and how they would like to be seen in a way that is consistent with our company's reputation.

When you craft your personal mission statement and translate it into behaviors that are consistent with your values, you will get into a "flow" so that you enjoy who you are and what you are doing. You will not be trying to be someone you are not. By avoiding needless comparisons, you will become more aware of your own strengths and limitations, and better able to set expectations that you can meet. This means you may say no to projects outside your limits and yes to projects within an appropriate stretch. Your personal reputation will affect how others treat you, how you treat yourself, and how far you can progress. Let me help make you known for your consistent reputation.

Accountability

We compete by being disciplined at getting things done, by meeting commitments, and by fulfilling promises. Customers trust us to do what we say. Each of our employees needs to master the skill of getting things done.

Getting things done as promised comes from setting priorities, learning that not everything worth doing is worth doing well, and realizing that some things are so important, they are worth doing poorly. To be accountable, you need to make and keep commitments to whatever you deem most important. When you make appropriate public commitments, you give both yourself and others confidence that you will accomplish tasks in a timely way. As you learn how to solicit and interpret feedback, you will constantly improve. Let me coach you so that you can get started now and use your early successes to build longer-term gains. Let me help make you a full contributor.

Collaboration

We compete through alliances, partnerships, joint ventures, and other forms of collaboration. To collaborate as an organization, our employees need to learn how to work with others and build relationships of trust.

Monitoring and improving your interpersonal skills helps others trust you. Your relationships will improve when you identify people who can help you solve problems and get work done. As you learn how to collaborate and delegate to others work that you should not do yourself, you become valuable to the relationship networks within your work unit. Perhaps I can assist you in discerning who is your colleague and friend and who is not, and tutor you in the skills for working through interpersonal difficulties. Let me help you become a team player.

Learning

We compete by learning and by creating knowledge that our customers can use. To learn as an organization, we need employees who demonstrate learning agility by letting go of the past and focusing on the future.

As an employee, you help the organization learn when you master the learning cycle—making choices, assessing consequences, and instituting corrections—and adapt it to yourself and your job. If you can accurately assess your learning styles and open your mind to experimentation, benchmarking, and competence acquisition, you will generate new ideas within your work unit and generalize those ideas across boundaries. My role is to encourage you to discover ideas with impact by mastering the disciplines of learning. Let me help you be a learner.

Leadership

We are known for the quality of our leadership brand. Leaders at each level act responsibly to serve customers and investors. To maintain a firm-wide leadership brand, each leader should possess a personal leadership agenda consistent with our organization's leadership brand.

When you master the following steps in becoming a more effective leader, you manifest your acceptance of the opportunities and responsibilities of leadership, regardless of your position in your company.

1. Define the strategies and goals of your organization.

2. Turn those strategies into behaviors leaders must demonstrate.

3. Clearly articulate the results that leaders must produce.

4. Create a personal leadership brand that incorporates what you must know and do and what you must deliver.

5. Build a leadership action plan to deliver results.

As a leader, you should be able to craft a vision, set goals, take action, and follow up. Even when you are not in a formal leadership position, you can lead others by asking questions, setting an agenda for getting things done, and influencing upward. Let me help make you a leader.

Customer Connection

We compete by gaining customer share from our targeted customers. To serve these customers, all employees must align their work with the needs of customers.

Serving customers begins by understanding who your real customers are. Then, you need to prioritize the most important customers and learn how to discern what they need and want from you. As you find ways to form alliances and relationships, you will better meet their needs and increase their desire to do business with you. It is important to continuously monitor how well you serve your key customers, so that you can break down the boundaries between you and them to form a lasting partnership. Let me help you become customer-expert.

Innovation

We compete by offering new products or services, defining new markets, or creating new ways to manufacture or distribute products. To innovate, we need employees who are able to create and try new things.

Individual creativity leads to organizational innovation. Creativity comes from identifying and solving problems, looking for alternatives, brainstorming, learning from failures, thinking divergently, and taking risks. Your personal creativity will flourish when you develop an innovation protocol for your work that encourages you to generate ideas, assess their impact, incubate and experiment with them, invest and commercialize them, and integrate new products or services into the existing business. Such creativity will help you ask and find answers to "What's next?" and "What can be?" Let me help you become an innovator.

Strategic Unity

We compete by having a vision or mission that distinguishes us in the marketplace. Our unique organizational vision should be consistent with an employee's personal vision or mission.

A personal mission begins with clarity about your criteria for personal success—what you want and what matters most to you—and turns those criteria into a vision of who you are and who you want to become.

This vision allows you to accept who you are and who you are not. It helps you eliminate the clutter in your life and focus on relationships and actions that matter most. Your personal vision should be visible in actions and results. Let me help you become personally vision-driven and teach you how to align that vision with your organization's mission statement.

Efficiency

We compete by maintaining lower costs and using our resources efficiently. Efficient organizations have employees who are wise stewards of time, resources, and energy.

Despite best intentions, you cannot be all things to all people. You can conserve personal resources by determining how much of your time an activity deserves, establishing a return-on-time-invested index to monitor your efficiency, and by conducting personal time audits. Personal efficiency comes when you identify resources that can help you get things done and retain energy so you can be emotionally and intellectually engaged. Let me help you be disciplined.

The Value Proposition as Defined by Line Managers (Capabilities) and Employees (Abilities)

HR adds value for line managers and employees. HR leaders can help line managers revise common HR misconceptions, build relationships of trust, and identify and create capabilities required for success. With employees, you create an employee value proposition, represent employee interests to line managers, deliver reliable administrative support, and help employees develop their abilities to deliver the capabilities the organization needs if it is to survive and prosper.

5

HR Practices That Add Value

Flow of People and Performance

---

*To what extent do our HR practices that focus on people
(staffing, training, development) add value?*

*To what extent do our HR practices that focus on performance
(setting standards, allocating rewards, providing feedback) add value?*

PICTURE THIS: you—an HR generalist—sit down with your line manager or your leadership team to present overall options for investing in HR practices. What value will you create? Or you—an HR specialist—want your group to revise or adapt HR practices to create additional value. On what will you focus? Or you—a senior HR executive—get together with your HR team with a view to upgrading your HR practices to add more value. Where should your team focus?

To answer these questions, you need a clear mental map for what HR practices are and do. We suggest four general groupings of HR practices that follow the flows or processes central to organization success.

1. *Flow of people.* What happens to the organization's key asset—its people—including how people move in, through, up, and out of the organization. Proper attention to people flow ensures the

95

availability of the talent the organization needs to accomplish its
strategy.

2. *Flow of performance management.* What links people to work—
   the standards and measures, financial and nonfinancial rewards,
   and feedback that reflect stakeholder interests. Proper attention
   to this flow promotes accountability for performance by defining, noting, and rewarding it—and penalizing its absence.

3. *Flow of information.* What keeps people aware of the organization and their collective knowledge resources. Proper attention
   to information flow ensures that people know what is happening
   and why, and can apply themselves to what needs doing to
   create value.

4. *Flow of work.* Who does work, how work is done, and where
   work is done combine individual efforts into organizational
   outputs. Proper attention to work flow provides the governance
   processes, accountability, and physical setting that ensure high-
   quality results.

This chapter deals with the flows of people and performance management, more traditional areas for HR practices. Chapter 6 continues
the story, covering the flows of information and work—emerging areas
for HR attention.

Working with the Flows

Designing and delivering HR practices that add value in each of the
flows involves a three-step process: *theory*, *choice*, and *action*. HR theory
is the first step in creating a line of sight between a practice and the
value it will create for investors, customers, line managers, and employees. Theory explains *why:* why this investment in training (or staffing,
rewards, communication, organization design, workplace design) will
create value for the organization's key stakeholders. Chapters 3 and 4
provide the basic theoretical framework, so we'll just sketch the highlights here to put them in context.

Second, as an HR professional, you need to construct a compendium
of choices about possible HR practices that might be used to create
value as well as assess the relative value each will contribute to key
stakeholders. Many books lay out the myriad choices of things to do in

HR; here we list and discuss only some of those most likely to be effective—that is, to add substantive value for target stakeholders.[1] Our metaphor for defining these choices is a *menu*. Menus in restaurants present what is offered and what can be selected, but obviously not all items are selected at once. HR professionals create menus of choices. In this chapter and in chapter 6, we propose templates and selected items for menus pertaining to people, performance, information, and work. Seasoned HR professionals can skim these menus and affirm that they are competent in each HR practice and identify areas to improve. Less experienced HR practitioners can use these menus as a baseline of HR practices they should master. In chapter 7, we review the process for selecting and prioritizing which HR practices to choose from these menus.

The third step is to craft an action plan to implement the HR practices you choose. Action planning assesses what can and should be done, then proceeds with specific plans around AR^2T^2 that involves answering these questions (see exhibit 5-1):

- *Action.* What will be done?

- *Resources.* What resources are required to do it?

- *Responsibility.* Who will do it?

- *Timing.* When will it be done?

- *Tracking.* Who will follow up and how?

EXHIBIT 5-1

Template for action planning

HR practice
Define the HR practice to invest in

Action: What will be done?	Resources: What resources are required to do it?	Responsibility: Who will do it?	Timing: When will it be done?	Tracking: Who will follow up and how?

As you apply this framework to targeted HR practices, they will move from theory to action, as demonstrated in chapter 7.

These three steps apply to each of the scenarios sketched in the opening paragraph. In each case, you would articulate how HR practices create value to investors, customers, line managers, or employees; define choices or alternative investments that could be made in the form of a menu; and finally, audit to help create an action plan for investing in HR practices that add the most value.

Flow of People

The war for talent may rage or simmer, but it's always there.[2] Any position from executive level to frontline employee that is difficult to fill becomes a potential battleground. Simply stated, firms with better talent will be more successful than firms with lesser talent.

Talent comes from the flow of people in an organization: how they enter, develop their skills, and move through (up or out). Talent management involves not only getting and keeping the good but identifying and removing the nonessential and outright bad. After all, the most strategic HR move a leader could ever make would be to place the firm's worst-performing employees with a competitor and hope they stay there for life.

Theory of Flow of People

While people practices add value to all stakeholders, employees are most directly affected. The deployment of people practices sends messages to employees about what matters most and that they can be successful. Most employees come to work wanting to do a good job. People practices communicate to them what doing a good job really means. Are the right people being hired? Are the right people being promoted? Are the right people going to training? Are the people who return from training doing the right things? If the answers are positive, everyone will be more likely to act in the organization's interest—and acting in the organization's best interest brings benefits to all stakeholder groups. Because of investments in people, investors will have more confidence, resulting in market value; customers will have relationships that create customer share; line managers will emphasize capabilities that deliver strategy; and employees will demonstrate the abilities expected of them.

Choices Around People

It's useful to regard the range of available people practices as a menu with six sections: buy, build, borrow, bounce, bind, and boost. Your job in HR is to prepare this menu of choices, then to help managers choose items from the menu that will work best for their situation. In the next few sections, we present templates for these menus. The menu that works for your organization will be formed from your experience with these HR practices, from learning what other leading-edge companies have done, and from research on HR best practices. Good menus list many alternatives, each of which can be delivered if selected. Chapter 7 deals with the process of picking the right item from the menu; here we synthesize practices related to people to create the beginnings of the people menu.

Buying: Choices in Staffing

Staffing brings people into the organization. It is probably the single most important HR practice, because if you have inadequate personnel, all the training, incentives, and communication in the world will not complete their makeover. Your people must have the abilities needed for today's job as well as tomorrow's. Staffing involves three major processes: expanding the candidate pool, hiring the best candidates, and orienting them to the work.[3]

Expanding the candidate pool improves your firm's chances of getting the employees it needs. Here are some ways to widen the pool.

- *Build relationships with key sources of talent.* Recruit on targeted campuses, develop relationships with key faculty members and with search firms who know your industry, and show up at technical conferences or trade shows.

- *Use referral hiring.* Ask current employees to suggest people they think might fit in, and pay a bounty for referrals who stay with you for a set period (a year or more). It's also useful to ask customers or suppliers for similar referrals.

- *Build an Internet hiring strategy.* Maintain a strong online presence with an attractive Web site linked to recruiting services; make it easy to apply for a job online; provide rapid feedback to let candidates know where they stand.

- *Target potential employees.* Use radio and TV ads; participate in job fairs; sponsor open houses; offer apprenticeships to strong prospects who are still in school; reach out to downsizing companies; recruit former employees who would be welcomed back. Build dossiers on candidates who reject offers, tracking events such as changes in their current company, marriage or the birth or graduation of a child, and salary reviews and project terminations that might make them interested in moving.

No matter how large the pool, it's still critical to fish out the right candidates and keep them hooked. Your "hit rate" will never be perfect, but if you do the right things, you will increase your ratio of offers to acceptances. Here are some ideas for increasing the hit rate.

- *Interview with intent to hire.* Communicate commitment to qualified candidates by including key line managers, customers, and coworkers in the interview process. Respond quickly after the interviews. Ask senior and visible line managers to invite the chosen applicant to join the firm (a call from a CEO or senior line manager sends a clear signal of how valuable the candidate is).

- *Create and market your employee value proposition.* Show what employees get from working at your company; brand your firm for future employees; advertise this value proposition to current and potential employees; communicate this value proposition in interviews and screening; personalize or tailor the employee value proposition to the needs of top candidates.

- *Offer financial assistance.* Financial assistance for new hires might include a sign-up bonus (cash or stock), help with student loans, relocation assistance (moving or home loans), and home office setup (a computer and connection to the workplace).

- *Communicate realistic but enticing opportunities.* Describe international assignments; review first posting and projects; discuss teammates and how the candidate will fit in with the team; highlight factors that tend to influence prospective employees (pay, benefits, vacation, work hours and policies); preview training opportunities for the first three years; discuss mentors and encourage mentorship of new employees.

- *Pay attention to personal issues.* Talk about spouse and children if relevant; review company culture around personal lifestyle; market the quality of life that the company creates; show how the company will attend to an employee's personal issues.

- *Be persistent.* The best candidates will have multiple job offers. Don't give up on them. Make them feel wanted by frequent contacts, even hokey kitsch (e.g., a shirt, jacket, or flowers from the company). Ensure that the targeted employees have daily contact with key people inside the company.

- *Form relationships.* Most work revolves around interpersonal relationships. Surround desirable candidates with a sense of being wanted and of fitting in. Help them sense that their future relationships at work with leaders and coworkers will be positive.

Once someone is hired, orientation is crucial in getting the candidate quickly up to speed and productive.[4] Sample orientation efforts include the following:

- *Administrative necessities.* Efficiently and quickly cover the administrative details (company ID, parking, official forms, computer hookup, and so on) to make a good first impression.

- *Early feedback.* Within thirty, sixty, and ninety days, offer direct and honest feedback about work to date. This sets a positive tone and makes any course corrections early in the employment.

- *Quick success.* Find an assignment where the employee can take responsibility for a task and accomplish it. Letting the new employee achieve success early creates a can-do feeling.

- *Orientation to the entire value chain.* Arrange contacts with suppliers and customers who will generate and use the output of the employee's work; show how the job fits into the overall strategy of the company.

- *Team assimilation.* Share team history, norms, expectations, and required performance. In order to build mutual acquaintances, have the team talk to the new employee and the new employee talk to the team.

- *Listening.* New employees often have insights on how to improve operations. Invite new employees to meals or other informal sessions with a leader to share their observations and ideas.

These days, we face an apparent paradox: hiring the right people is more critical than ever, but hiring is declining as a differentiator of performance. This is logical though somewhat counterintuitive. If you do not try to get the best people, your company will fail. However, your competitors are also trying for the best, and they're probably doing about as well as you are. So what makes the difference is not *who* you hire (unless, of course, you bring in people who can't do the job)—it's what you do with them afterward. And that does not mean simply retaining them. It means providing the environment, direction, and training for them to contribute optimally to business success.

Building: Choices in Training and Development. *Building* means unleashing latent talent by focusing on either training or development.[5] To make informed choices about training, HR leaders should address the following questions:

- *Who should attend the program?* Do you want to invite employees at one level or multiple levels, by themselves or in teams? Do you want to invite customers, investors, or suppliers to participate?

- *Who should present the program?* As program facilitators, will you use professors, consultants, or line managers who may be better at running a business than teaching, but who have enormous credibility and real-world experience? Do you want to include customers or investors in the teaching role as living case studies, role plays, or presenters?

- *Who should design the program?* Will you involve outside experts who have a point of view and experience in other companies? Will you enlist line managers, customers, or investors who want to design the training to accomplish their goals? Who will be on the program steering committee?

- *What should the program cover?* Will you build it around abilities individuals need to have? Around capabilities required for the organization to succeed? Or around results that key stakeholders need from participants? How will you build in action planning for individuals or teams? How will you ensure a transfer of learning from the training experience to the work site?

- *How will the program be delivered?* Will it be conducted on-site, off-site, or in a number of places? Will you use cases or action learning?

Will it focus on individuals, small groups or large organizational units? Will the course be self-directed or other-directed? How will technology (e-learning) contribute to the design and delivery of the course? Will it occur in a short time period (three days or a week) or over time (two days a month for six months)?

- *How will the program change the participants?* What will you do to measure the impact of the training? Will you look at reactions to training, knowledge received, behavioral change, actions taken, or business impact?[6] How will you be accountable for results? How will you follow up with action plans? How will you create a measure of financial return for the training investment?

The other half of the build menu comes from development—from opportunities to learn from experience.[7] Development may take a variety of forms:

- *Mobility.* Employees learn from new assignments that stretch them to learn new skills. Some firms have sponsored international job swaps to develop global sensitivity, functional rotations, or postings such as "deputyships" to encourage learning.

- *Mentoring or coaching.* Programs such as 360-degree feedback, assigned mentors, or formal coaching help employees learn, as do informal mentoring or coaching from leaders in day-to-day interactions with employees. Those who serve as mentors or coaches also learn from the experience.

- *Outside experience.* Participation in community service can help employees build both relationship networks and leadership skills. Sabbaticals allow time to explore ideas and concepts that may be only tangentially related to their current role. Fellowships to universities or think tanks often engage employees and orient them to new perspectives. Time off from work to explore personal issues may enable employees to return refreshed and engaged.

- *Personal development plan.* Creating a plan that includes reading, attending professional conferences, visiting other companies and individuals, or engaging in experiences designed to broaden perspectives (anything from singing in a choir to biking in the Himalayas) can help employees take responsibility for their own development.

- *Temporary assignments.* Ad hoc teams—projects taken on in addition to regular duties—often promote employee development. Internships (i.e., full-time temporary assignments) have a similar effect, allowing individuals to improve their understanding of the firm and vice versa.

Borrowing: Choices in Contracting for Talent

A firm need not own all the human capital it uses. It can take advantage of the talents of individuals who are not its full-time employees. Here are some options for accessing talent without ownership.

- *Form joint alliances.* Trade associations exist for almost every industry, allowing members to learn from others. Groups like the Conference Board, for example, have forums focused on performance within their industry. Consulting firms often team up with similar firms. Some industries codevelop new technology through alliances, as with the consortium (Apple, IBM, Microsoft, and other companies) that established the DVD standard.

- *Do site visits.* Visiting other companies often provides benchmarks and insights. This means going beyond the PowerPoint presentations to see how other companies really work.

- *Retain consultants.* Using consultants wisely brings new ideas into the company. Work to *adapt* rather than adopt their ideas, tailoring them to your business and making sure you own the results. Hire a specific individual rather than a firm; create a clear contract with expected outcomes and processes for delivering those outcomes; and continually monitor both the performance of the consultant and the impact of the ideas and tools. Assign permanent employees to work with the consultant to transfer knowledge into the firm at the end of the project.

- *Outsource work.* Figure out where you want to excel to win and where you are willing to accept industry average. When industry average is good enough, consider outsourcing the work to vendors who become your partners. Their expertise enables you to focus on your expertise—but you still need to manage the contract carefully, maintaining clarity about service levels and payments for performance (see chapter 8 for ideas on outsourcing).

- *Maintain relationships with former employees.* Former employees can be a source of enduring talent, either as vendors or as part of their new organizations. This works both ways: former consultants often channel business to their old firms when they move into line manager positions. And former technicians and managers often find ways to be of use to previous employers while working in consulting or supplier organizations.

Bouncing: Choices in Shrinking the Workforce

Although the term *rightsizing* makes language mavens howl, it expresses an important concept. In the current business environment, a firm needs a workforce of the correct size for its immediate and near-term output—and few firms can find ways to increase output (and sales) to absorb excess workforce capacity. Firms need to cut back to bring things into balance. And size isn't the only factor: any firm, no matter how lean its workforce, needs the right people—those with the will and ability to pursue its goals. It doesn't matter whether poor performance comes from a bad hire or from failure to update the knowledge and skills of current employees; the firm will suffer as long as it is allowed to continue. We refer to both types of cutback as *bouncing.*[8]

The risk of keeping poor performers is magnified because their scanty or damaged output is often the least of the problems they cause; the perception that poor performance is acceptable can be devastating. In bad economic times, having a poor performer in a chair is worse than having an empty chair, because they use resources and do not contribute. In good economic times, weaker performers may produce, but they still cause problems, because tolerance for their poor performance may become a standard. For best results, deal with performance problems openly. Just sliding a poor performer out the door will eliminate inferior output and make the firm more efficient by relieving coworkers of the ex-employee's drag—but it ignores a third and far more powerful benefit: setting an example. Instead of explaining the firing of a specific individual, most firms simply lie. They say something like "Bob Leblanc is seeking more attractive career alternatives consistent with his long-term goals and aspirations"—even if Leblanc was caught cheating customers. The inhibiting factor may be threat of legal action, a tradition of avoiding harsh messages, or lack of clear criteria and evidence. Whatever the reason, the decision to gloss over the departure costs the organization a valuable opportunity to signal its behavioral and achievement standards.

Removing employees for any reason should be difficult. It should be personally painful for the responsible leader and require reflection on what went wrong. Communicating care for the employees who leave and who stay becomes important in any circumstance. The TV-cute tag line "You're fired!" is archaic and destroys employee goodwill. It's necessary to move decisively but to show care by offering performance and outplacement counseling and by considering the impact on the individual.

In the end, however, the decision to remove an employee should come from a system, not a relationship. Choices for paring back the workforce vary depending on the circumstance:

- *Involuntary downsizing.* When labor costs must be reduced, HR leaders should take care to ensure that the right people leave. Use strategic differentials (e.g., cut 15 percent in one department and only 5 percent in another, rather than 10 percent across the board) to focus the cuts where the slack is greatest. In addition to moderating the overall impact by encouraging early retirements, creating severance packages, and using outplacement firms to help employees find new jobs, make sure your top performers feel secure. Offer attractive jobs to employees who can be reassigned. After the downsizing, reassure people and help them stay engaged and focused on the work, rather than on protecting their careers.

- *Performance problems.* Employees who are not meeting expectations must be removed before they taint the rest of the workforce. Ensure fair due process, of course, and fulfill legal requirements and union agreements—but avoid the common regret of not having acted soon enough. Don't agonize over employees who cannot do the work. Be clear about what is expected, and then make it the employee's choice to stay and work or to not work and leave.

Binding: Choices in Retaining Talent

Retention—binding existing talent to your firm—matters at all levels.[9] Senior managers with vision and competence are critical to a firm's success, which is why they are hot prospects for rival recruiting. Many technical, operational, and hourly workers are equally critical. Investments in individual talent often take years to pay back. Often referred to as "A" players, an organization's top talent produces many times the value of average or poor talent. Here are some of the choices for binding top talent to your firm.

- *Find out why talented people leave.* Ask talented people why they have decided to respond to the eighty-fifth headhunter who called after not doing so earlier—and respond to the conditions they report. Be honest in looking at this data to figure out what you might have done differently. If high performers are leaving certain parts of the organization in disproportionate numbers, investigate conditions in those areas.

- *Offer financial inducements to stay.* Although money is rarely the dominant motivator when people leave, it can be a factor in the decision to stay. True pay-for-performance incentives send a clear message to top performers. Retention bonuses (cash or stock options for those who stay a designated length of time) also help keep top talent from moving.

- *Offer intrinsic rewards to stay.* For the people you most want to keep, the opportunity to identify and undertake high-value, challenging work is the biggest inducement to stay. Everyone wins. The company gets greater value per compensation dollar, and the employees are both happier on the job and more valuable on the market. Customers and shareholders are better off by having employees face the greater challenges of meeting customer needs or reducing hidden costs.

- *Offer other nonfinancial inducements to stay.* Perks help assure people that their employer values their contributions, and people who feel valued are likely to reciprocate. Sabbaticals, development experiences (especially when they include top management visibility and reputation), flexible work arrangements, family support, and other measures can help bind employees to their jobs, especially when they can choose the mix that suits their needs. Simply letting talented employees know they are valued is an amazingly simple but profound gesture.

Boosting: Choices in Promotion

Promotions not only put people in the right jobs, they show what matters to your firm. Care in this area ensures that the right signals are sent to all stakeholders. Here are some of the choices around promotion.

- *Establish criteria for the new job.* To match people and jobs, you need to know what the job will involve. To define clear requirements, translate the strategy into specific expectations: What do we want a person in this job to deliver? To be known for? To accomplish? Answering these questions enables you to evaluate candidates against an accepted standard.

- *Allow volunteers—but don't stop there.* Some people want to be promoted when their desire exceeds their capacity. Others hold back when ready for more complex jobs because of lack of confidence, or because of outside factors that seem to make it unfeasible to accept. Thorough and candid career discussions should help you know when someone is ready and able to take a promotion, and what (if any) adjustments need to be made to deal with work-life balance questions.

- *Evaluate candidate potential.* Few people promoted into a more senior job are really ready for it (or they would have had it already). Promotion practices need to include an assessment of the candidate's capacity to grow into the job, which requires willingness to learn and try new things. Be aware that what resulted in high performance in the present job may not be what is required in the next job. Include multiple assessors to gather different points of view about potential candidates.

- *Support new job holders.* Once the decision is made, throw your full support behind the chosen candidate. It is likely that two or more candidates could do the job well and that the winner will be only marginally preferable. Nonetheless, even someone who wins a new job with 51 percent of the votes needs to go ahead with 99 percent of the confidence.

Action Plans for People

In creating an action plan for the flow of people, HR professionals may need to audit their current state of managing people. The people flow audit in assessment 5-1 helps you determine how you are doing and on what to focus in order to get more from your people practices.

Once you've assessed the most productive categories, you can ask which of all the ideas on your people menu (and other menus) will create intangible value for shareholders, lead to customer share, deliver organization capabilities, and ensure individual abilities.

ASSESSMENT 5-1

Audit for people flow

1. What percentage of our market value is intangibles?

2. How has our price/earnings (P/E) ratio changed over the past ten years compared to our largest competitors'?

3. Who are our largest customers? What are their buying criteria? How important is relationship to their purchasing decision?

4. What are the most salient capabilities for strategy? How are we performing on those capabilities?

5. What is our productivity?

6. What is the employee commitment level as determined by:

   - Retention of our best employees
   - Departure of our worst employees
   - Employee attitude surveys

7. How aligned are our people flow practices with each stakeholder's value?

   Score low, medium, or high as 1, 2, or 3 in each cell in the following grid.

		STAKEHOLDER VALUE			
	Practice	Investor	Customer	Line manager	Employee
Buy	Expanding the pool	1 2 3	1 2 3	1 2 3	1 2 3
	Increasing the hit rate	1 2 3	1 2 3	1 2 3	1 2 3
	Orienting new employees	1 2 3	1 2 3	1 2 3	1 2 3
Build	Assessing the needs	1 2 3	1 2 3	1 2 3	1 2 3
	Offering training	1 2 3	1 2 3	1 2 3	1 2 3
	Offering development	1 2 3	1 2 3	1 2 3	1 2 3
Borrow	Forming alliances	1 2 3	1 2 3	1 2 3	1 2 3
	Engaging consultants	1 2 3	1 2 3	1 2 3	1 2 3
	Outsourcing	1 2 3	1 2 3	1 2 3	1 2 3
Bounce	Involuntary outplacement	1 2 3	1 2 3	1 2 3	1 2 3
	Performance-based outplacement	1 2 3	1 2 3	1 2 3	1 2 3
Bind	Keeping great people	1 2 3	1 2 3	1 2 3	1 2 3
Boost	Promoting the right people	1 2 3	1 2 3	1 2 3	1 2 3

8. Of all the people practices we could focus on, what are the top three in terms of their potential to create value?

9. Do we have action plans in place for these three priorities?

Flow of Performance Management

Without doubt, incentives change behavior. Inevitably, people do what they are rewarded for and leaders get what they reward, but not always what they expect. Without clear standards, measured against expected results and linked to the rewards people want, employee behavior may seem very strange.[10] On the other hand, when standards and incentives align with company goals, the goals generally come within reach. For example, 3M makes innovation a goal, and it ties meaningful financial and nonfinancial rewards to a *vitality index*—the percentage of revenue from products introduced in the last five years. The clarity of this index encourages experimentation, risk taking, and sharing of ideas.

Theory of Performance Management

As with people flow, the theory of performance management can almost go without saying. It is easy to convince managers that performance matters. But it becomes necessary to translate the desire for performance into practices that encourage and sustain performance from everyone—from the top management of the firm through the whole range of line and staff employees. A personnel system needs resources and leadership support to be applied in ways that reliably link performance to rewards. This assures investors that the firm's intangible value is secure, and it provides managers and employees with a clear line of sight between their behavior and their rewards, motivating them to provide optimal customer service.

Choices for Performance Management Flow

HR practices that drive performance include setting standards, offering financial and nonfinancial rewards, and follow-up, and we offer menus for each. Setting standards is itself a three-part process—HR leaders need to decide what to measure, then build systems for measurement and for appraising employee performance.

Setting Standards: What to Measure

People often measure what is easy, not what is right.[11] For example, consumer products firms often measure revenue per line but not profit per line, per customer, or per area (all of which are tougher to track)—then may fail to notice their fortunes declining behind the rising index. Learning how to define and measure what is *right* rather than what is easy begins the process of performance management. Here are some of the HR practices that create clear standards and measures.

- *Align standards and measures to strategy.* The line of sight from business strategy to personal expectations must be clear. To get effective standards, ask, "If this strategy works, what will we see more of? Less of?" That will lead you to measurable behaviors and outputs tied to your strategy. The balanced scorecard is a helpful discipline for defining standards related to value for investors (financial measures), customers (service and share measures), organization (capability measures), and employees (ability measures). Stakeholder-based standards and measures show employees how to add real value.

- *Balance behavior and output standards and measures for individuals and teams.*[12] Standards and measures fall into four categories, as shown in table 5-1. To decide what is worth most attention, divide one hundred points among the four cells. Some jobs carry more weight in some cells than others. Sales jobs would probably have more points dedicated to individual outcomes (sales per employee) than R&D jobs, which might place more weight on individual behavior (participation on a team). Nonetheless, each cell should have its own standards and measures.

- *Prioritize measures.* Not everything that can be measured should be measured. Concentrate on the standards and measures that matter most to each stakeholder. Balanced scorecards need to be focused to have real impact.

- *Identify lead indicators.* The best standards and measures are lead, not lag, indicators. Lead indicators affect future performance. Employee attitude, for example, can be a lead indicator of customer attitude.[13] So, in selecting standards and measures, it is important to pick items that will affect other items. In one organization, a sales review found that 7 percent of cold calls reached people who said they might be interested; 10 percent of those who expressed interest accepted a follow-up; 25 percent of those who accepted a follow-up said they were committed to using the product; and 50 percent of those who claimed commitment actually used the product. Because of the insights in this value chain, the leaders focused attention on increasing cold calls. They also worked to increase the success percentages of each step, but the lead indicator—the variable employees could control directly—was the number of initial contacts.

- *Set stretch targets.* Standards and measures should demand performance higher than current levels, without being unattainable. With a group doing similar work, a simple solution is to take the top of the current performance range and set the standard near there. That sends the message that the standard is attainable—someone has already beaten it—but meeting it will raise overall performance. In the sales example, representatives were averaging 5.2 calls per day in similar territories, with a range from 2 to 9.5. The new standard was set at 9, providing an attainable stretch target.

- *Measure what can be controlled.* When the goal is to influence customers and investors, it's tempting to use measures that focus on purchases and stock price. Unfortunately, those results are often too far removed from employee daily action to serve as a useful guide. Tracking stock price motivates employees to follow the market, but they feel like fans rather than participants because they cannot see how their work directly affects shareholder value. In the sales example, the contacts-per-day target was within the control of each individual employee, thus becoming a valuable standard and measure.

Setting Standards: How to Build Measurement Systems

Deciding what to measure communicates what matters; the process of setting and monitoring standards determines how well those measurements work. For example, two theater groups with the same script may get dramatically different reviews. Two firms with the same standards may get drastically different results. It all depends on how well they use the material. Here are some choices for setting and monitoring standards:

TABLE 5-1

Types of standards and measures

	Individual	Team
Behavior	Competences	Team processes
Output	Management by objectives	Unit performance

- *Who sets and tracks standards.* When employees participate in setting and monitoring standards, they accept more accountability for delivering results. One of the best leadership practices is to share data with employees, then ask what they think they can and should do. We have found that most of the time, employees set standards as tough as managers would have set—or tougher. And virtually all the time, results are better with employee-participation standards than with imposed standards.

- *What tracking means.* Standards and measures must have both positive and negative consequences. To produce action, the results must be more than mildly interesting—which means they must be tied to financial and nonfinancial rewards.

- *How results are tracked.* Ownership matters. When employees post their own results and observe how they are doing, the feedback loop is tight enough to influence their performance. It is useful to create dashboards—either online or paper-and-pencil—that allow employees at all levels to track their performance. Timely information helps people self-monitor and improve.

- *Frequency of feedback.* In addition to ongoing performance dashboards, it is useful to provide formal feedback at regular times. Quarterly, semiannual, or annual reviews give people a chance to step back and look at the big picture.

Setting Standards: How to Build Appraisal Systems

Combining standards and measures forms a performance appraisal process. This process answers a series of questions for employees.

- *What's my job?* Employees should see their individual job responsibilities reflected in the appraisal's performance standards and measures.

- *How am I doing?* Employees should learn how well they are performing on the job. Such feedback helps employees determine how they are doing in light of standardized expectations.

- *Does anybody care?* Employees should learn that managers care not only about accomplishing business results but also about employees' quality of life.

- *How do we fit in?* Employees should see how their personal work and how the work of their unit fit into the overall strategy of their organization.

- *How are we doing?* Employees should learn not only how they are doing individually but also how their unit is performing. High-performing individuals can often help bring up the level of low-performing units if they recognize the need, and low-performing employees in high-performing units can be inspired to improve their efforts.

Allocating Financial Rewards

Money may not be everyone's main motivator, but it does affect everyone—and its economic, psychological, and social implications matter more for some employees than for others.[14] Economically, money enables employees to develop a lifestyle that suits their needs. Psychologically, money provides a feeling of personal worth and self-esteem. Socially, money determines a pecking order and a role and legitimacy in peer groups. Choices around money can generally be clustered into four quadrants, as in table 5-2. (The short- or long-term time frame refers to the relationship between the effort and the reward.)

- *Short-term cash.* Base salary or on-the-spot cash compensation helps employees create and maintain a lifestyle. Payments should be equitable internally and externally—that is, those who perform better should be paid better, and pay should fit the range of market rates. Base salary generally reflects tenure with the organization, job title, and performance.

- *Short-term equity.* Equity awards make the employee an owner in the company. Stock grants (where the employee receives stock as

TABLE 5-2

Financial choices

	Short term	Long term
Cash	Base salary or on-the-spot rewards for milestones or exceptional performance	Bonus (a form of profit or gain sharing)
Equity	Restricted stock or stock grant	Stock option

compensation instead of cash) can be based on performance, title, or seniority.

- *Long-term cash*. Cash bonuses based on continuing performance (often for a three-year period) help employees focus on the lasting implications of their day-to-day work. Bonuses often make up from 10 percent to 50 percent of total cash compensation, putting enough pay at risk to reduce the common tendency to suboptimize for instant results.

- *Long-term equity*. Long-term equity in the form of stock options (the right to buy shares at a fixed price regardless of current market value) enables employees to gain wealth as the firm gains market value. The higher the price goes, the more an option is worth. Traditional accounting practices keep options off the books, expensing them only upon exercise because they cost the firm nothing until then—and may never cost it anything. This off-the-books value has made them a popular form of compensation. However, recent legislation calls for the expensing of options when offered, which may reduce their future use.

Depending on an employee's level and role, the financial incentives from each of the four cells may vary. Entry-level employees often receive the vast majority of their total compensation in short-term cash, as in their base salary. At the most senior levels, executives often receive much of their total compensation from long-term equity.

Owning stock helps employees become—and therefore act like—owners, which provides an incentive to promote stock ownership. Companies often match employee stock purchases, or they put some or all of the retirement fund in company stock. United Parcel Service (UPS), for example, promises hourly employees that if they work steadily for UPS and take advantage of employee stock purchase programs, they are likely to retire as millionaires through stock appreciation. Many firms require senior executives to hold at least a stated minimum amount of equity, often a multiple of salary. For example, we know one CEO who had to hold ten times annual salary in equity within three years of becoming CEO. Dividing one hundred points among the four cells in table 5-2 helps you determine which type of financial compensation would be most appropriate for each employee.

Financial rewards must be linked to meeting performance standards. That is, someone who falls short of the standards must lose financial opportunities; likewise, someone who meets the standards must see financial returns follow.

Designing and delivering a total compensation program requires a compensation philosophy: What are the goals of our compensation program? What percentage of compensation should be at risk and what should be base salary? How do we want to target the compensation of employees relative to market? The resulting compensation philosophy creates measurable standards for employees to follow and uses those standards to evaluate employee performance and allocate rewards. Since people do what they are rewarded for when the standards are clear and the rewards are meaningful, financial compensation deserves the attention it receives.

Unfortunately, financial compensation has some drawbacks as a motivating instrument. It is difficult to change quickly and awkward to tie to daily performance. In addition, it tends to create feelings of entitlement. As a result, many firms are relying more and more on nonfinancial rewards.

Allocating Nonfinancial Rewards

Money matters, but other things often matter more.[15] Too often, nonfinancial rewards are given out randomly or to everyone regardless of performance. When the allocation is based on meeting standards, employees focus attention and energy.

Nonfinancial rewards can include the entire array of what an employee receives from work, occupying each segment of VOI^2C^2E (the employee value proposition framework introduced in chapter 4) as follows:

- *Vision.* A strong vision gives employees a sense of pride in the firm, which is enhanced on one hand by symbols such as T-shirts or souvenirs and on the other by efforts to build the community through service and giving that are in line with the company's vision. One firm asked people to submit photographs of employees engaged in fulfilling the vision. These were posted to communicate the vision and build morale.

- *Opportunity.* The chance to shine—making presentations to senior management, attending training normally reserved for higher-level staff or designed to develop new skills, engaging in conversations through forums or meals—helps reinforce people's sense of value. Status in the firm is also a motivator, so promotions or chances for promotion provide rewards over and above any increase in pay.

- *Incentive.* Recognition and praise can do as much as cash—or more—to keep people motivated and confident of their value. Simply expressing gratitude is often the most important incentive of all.

- *Impact.* People like to make a difference. Shifting decision-making responsibilities to the employee, encouraging employee suggestions for improvement, acknowledging and rewarding good suggestions, and allowing an employee to represent the company to outside interests all build intrinsic rewards into the job.

- *Community.* Building community goes beyond company social events, though those can be welcome if you have a community to begin with. Consider inviting a team to participate in selecting future members. Or you might want to get together as a team for outside activities—10K runs, helping at a community center, and so forth.

- *Communication.* Sheer access to information is a reward. You can emphasize this by limiting some communication networks to high-performing employees so they're informed of developments earlier than other employees.

- *Experimentation.* Give high-performing employees flexibility on the job. The freedom to choose hours and location of work and other working conditions is a benefit people will strive to retain.

Firms also have extensive benefits and perks programs that financially and nonfinancially reward employees. Benefits may include more traditional things like time off, sick leave, medical benefits, insurance, and retirement planning, but may also include elder care, tuition reimbursement, scholarships for children, concierge service while at work, transportation subsidies, or other services. These nonfinancial benefits become useful when they are not just entitlements that employees expect, but benefits that employees earn because they meet standards. Often, benefits become standardized across an organization, to the extent that all employees come to expect the same level of benefits. Finding ways to link benefits to meeting standards helps make them more performance-based.

Follow-up

Follow-up (i.e., feedback on prior activities and "feedforward" on what's needed) is critical to performance.[16] Without honest self-assessment, no one can make progress. Here are some of the menu choices for providing follow-up.

- *Chat informally.* Informal conversations are often less onerous and more effective than a formal appraisal in an office with forms and procedures. In a casual setting—playing basketball or walking down the hall or over lunch—a comment about performance can raise the issue and lead to a productive conversation.

- *Supply data.* People can't fix what they can't see. Provide charts and graphs that show revenues, profits, customer share, or other data both companywide and as far as possible for individual work units. Offer specific examples of personal behaviors that need fixing.

- *Let people draw their own conclusions.* Data means more when the firm shares it and asks employees what they think. When employees assess the implications for themselves, they engage more fully and work to adjust results as needed. We encourage leaders to share the problem, not the solution; then let employees cocreate a solution that works for them. Questions often generate more thought than answers.

- *Explain the "why," not the "what."* When employees understand the "why," they generally accept the "what." Employees who understand why something needs to happen are more willing to work to make it happen than when they're simply told what to do.

- *Do it.* The most difficult part of follow-up is doing it. HR's role is to make sure that following up with employees is part of every supervisor's and team leader's performance appraisal.

Action Plans for Performance Management Flow

As with the flow of people, the performance management action plan should focus on two to four HR practices. The performance management audit shown in assessment 5-2 will guide your attention to the types of practices likely to have the biggest payoff. Once you select the top two or three performance priorities, you can follow the AR^2T^2 logic found in the grid in exhibit 5-1 to create an action plan.

ASSESSMENT 5-2

Audit for performance management flow

1. How clearly have we translated our business strategy into individual and organizational standards?

2. To what extent are we able to measure the standards that we have set in behavioral and outcome terms that can be monitored over time?

3. To what extent have we made our financial rewards contingent upon meeting our standards?

4. To what extent have we made our nonfinancial rewards contingent upon meeting our standards?

5. To what extent do we have regular follow-up with employees on how well they are meeting our standards?

6. To what extent do we have a consistent performance management process for all employees throughout the organization?

7. To what extent are leaders in the organization taking personal responsibility and accountability for the performance management process?

8. How aligned are our performance management flow practices with each stakeholder? Score low, medium, or high as 1, 2, or 3 in each cell in the following grid.

		STAKEHOLDER			
		Investor	Customer	Line manager	Employee
Setting standards	What to measure?	1 2 3	1 2 3	1 2 3	1 2 3
	How to build measurement systems?	1 2 3	1 2 3	1 2 3	1 2 3
	How to build appraisal systems?	1 2 3	1 2 3	1 2 3	1 2 3
Allocating financial rewards	Short-term cash	1 2 3	1 2 3	1 2 3	1 2 3
	Short-term equity	1 2 3	1 2 3	1 2 3	1 2 3
	Long-term cash	1 2 3	1 2 3	1 2 3	1 2 3
	Long-term equity	1 2 3	1 2 3	1 2 3	1 2 3
Allocating nonfinancial rewards	VOI^2C^2E	1 2 3	1 2 3	1 2 3	1 2 3
Follow-up		1 2 3	1 2 3	1 2 3	1 2 3

9. Of all the performance management practices we could focus on, what are the top three in terms of potential to create value?

Menus for People and Performance Flows

Value from HR practices will be defined by investors, customers, line managers, and employees. When HR professionals understand the theory and choices for people and performance, they will create action plans that invest in the most effective HR practices. Creating the people and performance menus is a first step in this work.

6

HR Practices That Add Value

Flow of Information and Work

*To what extent do our HR practices that focus on information
(outside-in and inside-out) add value?*

*To what extent do our HR practices that focus on work flow
(who does the work, how is the work done, and where
is the work done) add value?*

P EOPLE AND PERFORMANCE MANAGEMENT—the topics covered in
chapter 5—are the traditional province of HR, but HR professionals need to devote their attention to two additional areas as well: the
flow of information and the flow of work. These emerging HR activity
areas have great impact on the human side of the business and add value
to key stakeholders.

- *Flow of information.* Organizations must manage the inward flow of
  customer, shareholder, economic and regulatory, technological, and
  demographic information to make sure that employees recognize
  and adapt to external realities. They must also manage the internal
  flow of information across horizontal and vertical boundaries. HR

professionals, with their sensitivity to people and processes, are ideally suited to assist with both information flows.

- *Flow of work.* Organizations must manage the flow of work from product or service demand through order fulfillment, to make sure their obligations are met. To do so, they distribute work to individuals and groups, and set up a structure to integrate the varied outputs into a cooperative whole. They design work processes and set up a physical environment that promotes effective and efficient work. HR professionals are ideally suited to assist in all aspects of the flow of work.

Like chapter 5, this chapter sketches the underlying theory for each topic, then outlines the menu of choices open to HR. This chapter also discusses action planning, offering templates to help you implement the choices you make and to track your progress in implementing the chosen practices.

Flow of Information

Information is the stuff of which organizations are made, by which they function and through which they prosper or fail.[1] Information permits a company to identify and meet the demands of competitive markets, creates company value in the eyes of customers and shareholders, and enables a company to function within the ethical parameters of its communities. Through information, organizations share goals, craft strategies, make decisions, and integrate behaviors. Information enables innovation to proceed, change to occur, service and quality to improve, costs to stay under control, and productivity to increase. It determines who has influence over which issues and who does not, giving meaning and direction to work and purpose to the lives of managers and employees alike.

Theory of the Flow of Information

The flow of information drives the flow of value. Investors, customers, line managers, and employees all value the organization based on what they know about it, either from observation and personal experience or from reading and listening. And since firsthand information is frequently limited to relatively small subsets of stakeholders, it behooves the organization to make sure the word spreads.

This principle of information flow applies at all levels. Companies need to be meticulous both in financial record keeping and in preparing clear and accurate reports for investors and regulatory agencies. They need both to establish the basics of intangible value discussed in chapter 3 and to make sure capital markets learn about their intangible assets. They need both to treat customers and employees well and to make sure that current and prospective customers and employees confidently expect such treatment.

Information is also what binds supply chains and work flows together. The more an organization can do to make sure information passes smoothly to the places where people can use it, the better off it will be.[2] And since information is much of what creates culture, organizations that create and sustain effective cultures manage information effectively. Thereby, employees clearly understand the importance of their work to customers and to the organization as a whole.

Choices Around Flow of Information

Information choices fall into two broad categories: communication strategy and information transmission. Underlying both categories, however, is the mindset within the organization. It needs to be focused and receptive, or communication will fail. Building an organization with a focused and receptive shared mindset is a formidable challenge, but it can be done when senior management leads the way, modeling and legitimizing diverse and reality-based ways of thinking rather than clinging to an institutionalized dominant paradigm.

Communication Strategy

A comprehensive communication strategy creates value through messages designed to meet the needs of each stakeholder. All messages need to be based on a clear understanding of their immediate purpose and to reflect the company's overall leadership philosophy. For example, if the leadership style is "telling and selling," then messages will be directive. Employees will receive brisk statements of what they are expected to do. If the leadership style is "involving and empowering," then employees will receive messages designed to evoke personal action by sharing basic information about customers, competitors, company financial performance, and other strengths and weaknesses. Here are some other basic choices.

- *Ensure consistency between messages and reality.* Organizations need a seamless message that links internal and external stakeholders. With today's multiplicity of information channels, it's impossible to present one face to employees and another to the world. Brand identity, customer experience, and organizational capability must all be consistent.[3]

- *Codify commonly understood concepts, language, and logic.*[4] A key strategic element is the establishment of powerful and flexible concepts ("We focus on customers"), language ("When we talk about customers, we mean *external* customers"), and logic patterns ("Customers determine our products, not vice versa"). It takes time and discipline on the part of management to establish these foundational elements—but without them, communication remains problematic.

- *Choose an "integrity shepherd."* Designate a member of the management team to keep track of the company's concepts, language, and logic. Part of this shepherd's job is to help senior leaders give messages time to develop and take root, resisting the temptation to change too soon.

- *Select media consistent with the message and audience.* This choice may seem obvious, but people often get it wrong. They send out important and emotionally loaded messages through e-mail or memos; they hold expensive off-site meetings to plan cost reductions; they phone critical suppliers or customers instead of talking face-to-face.

- *Know and speak to your audience.* Communications must be designed to reach people in their frame of reference. If your concepts, language, or logic seems too alien, your message is unlikely to be grasped or accepted.

- *Ensure integration and alignment.* Virtually all HR practices have an important communication component; they reveal what the company really is and does. Likewise, top management needs one voice when it comes to policy and direction, and corporate communications. Corporate messages, leadership communications, and HR signals must be in sync with one another. It's a major problem if the leadership says the organization will go in one direction, while HR hires, trains, promotes, measures, and rewards people for going somewhere else.

- *Establish accountability.* Communication is everybody's responsibility. From the CEO to the janitor, everyone needs to be mindful of and effective at communication; otherwise, chaos reigns. At the same time, someone must develop a comprehensive strategy for everyone to follow. In small firms, this is generally the CEO, but larger firms tend to select a communications specialist to work closely with the top team. Increasingly, this specialist reports to the senior HR executive, which helps keep the organization's communications efforts and HR practices consistent.

- *Measure and improve communication effectiveness.* A comprehensive communication strategy establishes mechanisms for detecting and correcting errors.[5] Management by walking around is the most straightforward way to learn how well messages are being received, but in complex environments, formal and informal feedback meetings and statistical surveys can evoke more detailed responses. With such feedback, the organization can make sense of its communications processes and manage communications more effectively.[6]

Information Transmission

Information moves in five directions: from outside an organization to inside, from inside to outside, from the top down, from the bottom up, and across individuals, teams, departments, and business units. For each direction, the issues are similar (Who sends? Who receives? What is sent? How is it sent? When is it sent?), but the choices differ. There are so many permutations of these issues that the range of choices can seem overwhelming. The following sections outline the choices we have found to be most valuable to customers, investors, managers, and employees. Because our recent research suggests the central importance of HR in moving external information into the firm, we begin with that flow.[7]

OUTSIDE IN

- *Know the "what" and the "how much" of customer information.* Organizations need to know what their customers want. Many companies gather information from focus groups or interviews of existing customers. This is useful for what *current* customers want but doesn't indicate *to what degree* the total market has the same wants. Answering the "how much" questions requires market research on a large enough scale for statistical validity.

- *Know most about the most important customers.* As discussed in chapter 3, for most businesses, some customers matter far more than others—they buy more, they provide greater returns, or they are less costly. As a result, it is useful to segment the market into meaningful categories before devoting much time to research.[8] Most companies know much about current customers that have both large potential and small potential. They devote much of their attention to hanging on to current buyers both large and small. They often become complacent and ignore the greatest opportunity for growth—potentially large customers with whom your company currently does little business. Obtaining accurate information from this category is more difficult yet conceivably more important for sustained business success.

- *Gather comparative data.* Comparisons bring data to life. How do your customers compare you against your competitors? How do your customers compare you today to how you were doing a year ago? How do your customers compare you to their own expectations?

- *Create and gather information through joint interaction with customers.*[9] One powerful way to grasp the concepts, language, logic, and priorities of customers is to join them in mutually beneficial activities. Such activities might include joint R&D efforts, joint solving of production or distribution problems, joint training programs, and joint interaction with customers' customers.[10]

- *Expose management and employees to customer requirements.* Direct customer interaction can often change in powerful ways how managers and employees think and behave.[11] Invite customers to management meetings, disseminate videotapes of customers describing how their lives have been influenced by your products and services, involve production employees in market research, bring customers in to plant operations and company celebrations, or have employees visit customers' businesses or homes to see exactly how products add value.

- *Bring investor logic into the firm.* Key investors have much to contribute in management and employee meetings. Investors tend to be objective, blunt, and highly credible when they provide feedback on company performance.

- *Enlist vendors as additional sources of innovation.* Outsourcing innovation mitigates risks, accelerates innovation, and reaches otherwise inaccessible talent.[12] Some companies are going beyond calling for proposals from specific vendors. Eli Lilly's InnoCentive.com Web site, for example, lists difficult pharmaceutical and technical challenges—and awards from $5,000 to $100,000 to the scientists (and hobbyists) around the world who propose successful solutions.

INSIDE OUT

- *Create the substance of the brand, then communicate it.* The perception of quality products and services is essential, but it must be supported by products and services that, in fact, have high quality. In the appliance industry, for example, Maytag has worked to communicate its quality by emphasizing the loneliness of the Maytag repairman. First create the reality; then create the perception of reality. Ultimately, companies win on the basis of customers' positive perceptions that are backed up by positive realities. For example, Maytag wins on perceived quality that is supported by high-quality products.

- *Communicate the brand image and then work to sustain it.* The perception-reality tie works both ways. Brands can be powerful statements of aspirations. For example, one of the world's most famous corporate slogans is GE's "We bring good things to life"—the ongoing goal that GE continually pursues through its customer-focused products and services. To embody their brands, companies must hire the right people, give them the right training, provide the right measurement and rewards, communicate the right internal messages, and develop the right kinds of leaders.[13]

- *Create emotional ties with customers.* When customers move beyond valuing a brand's utility to *loving* it, the company gains tremendous traction in the marketplace. Consider Harley-Davidson, for example: its customers tattoo the Harley-Davidson logo on their arms! Harley works to embody its culture proposition of fun, counterculture, and outdoor camaraderie. It responds to customer feedback in product design and communicates that responsiveness through super-engagement events such as HOG (for Harley Owner's Group) rallies, where its executives mingle with customers.

- *Create ties of trust with customers.* The intangible value of trust is especially important to communicate, and that requires both behaving in trustworthy ways and being known for it. The Johnson &

Johnson Credo is perhaps the best-known example of how a company creates ties of trust with customers. J&J's handling of the infamous Tylenol tampering incident demonstrated its willingness to place customers' best interests first. The company has built a remarkable level of consumer trust in its brand.

Top Down

- *Present major issues in top management's voice.* The source enhances the impact of a message, or detracts from it. In one study, 62 percent of employees reported preferring to hear about major issues from top management—and only 15 percent of senior managers said they were doing so.[14] But talk alone backfires—messages must be communicated through actions as well as words. HR's role is to encourage top management to act consistent with their talk.

- *Present action items in the immediate supervisor's voice.* The most credible source for information aimed at frontline change is the first-line supervisor.[15] HR needs to make sure that supervisors are trained in communication skills, and that they have access to the messages that need to be shared and the information that is relevant for their respective departments or teams.

- *Balance the "whats" and the "whys."* Many managers and supervisors have a natural tendency to communicate what is happening, what is needed, and what is expected. They may be impatient when it comes to taking the extra time and effort to communicate the underlying reasons. Yet when people understand the "why," they are more likely to accept the "what" and do the "how."

- *Balance the big picture and details.* Employees need to understand how their individual jobs add value for the whole company. They need to understand capital market demands, competitive threats, and customer expectations.[16] At the same time, they need information about their own responsibilities and performance, the consequences of good or bad performance, as well as technical information and how to get problems solved.

- *Balance good news and bad news.* Some executives are effective at sharing bad news but do a poor job sharing good news. Others are excellent at sharing good news but hesitate to share bad news. Generally, what employees value most is honesty. Claims that the news is all good tend to create distrust—and may encourage complacency anyway. Unmitigated bad news can wreak havoc on morale; employees need to know what they have to work with as they begin urgent improvements. And if the outlook is uncertain, then that should be part of the message. People unfailingly sense unstated uncertainty, and the rumor mill takes over—almost always painting the worst possible scenario.

- *Apply multiple media.* Employees generally prefer face-to-face communication—"town hall" meetings, team briefings, two-way video broadcasts, management by walking around, corporate celebrations.[17] However, in increasingly cost-conscious and globally dispersed business environments, face-to-face communications are being augmented by videotapes, one-way video broadcasts, teleconferences, direct mail, intranets, company newsletters, and even local newspapers and radio.

Bottom Up

- *Acknowledge the importance of upward information flow.* Upward channels tend to be the most constricted in the internal communication system.[18] Given the perceived power differences, bottom-up information flow does not occur naturally. Employees frequently recognize problems but fear that senior managers will reject honest feedback with embarrassment or anger. The burden is on management to make it clear that even negative information is welcome.

- *Be where the action is.* As Jack Welch was fond of pointing out, "Those closest to the work know better what to do than those further away from the work." This understanding of and respect for people at the bottom of the organization is what led Larry Bossidy to visit with more than five thousand employees during his first two months as CEO of AlliedSignal.[19]

- *Collect and use empirical data.* It is easy to overreact to a few loud voices from the bottom when they're the only voices management hears. If an organization establishes a database of employee views on ongoing issues, management will be able to make judgments more rationally. Dell, for example, has established a database it calls the "Dell pulse" to collect regular feedback on key issues from a large number of employees.

- *Provide avenues for upward information flow.* In addition to welcoming upward communications, management must create channels to facilitate flow. Leaders can attend town hall meetings, sponsor employee breakfasts, eat in the employee dining room, visit employees in their workplaces, and involve themselves in employee suggestion programs. And they can make themselves available and respond to lower-level employees.

Side to Side

- *Remove obstacles to effective lateral communications.* Organizations need to get peers talking together. The problem is, sometimes the receivers don't want to receive (the "not-invented-here syndrome"). And the givers don't want to give ("When promotions occur, I want to look better than you"). GE has greatly leveraged lateral communications by understanding such obstacles, removing them, and putting incentives in place to encourage greater volume of side-to-side communications.[20]

- *Promote efficiency.* The more communications flow horizontally, the less information must flow up and down through hierarchical layers. Because the overall social and financial cost of communications is reduced, more information gets through, resulting in better coordination as well as a simpler and less costly organization structure. This dynamic has allowed Dana Corporation to move from twelve or thirteen layers of management to five or six.

- *Develop a system of integrated horizontal linkages.* Horizontal communications flow can best be viewed as a series of systems: interpersonal information sharing and also interteam, interdepartmental, interdivisional, and intersector sharing. An effective framework will account for and integrate all these levels. Such a framework strongly contributes to an effective learning organization.

- *Expand market opportunities.* In a diversified business, product integration can begin anywhere to create wealth all along the value chain. But it doesn't just happen. Disney, for example, outperforms most of its sector because of its mastery of information flow and cooperative ventures. By simultaneously leveraging themes from movies, video games, fast-food promotions, and theme parks, Disney characters keep earning.

- *Employ the full range of vehicles for horizontal information flow.* Information can follow an array of channels: working meetings, staff transfers, ad hoc committees and task forces, temporary work assignments, best-practice discussion sessions, and online exchanges. At Hewlett-Packard, Dave Packard found that one of his single greatest leadership challenges was to get people and businesses in one part of HP to willingly share information with their counterparts elsewhere in the company.[21] To meet this leadership challenge, he allocated top management time to ensure the utilization of the full range of horizontal communication vehicles.

Action Plan for Flow of Information

Communications flow can be approached on many levels, but it's apt to be counterproductive to try too much at once. Instead, select between two and four HR practices to focus on first. The communications audit shown in assessment 6-1 will guide your attention to the types of practices likely to have the biggest payoff.

ASSESSMENT 6-1

Audit for information flow

1. To what extent do we have a clearly articulated communications strategy that links external information with internal processes, procedures, and information flow?

2. To what extent do we build a shared mindset capable of receiving, understanding, and acting on different and challenging information?

3. To what extent has management established a common base of language, logic, and concepts?

4. To what extent do we ensure that senior management communicates consistent messages?

5. To what extent do we ensure alignment between communication flow and the HR function so that they send consistent messages?

6. To what extent do we have mechanisms for measuring the effective and efficient flow of information—and do we remove obstacles that get in the way?

7. To what extent do we move information from customers, shareholders, and vendors into the firm in a comprehensive manner?

8. To what extent do we create relationships of credibility and trust through our communications with customers and shareholders?

9. In messages to employees, to what extent do we balance good news with bad news, "whats" with "whys," and the big picture with the details?

10. To what extent do we establish mechanisms that ensure the free flow of information from the bottom of the organization to the top?

11. To what extent do we build an organization in which horizontal communications build knowledge and value everywhere?

continued

Audit for information flow *(continued)*

12. How aligned are our information flow practices with each stakeholder? Score low, medium, or high as 1, 2, or 3 in each cell in the following grid:

		STAKEHOLDER			
		Investor	Customer	Line manager	Employee
Establish a communications strategy	Ensure consistency of message and reality.	1 2 3	1 2 3	1 2 3	1 2 3
	Build a focused and receptive mindset.	1 2 3	1 2 3	1 2 3	1 2 3
	Build commonly understood concepts, language, and logic.	1 2 3	1 2 3	1 2 3	1 2 3
	Ensure consistency between medium, message, and audience.	1 2 3	1 2 3	1 2 3	1 2 3
	Align communications with HR practices.	1 2 3	1 2 3	1 2 3	1 2 3
	Remove communications obstacles.	1 2 3	1 2 3	1 2 3	1 2 3
	Measure and communicate communication effectiveness.	1 2 3	1 2 3	1 2 3	1 2 3
Manage the movement of information	From the outside in.	1 2 3	1 2 3	1 2 3	1 2 3
	From the inside out.	1 2 3	1 2 3	1 2 3	1 2 3
	From the top down.	1 2 3	1 2 3	1 2 3	1 2 3
	From the bottom up.	1 2 3	1 2 3	1 2 3	1 2 3
	From side to side.	1 2 3	1 2 3	1 2 3	1 2 3

13. Of all the information flow choices that we could focus on, what are the top three in terms of their potential to create value?

Once you've assessed the most productive categories, you can ask which of all the ideas you've listed will do most to build stakeholder value. You can then build an action plan by following the template in exhibit 5-1 in chapter 5.

Flow of Work

Work is what ultimately transforms ideas and raw materials into products and services. It is the mechanism by which organizations fulfill their purpose in society. Too often, HR professionals have not participated in work flow decisions. We believe that since work flow decisions at all levels organize people to deliver value, HR professionals should play an active role in this area. Three key questions warrant attention: Who does the work? How is the work done? Where is the work done?

Theory of the Flow of Work

Work flow adds value to all stakeholders. Investors can have confidence in a consistent flow of products and services at the right volume, cost, quality, and speed. The velocity with which products and services flow within the organization through appropriately structured and organized work directly influences the velocity of cash flow and level of margins. Customer experience emerges from the ways the company organizes work processes, ensures accountability for customer decisions, and establishes physical arrangements. Managers coordinate how work is carried out to ensure that critical capabilities (e.g., speed, collaboration, learning, efficiency) are embedded in the organization's culture. Through the flow of work, employees know their roles and what is expected of them. They are able to focus on high- rather than low-value-added work, and they know who is accountable for results.

Work Flow: The "Who" Choices

Structure must fit the firm's strategy. Structural decisions should be contingent on the intent to support and drive the business strategy. Making choices relative to who does the work requires four sets of decisions about the structure of the organization: overall corporate portfolio, differentiation, integration, and configuration.

Corporate Portfolio

The fundamental decisions for any company involve what businesses to be in and what relationship its business units will have to one another.

The resulting strategy can be refined with decisions about industry, customers, competitors, technology, products, and culture. These six strategy choices set the pattern for one of four portfolio structures—a single business, related diversification, unrelated diversification, or a holding company—as outlined in assessment 6-2. The worst of all worlds is to muddle along without clear choices about relationships among the composite businesses. Note that if you answer 1 or 2 to the six strategy questions in assessment 6-2, you should probably have a single business unit or related diversification structure. If you rated 4 on the six dimensions, you should have a holding company. In-between scores would indicate related or unrelated diversification.

The idea is to align strategy choices with structural responses—that is, to avoid moving toward a portfolio-based diversification strategy while clinging to a structure based on integration, or the reverse. HR professionals can frame and encourage conversations that promote alignment and raise concerns when misalignment occurs. Here are the essentials of each choice.

Single Business Unit

Frequently (but not always), companies sell a single product or service or a set of similar offerings from one business unit at one location. Marketing Displays International, for example, produces sign frames, light boxes, and picture screens for use in airports, gas stations, and retail outlets, and as fast-food menu boards. It employs 160 people in its single combined office and production facility, and it has one department each for accounting, HR, legal, engineering, and production. These departments are well integrated with each other through meetings, lateral communications, strategic planning, and physical proximity of their offices. But this single–business unit approach isn't limited to small companies. Herman Miller, with around six thousand employees worldwide in the office furniture business, also has a strong central office with centrally coordinated staff functions.

Related Diversification

A company may consist of a set of relatively similar businesses with common products, services, customers, culture, or competitive criteria, and with explicit and extensive mechanisms to take advantage of these commonalities. Wal-Mart Stores and Sam's Club, for example, form a company whose similarities outweigh its differences. Its management works intensely to share and leverage insights about logistics, consumer

ASSESSMENT 6-2

Strategy choices and structural responses

Strategy choices	STRUCTURAL RESPONSES		
	Similar		**Different**
Industry	To what extent do we ...		
	Operate primarily in one industry		Operate in diverse industries
	LOW 1 2 3 4 5 **HIGH**		
Customers	To what extent do we ...		
	Serve a single customer or customer types		Serve diverse customers or customer types
	LOW 1 2 3 4 5 **HIGH**		
Competitors	To what extent do we ...		
	Compete against a dominant competitor in all markets		Compete against different competitors in different markets
	LOW 1 2 3 4 5 **HIGH**		
Technology	To what extent do we ...		
	Use or create similar technologies		Use or create different technologies
	LOW 1 2 3 4 5 **HIGH**		
Product	To what extent do we ...		
	Produce a similar product or service		Produce different products or services
	LOW 1 2 3 4 5 **HIGH**		
Culture	To what extent do we ...		
	Have a common or shared culture in all organization units		Encourage a different culture in each organization unit
	LOW 1 2 3 4 5 **HIGH**		
	Scores lead to structural responses:		
Organizational response	Single business unit	Related diversification	Unrelated diversification	Holding company

trends, real estate purchases, labor requirements, competitors, pricing, and inventory management.

Unrelated Diversification

Under unrelated diversification, differences across business units—in products, services, customers, competitors, and requirements—outweigh similarities. Shared learning, management, values, and brand may promote overall corporate success. However, such companies must resist the temptation to treat the disparate businesses alike, because a one-size-fits-all approach can impair business unit wealth creation. Cardinal Health, for example, derives its primary revenues from its wholesale pharmaceutical distribution business. It also manufactures and sells surgical equipment and pharmaceutical technologies and services, and it provides health care automation and information services. Despite some common threads, the differences in product and service offerings, customer demands, and competitive constraints result in substantial cross-business differences. Cardinal Health prospers by allowing its businesses to function as independent units with a modest level of coordination and synergy.

Holding Company

A holding company manages businesses that have almost nothing to do with one another. It is likely to have central finance, accounting, and legal functions for oversight, but most support activities are embedded within the business units. The Tata Group (one of India's largest private employer), for example, includes engineering, materials (predominantly steel), energy, chemicals, communications, retailing, information systems, and consumer products and services. For most of its history, these businesses have functioned almost autonomously under a strict set of ethical and legal values, but initial efforts are now under way to examine options for sharing relevant insights from different businesses for the benefit of all.

Differentiation

Companies can organize themselves primarily around products, markets, technology, function, or geography, or a formal combination called a matrix. Most use various combinations to one degree or another. For example, a company that relies on sensitivity to local markets generally organizes itself around geography. Within local regions or countries, it then organizes around function, product, or technology.

- *Product structure.* Organizing by product offerings works best when competitive advantage requires fast development and when product life cycles are short. Intel is one of the world's best examples of a product-driven company.

- *Market structure.* The increasing purchasing power of buyers and the shift toward service-based economies can drive a company to organize around markets.[22] Many professional service firms take this approach as they organize by industry segments.

- *Technology structure.* Companies organize around technology to allow new technology-based business propositions to take shape. This structure removes innovators from the mainstream of the company and protects them from other business units that may feel economically, politically, or culturally threatened. The Apple Computer Strategic Investment Group, the Lucent Technologies New Ventures Group, and Philips External Corporate Venturing exemplify this approach.

- *Functional structure.* Most small firms organize around functions such as finance, manufacturing, and marketing. However, this pattern works best in large firms where most tasks are simple or predictable, products or services are standardized, economies of scale are paramount, or functional knowledge is critical for success. Most utility companies are functionally organized.

- *Matrix structure.* Matrix structures combine criteria. They can be effective at processing large volumes of information.[23] However, they require extensive collaboration and negotiation before reaching final decisions, and this comes at a high price in terms of lost clarity, slow decision making, and internal conflict. Their redundant systems make them costly to operate. In the late 1980s, Imperial Chemical Industries (ICI) in the United Kingdom was structured as a five-dimensional matrix. Its costs escalated, while lack of innovation and slowness of decision making proved fundamental sources of competitive disadvantage. The company almost failed before new management stepped in and resolved the question "Who calls the shots?"

- *Outsourcing.* For activities that are essential but not central to the core mission or value proposition, the trend is to hand them off to a specialist that can enjoy economies of scale—either a central processing unit owned by the company or an external supplier. The decision to insource or outsource is often hotly contested. The British Petroleum Company (BP), for example, has gone the outsourcing route, whereas Shell has proceeded with insourcing. Regardless of outcome, the mandate is clear: reduce the costs of noncore activities while maintaining acceptable service quality.

Integration

Differentiation may create as many problems as it solves, and regardless of who does the work, a differentiated organization must be reintegrated. For example, a product-line company still has to encourage unity and cooperation—products from different divisions sold under the same company banner need to work together. Multinationals refer to this mandate as *local responsiveness and global integration.*[24] Companies have developed a long list of mechanisms to compensate for the tendency of differentiated units to diverge.

- *Hierarchy.* The traditional mechanism for binding together a disparate organization is a hierarchy of supervision. A boss sets a shared direction, encourages collective performance, and resolves conflicts. But that central boss has severely limited information-processing capacity (especially in the midst of the environmental turbulence as described in chapter 2), the hierarchical infrastructure is costly, and the centralized decision making erodes commitment among employees.

- *Meetings.* Bringing people together for meetings may facilitate common understanding, whether in person, by phone, or by videoconference. With a clear agenda and focus, meetings enable people from different units to collaborate effectively; without focus, meetings waste endless hours and breed antagonism among the participants and for the organization. Without meetings at all, people waste endless hours doing their own thing and not learning from each other.

- *Corporate staff.* Accounting, finance, HR, IT, legal, and marketing staff can promote information sharing and provide common rules and processes that encourage horizontal coordination. They can also discourage it and build silos exclusively within their function if not properly guided.

- *Measurement and rewards.* Measurements and rewards that focus on and reinforce collective performance can promote cooperation among otherwise competing units. They require careful design, or the behaviors and performance they shape may not be what you want.

- *Values, goals, and strategy.* Declaring values and setting shared visions and goals can reinforce the need for teamwork, respect, and cooperation—or undercut it, if not wisely chosen and communicated honestly.

- *Recruitment, promotions, and lateral transfers.* Personnel moves can tell the rest of the organization what behaviors are really valued and can move people into positions that facilitate the sharing of information from one part of a company to another. When the wrong people get ahead, that sends an equally vivid but negative message.

- *Cross-training.* Cross-unit project work, backed up with training about activities, processes, and needs in other units, builds broad company perspectives. But such projects must add real value. Make-work activities often produce cynicism and apathy.

- *Best practice and information sharing.* Effective mechanisms for identifying best practices and sharing information across company units build unity while enhancing the composite business. If there's too much red tape, however, people lose faith in the process.

- *Rules and roles.* Rules and policies can encourage knowledge transfer and cooperation, creating roles and positions that link one department with another.[25] For example, a *sales engineer* is part engineer and part sales rep, and works directly with both departments to communicate their respective needs back and forth. Similarly, policies can build walls where none need exist.

Configuration

HR also contributes to discussions of work configuration: the number of organizational layers, the proportion of staff to line, and locus of authority.

- *Organizational layers.* Companies are reducing layers and increasing span of control. This yields organizations that are nimbler and more responsive than their predecessors, with stronger quality and customer focus and a redefined management role. When Dana Corporation removed two-thirds of its management layers, for example, the remainder switched from telling people what to do to establishing shared goals, solving problems, providing information, and training, coaching, and inspiring employees.

- *Corporate staff.* As the workforce becomes more educated, better trained, and better informed, its need for rules and monitoring is reduced. Meanwhile, technology and outsourcing accomplish many transactional activities of traditional staff functions. As a result, staff-to-line ratios have reduced significantly.

- *Locus of decision making.* A central work flow question is which people at what levels get to make which decisions. In today's leaner, faster, and more innovative organizations, decision making moves toward the front line—toward employees who know the customers best, have the most information about products and services, and understand competitive realities. Besides producing better decisions, this trend makes employees feel more valued, less likely to leave, and more committed to implementing the decisions.[26] When Air Products and Chemicals reduced its corporate staff by 30 percent, frontline supervisors and employees took responsibility for improving processes, eliminating low-value-added activities, and achieving their targets.

Work Flow: The "How" Choices

Companies transmute raw materials and ideas into products and services through three sets of choices: human interaction patterns, focused governance, and levels of customization.

Human Interaction Patterns

The basic patterns of who does what, when, and with whom make a big difference in what gets produced. Depending on the desired outputs, different interaction patterns will produce optimal results.

- *Individual production.* Some tasks need little or no work-related interaction. Individual employees can be set to work without trying to form them into teams. Piece-rate production exemplifies this work pattern.

- *Sequential production.* Assembly-line production processes, where each worker does one thing to the product and passes it on to the next, who passes it on to the next, and so forth, accelerate productivity. The assembly line augments individual strength and skill with equipment and rigid procedures.

- *Interactive teams.* With still more equipment but flexible procedures, modern companies are applying teamwork rather than lines to large-scale assembly processes—and further accelerating productivity, lowering costs, and boosting productivity.

- *Sequential teams.* Sequential team production merges assembly-line production with teamwork. Teams complete substantial subassemblies and then pass the completed subassemblies to the next team. This combines the efficiency of sequential production and the integration and motivation of teamwork.

- *Virtual teams.* Some tasks need the skills of people who work in different units and even in different locations. With modern communications, teams can form to address these tasks, and disappear just as quickly, without their members' meeting face-to-face for any length of time, if at all.

Focused Governance

The main choice here is between vertical functional silos and horizontal processes driven by customer requirements.

- *Vertical organization.* In a vertical organization, functional departments dictate effectiveness criteria. The problem is that departments take on a life of their own and can lose track of customer needs. Information tends to flow down and up the functional hierarchy rather than across functions. This occasionally results in customers and products falling between the cracks.[27] Decisions come from the top of the hierarchy rather than from the levels at which customer information is most available.

- *Horizontal organization.* The horizontal organization begins with customer inputs and ends with customer utilization of products and services. It organizes work to fit smoothly in between. Its most influential individuals own processes rather than functions. The corporate culture places a premium on openness and collaboration. The organization reinforces this outlook with measurements and rewards for total process results, and with substantial cross-training and broad job expectations.

Customization

The next choice involves the extent to which processes are standardized or customized.

- *Standardized processes.* Standardized processes tend to be designed for fast order fulfillment for uniform products with few options and extensive automation. Quality is achieved through standardized service levels. Providing low-cost throughput dominates the process logic.

- *Customized processes.* Customized processes tailor product and process specifics through intensive interaction with customers, who derive value from the personalized output and delivery. Costs tend to be passed on to customers. A modified version offers the assembly of customized units out of standardized parts.

Work Flow: The "Where" Choices

Physical space communicates explicit and implicit messages about what matters to an organization.[28] HR professionals' expertise in culture, productivity, and employee value propositions can be useful in discussions with facility managers and architecture and design specialists. Physical settings may shape culture and increase productivity through facilitating the flow of work, engaging employees, and sending powerful signals about values, leadership, and status.[29]

Space

The arrangement of walls, seating patterns, and meeting rooms have direct influence on the flow of work.

- *Modularity.* Modularity enables organizations to reconfigure space quickly and flexibly depending on business needs. For example, conference rooms can become temporary offices or house task forces assigned to a project. SEI Investments has taken this to its logical conclusion, eliminating interior walls and cubicles. Each employee has a suite of furniture on wheels. When teams form, members roll their "offices" into a clump, plug in their voice and data ports, and go to work.

- *Physical proximity.* Proximity encourages trust and enhances the flow of information. If you want closer cooperation between sales and engineering, put their offices next to each other. If you want to boost creativity among your innovative "sparkplugs," move them near each other. Pixar, the computer animation studio, recently consolidated its staff in one building to facilitate greater synergistic creativity and collaboration.

- *Meeting rooms.* Space and furniture in meeting rooms speak volumes about expectations: a U-shaped table implies a two-way dialog between presenter and participants, while a round one implies team problem solving with influence based on personal insight. Or consider flip charts and overheads versus LCD projectors—the former encourage interaction, the latter passive listening.

- *Customer contact.* If you want employees to know what customers need, put them where they see customers. GE Aircraft Engines, for example, locates many of its service personnel in its customers' facilities.

Environment

Physical setting influences the motivation and productivity of individual employees.

- *Lighting.* Natural lighting in office space helps people connect with the world outside the office and prevents the irritation caused by long sessions in closed rooms. (We often see this in seminars; after a few days in a hotel ballroom, participants become edgy—without knowing why. After a half day of training outside, they generally revive.) However, glare makes effective lighting for computer-based work a particular challenge. Four types of lighting may be used in the office environment:[30]
  - Daylight from windows, skylights, and glass doors
  - Ambient light from ceiling or furniture-mounted light sources
  - Task light from lamps focused on a particular area
  - Accent or display lighting to add visual interest and define space

- *Color.* Color evokes mood and action. Some companies pick light colors for an open feeling; others equate social status with darker colors. Red, orange, and yellow tend to stimulate and excite. Pale greens, light yellows, and off-white (think doctors' offices) tend to calm. Watercolors seem cool, fire colors seem hot by association. Whatever color you choose, there's a message.

- *Involvement.* Humans tend to be strongly territorial. People like to personalize their work space. Even in temporary "hotelling" offices where employees share space and furniture, some personal touches appear. Companies that ban personalization not only reduce ownership in office space, they also risk reducing ownership in the company as a whole.

- *Ergonomics.* Attention to the physical demands of work pays off, both in a healthier workforce and reduced workers' compensation claims and in increased morale. Seating and working surfaces that fit the individual worker may be more costly than one-size-fits-all office furniture, but it can pay for itself in workers' comp alone—where back pain amounts to almost a quarter of the claims and a third of the dollars spent.[31] Simply encouraging employees to move around during the day rather than spend unbroken hours at their desks can make a difference.

The physical work environment can even serve as a vehicle for attracting and retaining key talent.

Symbolism

Because of the durability and relative costliness of physical things in the working environment, people tend to attribute symbolic meaning to physical stuff. Companies intentionally and sometimes unintentionally signal powerful messages through physical symbols.

- *Physical setting signals values.* The first impression sticks: a traditional stone chalet in a forest communicates a different message from a modern glass office building in the downtown. The whole physical plant—architecture, location, landscaping, signage, maintenance—will be read as an indication of the company's values. "No message" is also a message.

- *Physical setting signals leadership style.* Office layouts communicate management style and culture more clearly than any speech or culture change program. A top-floor corner office communicates a different leadership approach from a bottom-floor office near the main entrance. We know one leader who sits behind a desk that takes up almost half his office—and another who had the desk removed entirely and works at a small table in one corner. The former meets visitors across an imposing barrier; the latter turns and interacts directly with his guests.

- *Physical setting communicates the value of people.* Is the workplace clean, freshly painted, and safe? Are the gardens kept up? Are the windows clean? These tangible details of the workplace signal management's commitment to employees.

- *Physical arrangements communicate status.* Larger offices, customized wall hangings, plush carpets, richness of paneling, and office location send powerful messages that fit the needs of hierarchical organizations very well. Retaining such physical accoutrements in a theoretically flat and agile organization sends the unintended message that influence is a function of position rather than a function of insight, information, and contribution.

Action Plan for Flow of Work

When you address work flow, select between two and four HR practices to focus on first. The audit shown in assessment 6-3 will guide your attention to the types of practices likely to have the biggest payoff. You can then build an action plan by following the template given back in exhibit 5-1 in chapter 5.

ASSESSMENT 6-3

Audit for work flow

1. To what extent have we clearly articulated the logic of our business portfolio?

2. To what extent have we selected a high-level organizational structure consistent with our strategy?

3. To what extent do we apply the full range of integrating mechanisms appropriate for our business?

4. To what extent have we rationalized layers of management and corporate staff and moved decision making to those closest to the customers, information, and core work processes?

5. To what extent do we employ interaction patterns that enhance productivity and employee motivation?

6. To what extent have we organized ourselves to achieve the optimal balance between customer responsiveness and cost efficiency?

7. To what extent have we arranged the physical setting to promote the desired interaction patterns and flow of work?

8. To what extent is the physical work space arranged to engage employees?

9. To what extent does the physical setting send the desired messages concerning company values and the nature of company leadership?

continued

ASSESSMENT 6-3

Audit for work flow (continued)

10. How aligned are our work flow practices with each stakeholder? Score low, medium, or high as 1, 2, or 3 in each cell in the following grid:

		STAKEHOLDER			
		Investor	Customer	Line manager	Employee
Who does the work	Define corporate portfolio.	1 2 3	1 2 3	1 2 3	1 2 3
	Set criteria for top-level organizational differentiation.	1 2 3	1 2 3	1 2 3	1 2 3
	Establish horizontal integrating mechanisms.	1 2 3	1 2 3	1 2 3	1 2 3
	Configure the organizational structure.	1 2 3	1 2 3	1 2 3	1 2 3
	Place decision-making authority for maximum impact.	1 2 3	1 2 3	1 2 3	1 2 3
How the work gets done	Develop patterns of human interaction.	1 2 3	1 2 3	1 2 3	1 2 3
	Focus on internal hierarchy or on customer requirements.	1 2 3	1 2 3	1 2 3	1 2 3
	Balance standardization and customization.	1 2 3	1 2 3	1 2 3	1 2 3
Where the work gets done	Define influence of physical setting on work flow.	1 2 3	1 2 3	1 2 3	1 2 3
	Engage employees through the physical setting.	1 2 3	1 2 3	1 2 3	1 2 3
	Signal values and leadership style.	1 2 3	1 2 3	1 2 3	1 2 3

11. Of all the work flow choices we could focus on, what are the top three in terms of their potential to create value?

Menus for Information and Work Flow

For any company, information and work flow represent an intrinsic part of the value proposition. They have great influence on organizational capabilities and determine much of the human experience at work. Many HR professionals are beginning to add value in these areas. Now is the time for them to expand their roles by contributing even more to these important emerging HR activities.

7

Building an HR Strategy

*To what extent does our HR strategy process
turn business goals into HR priorities?*

MOTOROLA HAS BEEN RIDING a roller coaster for two decades.
Through the 1980s, the company's market share was up. Profitability was excellent. But in the early 1990s, the world of consumer electronics changed dramatically, as people began spending more and more time out of the office—working from home, on planes, in hotel rooms. They demanded faster, smaller, more integrated and energy-efficient electronics. At the same time, competition for their business grew more and more intense. Major competitors sprang up in Europe and Asia, radically increasing the churn rate in product styling, feature integration, and speed of innovation. The crowded competitive space forced prices down and mandated operating efficiencies, just as the investment community increased its demands for consistent earnings growth.

It was under these conditions that the Motorola HR leadership team set out to create a more powerful strategy. Their goals:

- Link HR practices to customer and shareholder requirements.

- Help drive business unit strategy while promoting coordination strong enough to have a multiplier effect on Motorola's overall value.

- Position Motorola as a more effective competitor.

- Make Motorola's cultural capabilities consistent with its desired marketplace brand identity.

149

- Engage the enthusiasm and support of management and employees.

Motorola provides a vivid case. Its experience illustrates the logic and process for developing a powerful HR strategy based on the concepts and best practices we describe. The company built a line of sight from investors and customers to its management and employees through more powerful HR practices. Working closely with senior line management, the HR leadership team identified the culture that the increasingly competitive environment required. Through this means, the HR leadership provided a powerful agenda for integrating staffing, performance management, training and development, structure, and communications with common business focus and direction. This allowed HR to maximize its impact on performance.

The strategy recognized that HR's primary deliverable is organizational capability and that the most central aspect of organizational capability is organizational culture: the collective mindset of the company. Collective mindset—that is, shared ways of thinking or shared cognitive patterns—has two powerful outcomes. It defines the way people behave, and it also determines what information people will accept, interpret accurately, and adopt as useful knowledge.

One powerful definition of culture is, therefore, the shared ways of thinking that determine how people both inside and outside the firm collectively behave and what information they collectively accept and use. A firm whose culture cannot accurately perceive and interpret its environment—the requirements of its customers, investors, and regulators, the technological alternatives it faces, the moves its competitors make—and effectively translate those perceptions and interpretations into employee behaviors will have great difficulty staying in business.

This chapter is intended to be a very practical guide to HR strategy development. It is meant to overcome the problem in many books, articles, and presentations on HR strategy—they sometimes tell you everything you need to know except *how* to do it. In this chapter, you will encounter lots of specific tools so that you can implement the ideas on your own. This chapter represents our best attempt to "unpack the black box."

Framework

The business trends outlined in chapter 2 all reinforce the importance of the culture agenda. Speed of technological innovation, increasing global competitiveness, increasing customer choice, and increasing shareholder demands mandate that firms must innovate and improve to stay alive and prosper. They must concurrently reduce bureaucracy and low-value-added work whenever feasible while enhancing employee involvement and commitment. Any vestige of complacency or denial will lead to suboptimal performance—or outright failure. In placing the organizational capability of culture at the center of our HR strategic logic, we rely on extensive experience, as well as on research at the University of Michigan that clearly identifies the fundamental logic that leading companies use to connect their HR practices to business strategy.[1] The great majority of high-performing firms we studied center their HR logic on a clear understanding of their desired corporate culture (the Hewlett-Packard Way, the Johnson & Johnson Credo, General Electric's Speed, Simplicity and Self-Confidence). In addition, in the most recent iteration of the Human Resource Competency Study, we found that the HR agenda with the greatest impact on business performance is a culture-based HR strategy.[2] Meanwhile, in the course of teaching thousands of HR and line executives at the University of Michigan Executive Education Center and working with more than half the *Fortune* 200 companies, we have seen increasing attention to the cultural agenda. Figure 7-1 describes the strategy-building framework we have derived from our studies and experience.

The framework logic flow begins with a clear understanding of trends in your external business environment—among customers, investors,

FIGURE 7-1

Framework for a culture-capability-based HR strategy

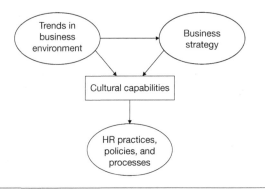

regulators, competitors, technology, and globalization—that shape the present and future external realities the firm faces. Then it makes a clear statement of the firm's sources of competitive advantage and their accompanying measurements. These insights make it possible to define the organizational culture required to implement the competitive strategy and promote success within the environmental context. It is then possible to design HR practices that will create the required cultural capabilities.

This logic is reasonably straightforward—so straightforward it looks like common sense. As in many such situations, however, the difficulty is not in the knowing but in the doing. Many sources of noise interrupt this logic flow, blocking out the voice of the marketplace and the business strategy.

For example, a company's past can be a source of noise. The culture that brought success in the past may not be right for the future. Union leaders can be a source of noise if they say, "Pay attention to me first. If there's time and money left over, then focus on customers." Consultants insert noise when they say, "Buy what I have to sell because this is what I have to sell." Even the necessary attention to competitors can be a source of noise because it's hard to watch their success while avoiding the temptation to copy them—and copying a competitor's culture will, by definition, not give you a competitive edge. And internal politics can be a powerfully distracting source of noise. Even executives following their self-serving agendas often block out critical messages from the business environment.

HR Strategy Development Process

A two-day workshop is almost always sufficient for fleshing out the basic HR strategy framework. Of course, it's also possible to hold a series of sessions running two or three hours each over a period of several weeks, but that approach tends to cost much more than an intensive off-site workshop, besides taking considerably longer. After the workshop (or series), the detailed implementation plan should be completed in no more than three months, and full implementation should take no more than nine months.

The process involves six steps:

1. Identify the organizational unit and organize the workshop.

2. Prioritize the trends in the business environment.

3. Specify the sources of competitive advantage and the measurements for each source of competitive advantage.

4. Define the desired cultural capabilities together with the behavioral expressions of these cultural capabilities.

5. Identify the HR practices that will have greatest influence on creating and sustaining the desired culture.

6. Develop an overall implementation plan.

Step 1: Identifying the Organizational Unit and Organizing the Workshop

To prepare for the workshop, begin by selecting the organizational unit for which the HR strategy is being developed, making sure it is the same one that is the target for business strategy development. That's the key initial decision. The remainder of the process can be applied to any organizational unit—the corporation as a whole or any business unit, region, or function. Having a clear definition of the organization unit affects both the choice of individual participants and the organization of the workshop.

Send invitations to the workshop to people who have an immediate interest in the results. One person can frame a workable HR strategy, but we have found that groups get better results. In most cases a group between twelve and twenty-four is ideal. You need enough redundancy to break up into at least three subgroups, each reflecting the full range of knowledge and concerns from both HR and line management. This distribution will help overcome groupthink, ensure breadth of perspective, and facilitate efficient decision making. Ideally, you will have both HR professionals and line managers involved. Ask the participants to prepare for the meeting by gathering information as follows:

- Read four analysts' reports about the company: two positive and two negative. If analysts' reports are unavailable, positive and negative newspaper or magazine articles should suffice.

- Read four analysts' reports about major competitors.

- Read an article or two about high-value-added HR practices.

- For the HR professionals, interview two or three line executives about the major competitive challenges facing the company, trends among key stakeholders, and major weaknesses that the company must address.

The physical layout of the workshop should reflect the kind of strategy you have in mind. For example, if you are developing an HR strategy for a holding company or an unrelated diversification, then arrange tables and name-tags so people will sit together with others in their own business units. On the other hand, if the target is a single business unit or an undiversified corporation, have people dispersed for maximum variety at each table. The former layout works from the assumption that the differences across highly diversified business units will outweigh the similarities and that those differences should be respected. The latter builds from the assumption that the similarities outweigh the differences and that similarities should emerge in the discussions.

Motorola takes a "related diversification" approach to its portfolio. Its business units differ in important ways, but their similarities generally outweigh their differences. The HR leadership therefore decided on the latter course, so as to develop a strategy that would be relevant for the combined business units while ensuring that the important differences across the business units would be respected.

Step 2: Prioritizing Trends in the Business Environment

Why begin with an analysis of the business environment? It may seem like unnecessary wheel spinning when the group could simply start with an existing business strategy. However, many strategies are by no means as fully developed as they could be, so it's always useful to take another look. The current strategy may have been based on errors, or business conditions may have changed, so that a once-effective strategy no longer applies. In addition, the finance, marketing, and engineering perspectives that dominate most strategy formulation processes may omit key perspectives needed for HR strategy development.

Sources of Trends

Have workshop participants address the following questions to help them prioritize and translate external business trends into HR implications:

- *What is going on in the economy? What is the demand for your products or services?* These questions help assess the number of people and the kinds of abilities required, and identify which business units will be growing and which diminishing. The resulting insights bear on the allocation of HR resources to create and sustain key growth-oriented cultural capabilities.

- *What are your customers' buying criteria? Your customers' customers' criteria? Are they changing?* Business success often starts with knowing what customers demand and then doing better than competitors at providing it. To identify the required cultural capabilities, HR professionals must know what is driving customer decisions. Are they buying on the basis of price, flexibility, responsiveness, innovative solutions, quality, on-time delivery, relationships, service, convenience, branding?

- *What is the nature of your relationship with your suppliers?* The mirror image of the customer-service logic holds true for a company's relationships with its suppliers.

- *How much competition do you face? What is the basis of competition? Are changes occurring in the amount or basis of competition?* Intense competition generally mandates a culture capable of commensurate intensity, focus, and accountability. Increasing numbers of competitors generally require the firm's culture to become more efficient, lean, and productive, and at the same time to develop greater agility and speed in innovation, responsiveness, and adaptability.

- *What is the nature of your technology? How fast is technology in your industry changing?* Look at three types of technology: process, product, and information.

  - *Process technology.* Manufacturing or services that involve substantial teamwork (as at Toyota) require a culture of collaboration, trust, and cooperation. Those that emphasize individual effort (as at Avon) require a culture of individualism, personal initiative, and self-confidence.

  - *Product technology.* If the design of products and services is changing quickly (as at Intel), then cultures of speed, nimbleness, and creativity will be required. If the design is moving toward technological integration on a common platform (as at Motorola), the culture needs to emphasize collaboration and synergy.

  - *Information technology.* As the speed and breadth of information exchange creates ever more turbulence in the technological environment (as at Microsoft), the culture needs the capacity to change and learn quickly, adapt before being compelled to do so, and maintain its integration.

- *What is your relationship with your regulators?* Across the world, nations and industries are becoming generally less regulated. National economic borders are breaking down with reductions in tariffs and increases in international trade. (See chapter 2.) When regulators reduce their influence and competitive intensity increases, company cultures need to emphasize performance, accountability, efficiency, service, and innovation. Some aspects of some industries, on the other hand, are becoming more regulated. You need to be aware of which is occurring in your industry and account for the trends as they appear.

- *What are your owners' expectations?* More people own stock now than ever before, so the dispersion of shareholding has never been greater. However, practical control over those dispersed shares has seldom been so concentrated—mutual funds and pension funds control large blocks of stock in many companies. As discussed in chapter 3, institutional investors increasingly focus on economic intangibles along with financial performance as the basis for buy or sell decisions.

Each of these issues will matter more to some companies than to others. Participants in the HR strategy development process will need to select and appropriately weight each trend as they complete this step.

Workshop Process

We have found it useful to divide the workshop into three subgroups and have each subgroup work through each step concurrently.

1. Brainstorm the external environmental trends that influence your selected business unit. We have found that subgroups will frequently identify fifteen to twenty trends based on the questions outlined earlier.

2. Identify the top three or four trends. It's essential to pick the ones that matter most to business success, as it is difficult—if not impossible—to define a culture to cope with fifteen to twenty different trends simultaneously. Since "the enemy of the great is the good," clear strategic focus at this stage of the process is critical.[3]

3. Allocate one hundred points among the selected trends, based on their respective importance as external threats or opportunities. If you do not allocate these one hundred points, you must

logically assume that the trends are equally important, and they are not; some are more important than others. Therefore, make sure each gets a different number of points.

4. Report results back to the plenary group. The facilitator works with the plenary group to identify the commonalities and differences among the results from the three subgroups. (Exhibit 7-1 provides a useful worksheet for this step.)

At the Motorola workshop, the plenary session came up with the distribution of trends shown in exhibit 7-2.

EXHIBIT 7-1

Environmental trends worksheet

Trend	Group 1	Group 2	Group 3	Total
	100%	100%	100%	100%

EXHIBIT 7-2

Motorola worksheet for step 2: environmental trends

Environmental trends	Total
Productivity initiatives and global competition have forced substantive cost pressures on the industry.	40
New entrants are entering the industry on a global scale, especially in China.	30
Partnerships and alliances are becoming more critical for reasons of scale, market entrance, and access to innovative technologies.	20
Services component of the relevant business is growing.	6
Disruptive technologies increasingly provide threats and opportunities.	4
	100%

Step 3: Identifying Sources of Competitive Advantage and Relevant Measures

Even though the existing business strategy probably identifies what the company regards as its competitive advantage, the workshop should still go back to first principles at least briefly. The group should take a fresh look at potential advantages and figure out whether those advantages are being realized.

Sources of Advantage

Twelve general areas can provide sources of competitive advantage:

- *Innovation.* Be the best at developing new products and services, continually improving existing processes, and identifying new markets. (Examples: 3M, Intel.)

- *On-time delivery.* Be the best at getting goods into customers' hands in a timely manner. (Examples: FedEx, any firm doing business with Wal-Mart.)

- *Convenience.* Be the easiest for customers to deal with. (Examples: McDonald's, Amazon.com.)

- *First to market.* Bring out new, modified, or repackaged products and services before anyone else. (Examples: Microsoft, Eli Lilly.)

- *Quality.* Offer the products or services that best meet customer expectations. (Examples: Toyota, Motorola.)

- *Cost.* Offer the least expensive products or services. (Examples: Wal-Mart, Southwest Airlines.)

- *Relationships.* Have the most satisfactory ongoing interactions with customers who place high value on such interactions. (Examples: Private Banking at United Bank of Switzerland, Disney.)

- *Mergers, acquisitions, and alliances.* Be the best at identifying, consummating, and integrating deals that combine company operations. (Examples: Cisco, Vodafone.)

- *Synergy.* Be the best at sharing knowledge and experience across otherwise disparate business units. (Examples: Wyeth, University of Michigan.)

- *Branding.* Develop the most powerful identity in the minds of consumers. (Examples: Coca-Cola, Intel.)

- *Distribution.* Dominate channels, thereby effectively blocking the competition. (Examples: Unilever, Kellogg.)

- *Service.* Provide the best customer support before, during, or after the sale. (Examples: Marriott, Virgin Atlantic Airways.)

Notice that these categories can often overlap. For example, service and quality would be the same at Marriott but different at GE Aircraft Engines. Almost any competitive action or business tactic will be a subcategory of one of these sources of advantage.

Measuring Advantage

Besides identifying and prioritizing the desired sources of competitive advantage from among these categories, it is also essential to figure out how to tell whether or not the chosen sources of competitive advantage are being achieved. Measurement is important for four reasons:

- To know exactly what is meant by the key words—quality, cost, first to market, and the rest—which take on precision and exact meaning when expressed in hard numbers.

- To know how the company is doing and how much improvement it needs.

- To be able to measure the effectiveness of HR.

- To establish a contract between HR and management. In return for the time, effort, and money that management invests in HR, HR should guarantee that the chosen measures of competitive advantage will be higher in the future than they have been in the past.

Table 7-1 provides a list of measures of competitive advantage.

Although measures such as profitability, market share, and repeat business are also important, they are not useful at this stage of the process. These overall outcome measures reflect a firm's ability to do everything, and thus do not discriminate among specific sources of competitive advantage.

Workshop Process

The goal here is to select sources of competitive advantage with the greatest potential impact within the context of the business environment that the plenary group described in step 2. Advise the subgroups to look for sources of competitive advantage the organization should

TABLE 7-1

Sample measures of competitive advantage

Advantage	Measurement
Innovation	• Number of new products per time unit • Percentage of revenues from new products • Number of patents • Customers' perceptions of innovativeness
First to market	• First to concept and prototype • First to internal utilization • First to external utilization • First to profitability
Synergy	• Corporate value compared to sum of subunit values • Revenues generated from joint activities
Mergers, acquisitions, and alliances	• Achievement of preset goals • Perceptions of fairness and cooperation
On-time delivery	• Percentage of deliveries on time • Lag time from empty to full shelf
Distribution	• Percentage of premium shelf space • Percentage of markets where competitors are locked out • Percentage of population having access to products
Quality	• Percentage of rejects • Six Sigma metrics • Customers' perceptions of quality
Service	• Customers' perceptions of service • Time from complaint to resolution • Number of telephone transfers
Convenience	• Distance from traffic flow to purchase • Time in line • Customers' perceptions of cost of doing business
Costs	• Margins • Corporate overhead costs • Number of management layers
Branding	• Brand recognition and meaning attribution • Premium that can be charged above that of competitive products of similar composition
Relationships	• Time from placing a phone call to a key customer or government official to when it is returned • Customers' statement of loyalty from a customer survey

have rather than limiting themselves to what it has at the moment. The subgroups should proceed with the following steps:

1. Identify the four to five sources of competitive advantage that the company needs to have to be more successful.

2. Allocate one hundred points among the top choices to identify their relative importance. Again, make sure that no two sources of competitive advantage receive equal numbers of points.

3. Report back to the plenary group to discuss similarities and differences and select advantages to pursue. Exhibit 7-3 is a useful worksheet for this stage.

4. Break up into subgroups, assigning a specific source of competitive advantage to each subgroup.

5. Identify two to four measures of success for each source of competitive advantage.

6. Report back to the plenary group to discuss the measures with a view to reducing redundancies and inconsistencies, preparing a worksheet like the one in exhibit 7-4.

Motorola came up with the list of competitive advantages, weightings, and measurements shown in exhibit 7-5.

EXHIBIT 7-3

Summary of competitive advantage

Competitive advantage	Group 1	Group 2	Group 3	Total

EXHIBIT 7-4

Measurements for competitive advantage

Advantage	Measurements
1.	1.
	2
	3
2.	1.
	2
	3.
3.	1.
	2.
	3.
4.	1.
	2.
	3.

EXHIBIT 7-5

Motorola's competitive advantage chart

Competitive advantage	Weighting	Measurements
Cost control	27	1. Yield rate 2. Margins 3. In-house efficiency measures
Innovation	25	1. Percent of profit derived from products less than one year old 2. Ratio of number of new patents to revenue 3. Published acknowledgments of innovativeness
Relationships	30	1. Percent of product development initiatives that involve customers 2. Predefined targets for joint ventures 3. Quality of relationship as measured by customer survey
First to market	18	1. Time to targeted profitability 2. Percent of revenue from products that are introduced to the market ahead of competition 3. Time to have products off the production line

Step 4: Defining Desired Cultural Capabilities and Behavioral Expressions

The culture management agenda has two components: the description of the required culture and the specification of how people behave within it. These are not at all the same thing. Consider a Disney theme park, for example. Suppose that at the end of a visit to the Magic Kingdom, someone asks you to describe the Disney culture. One word that would probably come to mind is *friendly*. You might be tempted to say that Disney has a friendly culture.

But *friendliness* does not exist at Disney. Like other culture words, it describes something that exists in the mind of the observer rather than something inherent in what is being observed. What you saw going on at Disney was not people being friendly; what you saw was Disney employees smiling, making eye contact, answering questions cheerfully and accurately, offering help to people who looked lost, or trying to bring laughter to tired or irritable children. When you saw Disney employees doing these things, then *you* concluded that you were in a friendly place.

A lifetime of linguistic socialization ties culture words to sets of behaviors. When people smile, make eye contact, and answer questions readily, we have learned to refer to that set of behaviors as *friendly*. The same reasoning holds true for any culture word: *collaborative, aggressive, creative, disciplined,* and so forth all represent a variety of behaviors. Culture words are powerful linguistic constructs that promote efficient communication. But they are abstractions from the behaviors that they represent. Therefore, to be rigorous and complete in specifying the desired culture, it is essential to specify both the words you would use to describe your ideal culture and the behaviors that reflect that culture.

Defining Culture

In recent years, companies have been becoming more sophisticated about culture definition. They have come to recognize that they can't try to do everything. In our cultural audits, we almost always find that a firm is best off with no more than two or three cultural targets or pillars. It makes sense—after all, how many major messages can a company send and internalize over a year or two? The answer is rarely more than three. Beyond that, the more cultural attributes a firm tries to create, the less likely it is to succeed.

Firms are also defining their cultural attributes in more rigorous and competitive ways. Some examples:

- Disciplined risk taking (Deutsche Bank)

- Restless creativity (Unilever)

- Teams passionate about winning (AstraZeneca)

- Resourceful agility (BAE Systems)

- Customer-focused innovation (Texas Instruments)

It's essential to define the culture to support and sustain the chosen sources of competitive advantage and improve company results. That is, the group should address this question: What is the culture we need to have to achieve better performance in our measures of competitive advantage in the future than we have today?

Workshop Process: Culture Specification

The following process is one we have found useful for identifying a desired culture. It can and should be modified to fit the logic and vocabulary of your firm.

1. Rearrange the workshop into new subgroups, assigning each one of the identified sources of competitive advantage.

2. Prepare a laundry list of the words that most reflect the cultural capabilities needed to support that advantage. Exhibit 7-6 provides a starting point from which to list your desired words.

3. Select the six cultural capabilities most important to the group's assigned advantage, then consolidate them into two or three sets by either combination or elimination.

4. Report out to the plenary group. In plenary session, finalize a list of two or three dominant cultural capabilities.

5. Divide into new subgroups based on the selected capabilities and do a gap analysis to determine which will require the most improvement, assigning each a place on a 1–5 scale, with 1 being "Needs no improvement," 3 "Needs a little improvement," and 5 "Needs a lot of improvement."

EXHIBIT 7-6

Culture words

Adaptable	Cost-conscious	Multidisciplined	Passionate	Risk-inclined
Aggressive	Courageous	Nimble	Proactive	Sensitive
Agile	Creative	Individualistic	Prompt	Simple
Alert	Decisive	Ingenious	Rapid	Smart
Assertive	Disciplined	Initiating	Reactive	Stylish
Bold	Driven	Innovative	Reality-based	Team-based
Bright	Efficient	Integrated	Receptive	Tenacious
Brilliant	Fast	Intimate	Relational	Thoughtful
Clever	Flexible	Inventive	Relentless	Tough
Collaborative	Focused	Lean	Resourceful	Unencumbered
Commercial	Friendly	Opportunistic	Responsive	

Workshop Process: Scenario Building

Next, ask workshop participants to consider this question: How do you want people to behave in the future so that you get better results than you do today? The most effective process for this is something we call "behavioral scenario building." To lead up to the exercise, we suggest describing the following situation:

It is 20xx [a date three years ahead] and you have built the desired company culture. Your best friend comes to pick you up at work. As the two of you are walking somewhere through your company, your friend says, "I don't get it. You have been talking about [your targeted cultural capability] for years now, and I still don't know what you are talking about." At that moment, you see an incident where people really have it right. You turn to your friend and say, "Look over there. Do you see what is going on? That is exactly what I mean. People all over the company are behaving like that." Your friend asks, "So just what am I supposed to be seeing?" Then you describe what's happening, so your friend can tell what to look at. Write what you say to your friend, in a paragraph of four or five sentences.

As people write, they should remember the following principles:

• Make the scenario rich in description. The more detail you provide, the better.

- Make it clear that the greater the degree to which people in your company exhibit the described behaviors, the more successful it will be in achieving its numbers and in winning its competitive battles.

- Describe specific, observable behaviors: what people do, not what they think or what they value. Action matters here, not attitudes. Avoid using culture words to describe culture—that is, say "making eye contact and answering questions clearly and constructively" rather than "being friendly and helpful."

  1. Begin by having participants each write their own individual scenario: a short story or situation in which people use the redesigned cultural capabilities in ways that can be seen or heard. It helps to have the following questions posted prominently: Who is doing what? Who are they with? Where are they? What is being said or done? What are the desired outcomes of this situation? What follow-up occurs?

  2. Share the scenarios within the subgroups, preferably by having each participant read aloud. (If people read their own scenarios, it will avoid problems with handwriting and will focus everyone's attention on the material.) Resist the temptation to let people generate the original scenario as a group. You will get richer and more complete scenarios if people do the exercise first as individuals and then share their results with their teams.

  3. Have each subgroup note the most useful and powerful ideas that come out of the individual scenarios. We normally recommend using flip charts to record between four and six detailed behaviors for each cultural capability. These are some samples:

     - "People in all functions constantly and actively track customer satisfaction and profitability through open, shared information systems. They reflect this in business projects and plans, taking action to exceed customers' expectations."

     - "People in meetings follow established ground rules, including time allocation, defined objectives and tasks, and monitoring benefit to customers and shareholders. People show up on time, fully prepared to contribute, and turn off their cell phones; otherwise, the meeting is dissolved or people leave. Tasks are followed up and people are held accountable for assignments."

4. Reconvene the plenary session and select the most appropriate behaviors for each of the chosen cultural pillars, recording them in a format along the lines of exhibit 7-7. When all teams have reported out on their respective behavioral scenarios, ask the group whether the proposed behaviors would produce better results than what the company sees now. In almost all cases, the answer will be a resounding "yes." If the response is less than enthusiastic, send the teams back to work.

Motorola came up with the following list of cultural capabilities and their accompanying behaviors.

HIGH PERFORMANCE ACCOUNTABILITY

1. People actively debate alternatives, express complete buy-in to decisions made, and execute flawlessly. Optionalism is not an option.

EXHIBIT 7-7

Cultural capabilities and supporting behaviors

Capabilities	Behaviors
1.	1.
	2.
	3.
	4.
2.	1
	2.
	3.
	4.
3.	1.
	2.
	3.
	4.

2. People receive regular feedback from their supervisors about performance. Areas for improvement are intensively reviewed, and positive or negative consequences occur according to pre-determined agreements.

3. People are regularly and candidly coached on improvements that are necessary for them to meet their targets.

4. People regularly engage in business scenario planning that includes descriptions of consequences for performance and nonperformance.

Fast Innovation and Execution

1. When bureaucratic obstacles are encountered, the root cause is immediately identified and removed, or the person finds the person who can remove it and encourages its removal.

2. Clear targets are stated and agreed upon, and deadlines are set. People develop plans for overcoming any obstacle that might result in suboptimal performance, reach agreement as necessary with their immediate supervisor, and implement the plans quickly and accurately.

3. Cross-functional teams are composed of people based in different business sectors to resolve customer issues both as they exist and as projected. They meet to discuss and resolve customers' issues.

4. Teams regularly track best practices from across the company. They share and utilize both internal and external best practices and communicate to other divisions when a best practice is designed or discovered.

Passionate Collaboration

1. People intensively ask customers what their critical business problems are and question, listen, and interpret customers' comments in the context of Motorola's capability to resolve difficulties or to optimize opportunities.

2. People move freely across organizational boundaries. People are included in decision-making teams based on their exhibited

knowledge of business problems. Differences are leveraged for multiple and unique perspectives that result in creative solutions.

3. Teams are constructed based on strategic business needs instead of political expediency. People fully leverage the knowledge and experience of all team members. Teams work out specific action plans with deadlines. Follow-up meetings are held based on established timelines and requirements. Activities are completed and reported in a timely manner.

4. In cross–business unit teams, decisions are made based on what is best for Motorola as a whole. People complete all agreed-upon assignments independent of whether the outcomes are in the best interests of the whole corporation or are in the best interests of individual business units.

Step 5: Identifying Key HR Practices

With a clear idea of what they want to accomplish and why, the participants are ready to get down to the meat of the exercise: designing HR practices that will maximize the company's likelihood of success.

As noted in chapters 5 and 6, HR practices fall into four basic categories:

- *Flow of people*. Recruitment, promotions, transfers, outplacement, and training and development (especially leadership development)

- *Flow of performance management*. Measurement, rewards, and follow-up

- *Flow of information*. Keeping the organization in touch with key external realities, managing internal communications, and designing information technology infrastructure

- *Flow of work*. Organization structure, work process design, and physical arrangements

Selecting Targets

HR faces the same pressures as other departments to do more with less. The challenge is thus to identify those practices that will have the greatest impact on creating and sustaining the desired culture and behaviors. It won't be possible to improve everything in HR as you might like; as ever, "the enemy of the great is the good."

It is possible to move very swiftly when the mandate for change is strong enough. Recently at General Motors, HR and line management moved to develop a culture that focused on rapid improvement (Go-Fast). Over an eighteen-month period, the GoFast team implemented major or minor changes in work process design, classroom training, on-the-job development, individual and organizational measurements, organizational structure, transfers, internal communications, and leadership development. As a result of this intensive investment, strong results were visible within two years. By moving quickly and decisively in designing and delivering a set of mutually reinforcing HR practices, the GoFast team created a culture of greater speed in a remarkably short time—especially given GM's size, geographical spread, and history.

In our experience, however, most companies find it difficult to change more than three or four HR practices in the course of a year or two. In the absence of a driving mandate and massive support and resources, it's best to concentrate on the top candidates.

Workshop Process

The goal of this stage of the process is to look at the firm's current HR practices with a view to answering two questions:

- To what extent is each of the HR practices currently designed and delivered with a clear line of sight to the desired culture?

- To what extent does each of the HR practices have the potential for strong impact on the desired culture if they were designed and delivered with a clear line of sight to the desired culture?

Exhibit 7-8 provides a useful worksheet for this process.

The three-point scale in column 2, which addresses the question of current alignment between HR practices and the desired cultural capability, breaks out as follows:

- 1 = This HR practice is generally aligned with the desired cultural capability as the target.

- 2 = This HR practice is occasionally aligned with the desired cultural capability.

- 3 = This HR practice is always aligned with the desired cultural capability.

EXHIBIT 7-8

Identifying HR practices to improve

Cultural capability

HR practice	Aligned with cultural capability now *(1 = aligned; 3 = not aligned)*			Impact if practices were aligned *(1 = low; 3 = high)*			Priority *(column 2 × column 3)*
Recruitment	1	2	3	1	2	3	
Promotions	1	2	3	1	2	3	
Transfers	1	2	3	1	2	3	
Outplacement	1	2	3	1	2	3	
Training	1	2	3	1	2	3	
Development	1	2	3	1	2	3	
Measurement	1	2	3	1	2	3	
Rewards	1	2	3	1	2	3	
External connectivity	1	2	3	1	2	3	
Internal communications	1	2	3	1	2	3	
Information system design	1	2	3	1	2	3	
Organization structure	1	2	3	1	2	3	
Process and work design	1	2	3	1	2	3	
Physical setting	1	2	3	1	2	3	
Leadership (2×)	1	2	3	1	2	3	

For example, suppose "fast innovation" is the targeted cultural capability. The following questions address this capability:

- *Recruitment.* To what extent do we hire people on the basis of their track record of creating fast innovation?

- *Promotions.* To what extent do we promote people on the basis of their contribution to fast innovation?

- *Transfers.* To what extent do we transfer people around so that they can be exposed to excellent role models and practices of fast innovation?

- *Outplacement.* To what extent do we move people out of their jobs or out of the company if they do not exhibit fast innovation?

- *Training.* To what extent do we use formal training to build fast innovation?

- *Development.* To what extent do we use on-the-job development to build fast innovation?

- *Measurement.* To what extent do we measure fast innovation and give people feedback on the extent to which they exhibit it?

- *Rewards.* To what extent are people rewarded for fast innovation?

- *External connectivity.* To what extent do we use the voice of external customers and shareholders to communicate the importance of fast innovation?

- *Internal communications.* To what extent do our formal communication processes (newsletters, speeches by senior executives, in-house video systems) communicate the importance of fast innovation?

- *Information system design.* To what extent is the information system designed to provide the information people need to be fast at innovation?

- *Organization structure.* To what extent does the structure of the organization encourage fast innovation?

- *Process and work design.* To what extent are work processes designed to encourage fast innovation?

- *Physical setting.* To what extent does the physical setting (office layout and symbols) encourage fast innovation?

- *Leadership.* To what extent are leaders regular and consistent role models of fast innovation?

The three-point scale in column 3 addresses the impact of each of the practices, recognizing that the effect of each practice will be stronger with some capabilities than with others.

- 1 = If this practice were aligned with the desired cultural capability as the target, it would probably have little or no impact.

- 2 = If this practice were aligned with the desired cultural capability as the target, it would probably have medium impact.

- 3 = If this practice were aligned with the desired cultural capability as the target, it would probably have great impact.

Multiplying the scales in columns 2 and 3 will provide a quick index as to the practices where an investment will get the most mileage. A practice that scores a 3 in both, being seriously broken and of high impact if it were fixed, will get a 9, while those with less relevance or less impact will range down to 1. To use this tool, take the following steps:

1. Explain the scales and work through a sample.

2. Break up into subgroups, each addressing one of the chosen cultural capabilities.

3. In the subgroups, discuss what the company currently does in each of the HR practices listed in exhibit 7-8, and come to a consensus on the ratings for columns 2 and 3.

4. Report subgroup results to the plenary session, which then decides what HR practices to focus on. If the subgroups have identified more target HR practices than you have the resources to improve, do a gap analysis like the one used earlier to identify cultural capabilities for further work. HR practices with the biggest gaps should have greater priority than those where the gaps are less. (Note: this process provides reasonable discipline and rigor, but it can't be applied blindly. Before moving on, assess the degree to which the results make sense in the context of your company and your HR department.)

5. Break up into new subgroups based on the chosen HR practices. Discuss what initiatives need to be created or changed to build your desired cultural capabilities.

6. Report back to the plenary session, and prepare a chart like the one in exhibit 7-9 to list the changes that need to occur in each HR practice.

Motorola identified five HR practices to modify or create so as to build its desired culture:

- Leadership development

EXHIBIT 7-9

Summary of improvements in selected HR practices

HR practice	Improvement or change
1.	1.
	2.
	3.
	4.
2.	1
	2.
	3.
	4.
3.	1.
	2.
	3.
	4.

- Work and organization design
- Performance management (measurement and rewards)
- Promotions
- External reality check

These practices are currently in the process of being designed and implemented.

Step 6: Developing an Implementation Plan

At this stage, the implementation plan is relatively straightforward. It will later need to be fleshed out, of course, as parties outside the workshop become involved in the process, but the last two or three hours of the workshop should be sufficient to construct the bones of the program.

Key Questions

The following questions need to be addressed:

- What will we do?

- Who takes the lead?

- Who else needs to be involved?

- When are the interim reports due?

- When is the final report due?

- Who has final approval?

Workshop Process

The plenary group can move straight on from identifying the target HR practices to deciding how to attack them. The questions translate to the following steps in the process:

1. Agree to move on with the practices just identified.

2. Decide who will direct the process of translating the general approach into specific practices or policies. This role may be taken by someone in HR or by a line executive.

3. Identify other participants in the planning process or those who did not attend the planning sessions. Look for people with required technical skills who are knowledgeable about the key aspects of the business, and who are likely to be enthusiastic about being involved and will have authority to make it happen.

4. Set interim report dates. Three weeks is the optimal time for the first report—long enough for people to think and meet about the assignment but short enough to maintain focus and urgency.

5. Set a final report date. Final results should be presented to the appropriate management or HR team within three months.

6. Identify the go/no-go authority. In most cases, the changes in HR resulting from this process are important enough that senior line management should make the final decision.

EXHIBIT 7-10

Action planning form

Activity	Interim report date	Completion date	Who is responsible	Who is involved

A form like the one in exhibit 7-10 will provide a useful record of the final decisions.

Following the HR strategy off-site at Motorola, the outcomes of the process were presented to the senior line leadership of the company. After considerable discussion and a few modifications, the results were approved and implementation teams began their work.

8

HR Organization

To what extent is our HR organization (e-HR, service centers, centers of expertise, embedded HR, and outsourcing contracts) aligned with the business strategy?

E FFECTIVE HR LEADERS align their departments with the organizations they serve and match their resources with business requirements. At the top, HR needs to help make the whole corporation greater than the sum of its parts, and to implement practices that support corporate strategies, build shareholder value, and shape the corporate image. At the business unit level, HR needs to focus on strategic objectives, identifying and serving target customers, creating wealth in the marketplace, and delivering an employee value proposition.

As discussed in chapter 6, business structure should follow strategy. Based on the scale and scope of their products and services, firms set themselves up as single businesses, related or unrelated diversifications, or holding companies. To fit into these structures, HR generally assumes one of three generic patterns: HR functional organization, HR shared services, and embedded HR.

An HR functional organization has specialists in each practice area: people flow (staffing, training, succession planning, outsourcing), performance management flow (appraisal, compensation, benefits), information flow (information, HR information systems, employee relations), and work flow (organization design, work process redesign, and workplace design). These specialists create value by providing both theory and practice in their discipline.

An HR shared-services organization is a catch-all. In general, shared services divide into two parts: transaction work (the standardized administrative duties of HR) and transformation work (adding value for investors, customers, line managers, and employees). For HR transaction work, value accrues through efficiency—service centers, technology for employee self-reliance, and outsourcing. For HR transformational work, value accrues through balancing corporate control, which promotes standardization, and business unit autonomy, which encourages flexibility.

Embedded HR places HR work within a business unit as HR generalists, business unit HR, business partners, or HR account managers. Essentially, each business has its own HR resources for staffing, training, compensation, and so forth. Value occurs as each business tailors HR practices to its needs.

HR structure aligns with business organization as shown in figure 8-1. As this figure suggests, a single business calls for a functional HR organization, a diversified business (related or unrelated) for a shared-services organization, and a holding company for embedded HR.

FIGURE 8-1

Alignment of business organization and HR organization

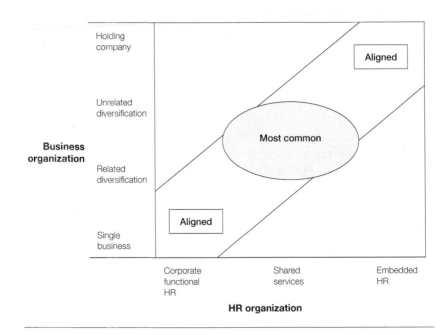

In practice, HR structure often has more to do with fashion (and the clarion call of consultants) than with strategy. The shared-services approach has been in vogue lately, and it has served many HR leaders well. But by no means has it served all who have used it, since real value depends on matching the HR organization to the business organization.

To figure out what type of HR organization will work best for you, start by diagnosing your business organization type. You can use the assessment tool on strategy choices and structural responses (assessment 6-2) to plot your firm along the vertical axis of figure 8-1 and place it in one of the generic business organization types.

This chapter reviews tips for creating each of the three HR organizations, with a greater focus on shared services, given the prevalence of diversified businesses.

Single Business: Functional HR

Start-ups and small companies have small HR staffs. Until a company has fifty to seventy-five employees, it hardly needs a full-time HR professional; a line manager can handle HR activities. As its workload grows, it eventually hires someone to oversee HR, setting basic policies and practices for hiring, training, and paying employees, and perhaps also running the office and administrative side of the business. This HR generalist will probably be part of the management team and will be consulted on organization changes.

As companies grow, their HR staffs grow as well. But as long as they stay primarily in one line of business, HR expertise often resides at corporate headquarters, with HR generalists in the plants or divisions who apply corporatewide policies.

Herman Miller, for example, was founded in 1923 as a home furniture manufacturer and branched out into office furniture and ergonomics, becoming the world's second-largest company in the field.[1] As mentioned in chapter 6, it now employs about six thousand people worldwide who work in functional departments. Its HR organization is led by Andy Lock, who also directs its IT operations. He has corporate specialists in recruitment, development, and compensation who design policies and practices that apply throughout the company. Thus the thought leadership for HR policies comes from corporate specialists, the responsibility for employee engagement rests with line managers, and local HR generalists tailor corporate policies to plant conditions and participate in employee-related decisions.

And Herman Miller is by no means the largest company to use this format. Bell Canada, with forty thousand employees, also has primarily a functional HR organization structure. Some of its emerging businesses have different HR policies, but most of its employees receive similar treatment because they are in relatively similar operations. The standardization and integration of services ensures efficiency, low cost, and consistency across the company, while the corporate HR specialists work to create policies that will work for each customer segment and help deliver the company's overall strategic agenda.

If you are in a single-business organization, you will want to create and maintain a strong HR functional organization. This means identifying staff specialists who can design HR practices that match the needs of the business and deliver them to all corners of your company. Employees who move from site to site want to find familiar terms and conditions of work. Managers want to know what is expected of them regardless of where they work. HR professionals in local plants or operations need a solid line to their HR hierarchy while supporting local business leaders. Therefore, it is important to make sure your HR organization avoids these common mistakes:

- *Hyperflexibility.* These days many HR professionals want their work to be flexible, not standardized, even though flexibility may do more harm than good when the basic business is similar across the organization. Flexibility in HR should match diversity of business operations. When a company has similar strategies, products, and operations, HR practices should likewise be similar.

- *Separating corporate and business unit HR.* As single businesses expand, the increasing workforce seems to create a need for business unit HR specialists. Both corporate and business units add HR staff, creating a financial and administrative burden and leading to unnecessary proliferation and redundancy of HR practices.

- *Isolation.* Corporate staff specialists who distance themselves from business realities respond slowly to business changes. Barricaded in corporate offices, they might design HR practices for the past and not the future.

- *Disintegration.* Functional HR specialists often settle into silos or functional roles that separate them from one another. When recommendations come from separate specialties, it may become difficult to weave the resulting practices into a unified whole. Too many companies hire based on one set of criteria, train based on a different set, and evaluate performance on yet a third. Then their leaders wonder why employees lack a common set of goals and objectives.

The HR functional organization suits a single business strategy. It should not be abandoned in favor of the more popular shared-services organization unless the structure and strategy of the business mandate the choice.

Holding Company Business: Dedicated HR

Pure holding companies house diverse businesses that operate independently. The Indian holding company Tata Group, for example, has an annual turnover of around US$11.2 billion—2.4 percent of India's total GDP. It is organized into eighty-five major companies in seven sectors (materials, chemicals, energy, and engineering products, as well as engineering services, automotive, and communications and information technology). Each of these independent companies has a business strategy based on its market and customer requirements, and therefore creates its own HR functional organization, with a leader who directs its HR policies and practices. Corporate has a small HR staff whose original task was simply to coordinate and share information across business units.

Recently Tata has looked to create greater synergy and brand unity among the component businesses. The corporate HR function now sets overall direction by crafting a general HR value framework and setting minimum standards, spearheading specific HR interventions in Tata companies, and linking their needs with the overall corporate vision. Specific corporate HR interventions are generally limited to learning, leadership development, performance and remuneration management for senior executives, succession planning, and strategic and high-potential recruitment. While corporate HR does not dictate business unit HR strategy, it does provide process tools for business unit HR professionals to design and implement high-value-added and business-focused HR agendas.

If you're organizing HR for a holding company, you will want to support and coordinate dedicated HR departments embedded in the business units. Here are the common mistakes to avoid:

- *Corporate interference.* A true holding company has limited corporate involvement in HR work conducted at the business unit level.

Corporate should set general directions and philosophy, but policies and practices belong to the business units.

- *Lack of sharing.* Diverse business units find it easy to slide from autonomy into isolation. HR leaders and professionals need to stay in touch with one another, sharing lessons through learning communities, technology, or other forums. Corporate HR can host and sponsor such meetings, but should not attempt to regulate them—the line between facilitation and interference is always narrow.

- *Repatenting the wheel.* Even when business unit HR departments are in touch with one another, they often prefer to develop programs on their own. The "not invented here" syndrome is alive and well in HR, and many professionals are reluctant to make a commitment to a program they didn't create. The corporate HR staff needs to help the business units recognize what is being done and to transfer learning across units when appropriate—not forcing units to adopt certain programs, but discouraging them from going off on their own when it isn't necessary.

While relatively few true holding companies exist, the closer a firm comes to that model, the more its HR work needs to be in dedicated business unit operations.

Diversified Business: Shared-Services HR

The choice between functional and dedicated HR often looks like an either/or question: HR exists at either corporate or business unit levels, and it is either centralized or decentralized, efficient or effective, standardized or flexible. Business units have similar HR practices or dissimilar ones, the flow is top down or bottom up, and so forth. In the kind of reorganization that only *looks* like progress, companies often shift from one extreme to the other, not realizing that the key is to align with the business organization.

Most large firms are neither pure single businesses nor pure holding companies. They lie somewhere in between, in either related or unrelated diversification. They create units to compete in different markets, yet try to find synergy among them. For these business organizations, a relatively new way to organize HR resources, called *shared services*, has emerged. From a distance, shared services looks a lot like centralization, but it is not. Table 8-1 marks some of the ways functional HR, shared services, and dedicated HR differ from one another.

TABLE 8-1

Functional HR, shared services, and dedicated HR

Dimension	Functional	Shared services	Dedicated
Business organization	Single business	Related or unrelated diversification	Holding company
Design of HR policies	Performed by corporate functional specialists	Alternatives created by specialists in centers of expertise	Designed and delivered by functional specialists within a business
Implementation of HR practices	Governed by corporate specialists	Governed by local HR professionals who select options from center-of-expertise menu	Governed by local HR specialists embedded in the business
Accountability	Corporate HR	Split between operations and HR	Local business leader
Services orientation	Standardized services across the corporation	Tailored to business needs with consistency through learning and sharing	Unique services for each business
Flexibility	Mandates use of internal resources	Has flexibility as governed by the centers of expertise	Each business creates what is required
Chargebacks	Business units pay an allocation of HR costs	Business units pay for use of service	Business units fund their own HR costs
Location	Strong corporate presence with HR generalists on-site	Wherever makes sense	Small corporate HR office, with HR staff at local level
Skills requirements for HR	Technically expert in design and delivery	Design expertise, but also consulting and support	Business expertise and technical specialty in business
Wealth-creation criteria	Corporate shareholder value	HR value creation for line managers, employees, customers, and investors	Business unit profitability

Source: Adapted from Booz-Allen Hamilton, "Getting Shared Services Right: Capturing the Promise." Accessed on the Internet at http://www.boozallen.de/content/downloads/viewpoints/5K_GettingSharedServ.pdf.

Shared services became popular among staff groups—not just HR—in the 1990s as a response to general cost pressures. Staff leaders couldn't simply choose the cheapest and most efficient approach—that is, centralize and standardize all processes—because centralized staff work cannot keep up with the needs of each unit of a diversified business. Shared services became a way to balance the efficiencies of centralization with the flexibility required for competing in different markets.

As the shared-services concept evolves, it is moving toward the need to ensure that output from staff functions adds value to the business. Cost savings and transaction work efficiencies remain important, but transformation work—designing and delivering business strategies that add value for multiple stakeholders—is gaining more and more attention.

Figure 8-2 diagrams the current transition in HR work. It captures the essence of emerging governance issues related to the major parts of HR.

The bold solid line represents the administrative, transaction-based work of HR. This line shows that HR work to support employees is a given—it has been, is now, and will be done. In any company, employees must be hired and paid. They will need benefits processed, roles assigned, and training offered. The service and support work of HR must be done, and done flawlessly.

The angled line shows that in the past, HR dedicated 70–80 percent of its resources to administrative work. At present, most diversified business organizations are in transition as they attempt to find ways to reduce that proportion to 15–20 percent without loss of quality—thereby creating efficiencies throughout the organization. In the process, HR will find ways to improve many activities and to do without others entirely.

FIGURE 8-2

HR's transformation journey

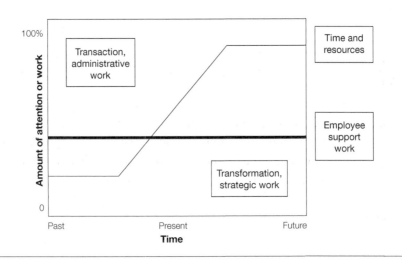

Some activities routinely part of HR may simply not need to be done anymore. For example, companies have sponsored day care, health clubs, picnics, fundraising campaigns, and so forth, then questioned the value these activities add to the mission of the company. The criteria for knowing which activities add value come from viewing them from a stakeholder perspective:

• Will this activity increase intangible value for investors?

• Will this activity help build customer share with target customers?

• Will this activity enhance organization capabilities that line managers need?

• Will this activity improve employee abilities or further an employee value proposition?

HR Transaction Work

Often, activities that build employee commitment do not translate to capabilities, customer share, or intangibles. In these cases, these activities may be discontinued. For those activities that should be continued because they add value, or are legally required, or are necessary to operations, the firm can turn to service centers, technology, and outsourcing. These three approaches are not discrete solutions to managing HR transactions; they combine to process administrative work better, faster, and cheaper.

Service Centers

Service centers emerged in the 1990s as staff leaders realized that many administrative tasks were more efficiently carried out in a centralized, standardized way. And there's no real limit to centralization. As one HR executive said, "If we move the HR work four hundred yards, we might as well move it three thousand miles." It works because employees are willing to find answers to routine, standard questions through a service center.

Service centers enjoy economies of scale, enabling employee concerns to be resolved by fewer dedicated HR resources. In addition, service centers standardize HR processes, thus reducing redundancy and duplication. For example, a global oil services firm had more than ten separate ways to register for training; its new service center created a standard procedure that both increased efficiency and reduced costs. Service centers can also be accessible twenty-four hours a day, seven days a week, from inside or outside the company, which enhances the service level for employees and retirees.

A service center setup has its own pitfalls:

- *Ignorance.* Firms sometimes forget to make sure employees know how to access the service center. In one company, employees could not find local HR professionals to answer their questions, so they began to ask line managers instead. This meant having relatively expensive people spending time running down questions or concerns that could have been resolved more cheaply by local HR professionals—and more cheaply still by the service center.

- *Loss of personal touch and ancillary data.* Service center employees miss out on the sort of tangential information that local HR professionals pick up in the course of answering administrative questions: how the employee feels, how work is going, and how the culture of the unit is adapting to business requirements. These questions are seldom dealt with in technology (computer or phone) based service centers. Service centers also inevitably remove some of the personal touch that comes from face-to-face interaction.

Even given these risks, service centers have permeated large companies. Their value is so great that it is worth finding ways around the associated problems.

Technology and Employee Self-Reliance

Properly designed technology enables employees to manage much of their own HR administrative work. They can access information on HR policy and usage, such as vacation days allotted and taken, retirement provisions such as 401(k) status, job or career opportunities and qualifications needed, and their own skill levels (via self-assessment surveys). They can also take care of many routine transactions whenever they wish, because automated systems don't keep office hours.[2]

We estimate that 60 percent of employee HR questions can be answered online by the employees themselves. If employees feel uncomfortable with the online response, they can contact a service center and talk to someone. Customer service representatives at service centers can usually deal with about 85 percent of the remaining queries. The remaining 15 percent can be allocated to a case manager who responds. Some estimates of the cost savings of these tiered solutions are as high as 50 percent of HR transaction costs.[3]

Relying on technology to perform HR transactions has many benefits. The HR practices involved must be standardized, which avoids duplication, reduces costs, and ensures consistency. Since employees can access HR transactions at their convenience, their perception of service quality also increases. In addition, accuracy improves because employees can update and modify their own records. Managers have access to personnel information (such as training and salary history) and may be able to make better decisions.

For example, Boeing has integrated its employee services through a personalized Web-based portal and phone center. Through this portal, called TotalAccess, Boeing employees have a secure and convenient system for accessing HR. They can find information to make decisions, instructions for performing transactions, and access to Web-based services to complete those transactions.[4]

As technology-based solutions to routine HR administration increase, a few trends are worth considering—and some emerging pitfalls are well worth avoiding:

- *Building from scratch*. Companies often regard themselves as unique, but it is best to avoid the temptation to design and implement a unique HR data portal and service. Many effective products are on the market, and adapting one of them is much simpler and less expensive than building something new.

- *Forgetting relationships*. With many HR transactions, the goal is to finish as quickly and painlessly as possible. Nonetheless, HR is not like mass-market banking, where customers happily manage transactions without building a relationship with the bank. It is more like high-end investment banking, where relationships still offer the best long-term approach to customer share. Relationship HR, designed to build loyalty between individual employees and the firm, likewise offers the best long-term approach to employee care.

- *Data without insight*. Data does not improve decision making unless it is collected with a purpose. If it's warehoused in files and never fully deployed, it might as well not exist. Good decisions start with good questions that require managerial insight and foresight. Then data collected through technology can be used to assess alternatives and test hypotheses.

- *Intrusiveness*. Concerns over privacy continue to be a major challenge. The more data accumulates, the more the firm knows about the employee, and the harder it is to keep the data secure. As useful and convenient as 24/7 access to employee data can be, it blurs the boundaries between work and social life. While each employee needs to find ways to manage this balance, technology may become increasingly intrusive and remove balance that gives employees purpose and passion.

Even with these concerns and challenges, technology will increasingly be used to deal with employee transactions. As the technology becomes more user-friendly, accessible, and secure, it will help employees to manage their personal careers and leaders to use employee data and resources to produce value for the company.

Outsourcing

Outsourcing draws on the premise that knowledge is an asset that need not be owned to be accessed. HR expertise can be shared across boundaries by means of alliances, where two or more firms get together to create a common service, or by outright purchase from vendors who specialize in offering it.

Vendors can take advantage of economies of both knowledge and scale. Economy of knowledge leads them to keep up with the latest research on HR issues and with the latest technology, so as to offer transaction work that accesses the most recent ideas and is delivered in the most efficient way. For economy of scale, vendors offer bundles of HR services and seek to move their clientele away from the traditional idea of outsourcing to multiple vendors—one for staffing, another for training, another for compensation, and so on, all taking somewhat different approaches to their work.

Increasingly, HR outsourcing will seek integrated solutions rather than isolated practices. For example, in hiring, HR systems can identify the skills required for certain jobs and then use these skills in sourcing and screening talent. However, when considered as an integrated solution, the skill requirements can be applied to training, compensation, and job assignments as well, not just hiring. Integrated solutions require vendors with expertise in multiple areas, not single HR practice areas. British Petroleum (BP), International Paper, Prudential, Bank of America, and others have pioneered the outsourcing of HR transactions.[5] Though outsourcing on this scale is too new for results to be definitive, these firms have encountered several potential benefits of outsourcing:

- *Cost savings.* Savings have been in the 15–25 percent range—a substantial amount for large companies, which spend an average of $1,600 per employee per year on administration. Firms with 10,000 employees, for example, could estimate saving $3,200,000 per year (20 percent of $1,600 times 10,000).

- *Standardization.* Outsourcing requires consistent HR transactions. Many large firms have grown through mergers and acquisitions, accumulating diverse HR systems. Simply contracting out this work compels consistency that might have taken years to accomplish internally.

- *Increased speed and quality of service.* Outsourcing vendors generally rely on technology, which permits 24/7 availability of HR data and advice. Employees perceive service as actually improving with effective outsourcing.

- *HR focus.* Outsourcing frees HR professionals to focus on more strategic work. We deal with how to prepare HR professionals to do this in chapter 11, but the act of outsourcing administrative work increases the likelihood that HR professionals will become strategic in thought and action.

These benefits do need to be analyzed over a longer time to ensure the value of outsourcing. Nonetheless, early indicators suggest that outsourcing offers positive returns.

Outsourcing also has its risks and pitfalls:

- *Picking the wrong vendor.* As with any new business, not everyone who offers the service is really able to deliver excellent work, keep up with the volume, and ensure continuity. However, it seems likely that increasing competition will winnow vendors to those who can meet these criteria.

- *Unbalanced contracts.* The contract between the outsourcing provider and the organization may be skewed toward one party or the other and may make dispute resolution impractical. It is essential to specify current and desired service levels in mutually agreeable terms, outline a procedure for dispute resolution that both parties find fair and equitable, and include incentives for performance for the vendor and cooperation for the company.

- *Lack of change management.* The changeover from internal to external vendors often upsets employees, line managers, and HR professionals. While some confusion is inevitable, companies can implement change processes that plan for alternative scenarios, engage employees and other affected parties in the process, and learn from self-correcting systems in order to enhance the probability of successful change.

- *HR role conflict.* Outsourcing changes HR's role in the company. Employees who used to know whom to see and how to get things done now have to rewire their expectations, work norms and information networks. HR professionals who had an identity based on doing the little things well and taking care of people now need to reorient themselves to different issues.

- *Loss of control.* The firm surrenders control of outsourced transactions—but the need for the transactions will not go away. If outsourcing vendors have business problems, they will dramatically affect the firm's ability to relate to its employees.

Despite these risks, we believe large firms will continue to outsource bundles of HR transactions to increasingly viable vendors. Smaller firms will probably outsource discrete HR practices. Both types of outsourcing reflect the kind of collaborative work across boundaries that will characterize the organizations of the future.

HR Transformation Work

In a shared-services organization, HR transformation work balances centralization and decentralization, standardization and flexibility, and corporate control and business unit autonomy. If it falls too near either end of these continuums, it becomes either functional HR or dedicated HR. Finding the middle ground requires an understanding of the four sources of HR delivery: corporate, embedded, centers of expertise, and line managers.

Corporate HR

HR professionals in corporate roles address five issues in a shared-services organization. First, they create a consistent cultural face for the corporation. No matter how diversified the business strategy, many external stakeholders form relationships with the entire firm. Shareholders tend to care mainly about overall performance, and large customers tend to engage with many different divisions. Likewise, the image of the entire firm is often what attracts potential employees to the divisions. Corporate HR professionals build the firm's culture and reputation by focusing on values and principles. Hewlett-Packard, for example, has diversified dramatically, but the guidance of the HP Way continues. Line managers own its principles, but corporate HR professionals are the ones who institutionalize them. It takes more than publishing a set of values; you have to use them in all interactions with shareholders, suppliers, customers, and employees.

Second, corporate HR professionals shape programs to implement the CEO's agendas. Most CEOs have corporate strategic agendas—for example, globalization, Six Sigma quality, product innovation, customer service, growth, and so forth. Corporate HR professionals build organizational readiness to deliver these agendas through the process described in chapter 7. Corporate HR will not do all the work, or even refine all the details. Instead, it will call on centers of expertise to create menus of specific choices, embedded HR professionals to tailor solutions to each business, and line managers to accomplish strategic goals through the HR service.

Third, corporate HR professionals arbitrate disputes between centers of expertise and embedded HR. The former naturally lean toward consistency and sharing of ideas; while the latter prefers flexibility. Corporate HR won't have a magic answer or uniform formula for deciding when to standardize practices and when to vary them, but it can focus on value creation for multiple stakeholders and shift HR practices to create that value in each specific instance.

Fourth, corporate HR professionals take primary responsibility for nurturing corporate-level employees—a role both like and unlike roles elsewhere in the firm. Like all employees, corporate employees should learn to perform their transaction HR work through service centers or technology. However, some corporate employees are unique in that their relationship with the firm is visible and symbolic. Public reports of executive compensation, for example, require extra care to ensure that the right messages are communicated. Senior HR professionals also frequently play significant coaching roles for senior executives, offering advice ranging from personal leadership styles to dealing with key employee transitions, to observations about the corporate culture.

Fifth, corporate HR is responsible for HR professional development. Too often, HR professionals are the cobbler's barefoot children—

designing learning experiences for others, for example, while forgoing learning experiences themselves. HR corporate staff can work to help HR professionals unlearn old roles and learn new ones. This may require hiring a new breed of HR professionals, moving HR professionals to different roles, and investing in HR development and training. (See chapter 11 for how this might be done.)

Embedded HR

In shared-services organizations, some HR professionals work in business units defined by geography, product line, or function, such as research and development (R&D) or engineering. These embedded HR professionals go by many titles: "relationship managers," "HR partners," "engagement managers," "HR generalists." They work directly with line managers and on the business unit leadership team to clarify strategy, perform organization audits, deliver supportive HR strategies, and lead their HR function.

Embedded HR professionals engage in business strategy discussions, offering insights and helping identify where the firm can invest resources to win in new business ventures. In strategy discussions, HR professionals also represent employee interests and highlight implications for employees when the workforce is to be retrained, reorganized, or resized. HR professionals help develop a clear strategic message that can be communicated to employees and translated into action. In the process, they watch out for the tendency for groupthink, encouraging everyone to participate and clearly valuing dissent while seeking consensus.

Once strategies are set, and even while they are being set, embedded HR professionals audit the organization to determine what will be required to reach the goals. Sometimes this is an informal process whereby HR professionals reflect on and raise concerns about strategy delivery. Other audits may involve a formal 360-degree review to determine what capabilities are required and available given the particular strategy (see chapter 4). In doing these organization audits, embedded HR professionals partner with line managers and collect data that lead to focused action.

Based on organization audit information, embedded HR professionals select HR practices that deliver strategy. In light of the unique needs of the business, HR professionals select practices from the choices in chapters 5 and 6 concerning people, performance management, information, and work flow as well as from the processes in chapter 7 that add value. They integrate these practices in order to deliver capability and sequence them to ensure implementation. Embedded HR professionals draw upon the centers of expertise and adapt that input to their unique business requirements. This process of accessing resources rather than owning them means that embedded HR professionals must be adept at managing temporary teams. They must also be able to measure and track performance to see whether HR investments deliver their intended value. In essence, they diagnose what needs to be done, broker resources to accomplish it, and monitor progress to make sure everything is completed.

The embedded HR function may be small or large, but the HR professional in a business unit must treat the function itself as a business. It needs its own strategy, budget, and action plans, and it must invest resources to deliver on that strategy. Accountability for HR means that HR professionals also need indicators or measures to track their performance.

For embedded HR professionals to perform these tasks, they need to let go of the administrative routines that define traditional HR. In the new HR, service centers and technology meet employees' administrative needs, while HR professionals apply organization development and organization effectiveness skills to partner with line managers and solve business problems.

Centers of Expertise

Centers of expertise operate as consulting firms inside the organization. Depending on the size of the enterprise, they may be corporatewide or region- or country-based. They operate like businesses with multiple clients (business units) using their services, funded by a fee for use plus an overhead charge for basic services. The per-use fees are sometimes set to recover costs and sometimes comparable to market pricing. Business units must go to the center before contracting for independent work. If the center experts decide to go to outside vendors, the new knowledge will then be added to the menu for use throughout the enterprise. Centers are demand-pull operations—if businesses do not value their services, they will not continue.

Royal Dutch/Shell, for example, uses centers of expertise that operate on two dimensions: setting strategic direction for each specialty and designing the conceptual architecture and processes for its implementation. Design experts master the latest trends in a particular area, such as rewards or leadership development. They know best practices and create strategies and objectives that would work at Shell. Then experts in process design and delivery consult with embedded HR professionals, contract for delivery of programs to businesses, and lead implementation teams to apply HR expertise to business problems. These roles enable Shell's centers to respond to requests in a timely and cost-effective way. To accommodate Shell's global reach, HR service centers are established regionally so they can respond quickly and with sensitivity to local customs.

As internal design and process consultants, HR professionals in centers of expertise create menus of what can be accomplished. Embedded HR professionals must choose from the menus, which legitimates the HR practices in use companywide. Process experts consult with embedded HR to help pick the options that best solve specific business problems.

For example, say an embedded HR generalist realizes a need for a first-line supervisor training program. The center of expertise should already have a menu of choices, perhaps including an in-house workshop, external workshops, a video program, a self-paced computer learning exercise, a 360-degree feedback exercise, and other development experiences. (If one doesn't exist, the design experts will assemble a menu based on their knowledge of the field and the company.)

A process expert takes this menu to the embedded HR professional and helps select the items most appropriate for that business, offering advice on how to implement the selected choices. The embedded HR professional is responsible for making the selections and for implementing the right development experiences for improving first-line supervision. If the process expert agrees that existing menu items are insufficient, the design experts are invited to create new solutions that will then be added to the menu for the entire enterprise.

The size of the menus depends on the degree of business diversification. In related diversification, the menus will be smaller, ensuring that different businesses use similar management practices. In unrelated diversification, the menus will be larger, allowing more flexibility.

Centers of expertise also shepherd the learning community within the enterprise. They initiate learning when design experts generate new ideas for the menu; then process experts generalize learning by sharing experiences across units. For example, they share the experiences of supervisory training from one unit to another so that each business does not have to re-create its own training programs. The process experts may transfer the learning or they may have the requesting organization unit communicate directly with those who have previously done the work.

Centers of expertise are relatively new to organizations, and they have a number of risks:

- *One size fits all.* Center experts tend to fall into routines and push programs that are familiar to them. Left to themselves, they may fail to adapt their programs to the needs of each business. It takes careful attention to make sure the menus continue to evolve and multiple items are selected from the menus

- *Out of touch with reality.* If the center experts isolate themselves from day-to-day business problems, their menus are apt to offer solutions that are academically rigorous but irrelevant. Design experts must bridge future ideas to present problems. They need to turn theory and best practices into effective action.

- *Canned solutions.* It is much easier to have a solution in search of a problem than to design a solution for a problem. Like independent consultants, center experts are often tempted to craft single solutions that they sell to multiple businesses.

- *Not invented here.* Embedded HR professionals who worry more about personal credibility than impact are reluctant to use the best practices proposed by center experts. If either center experts or embedded HR professionals declare themselves more important to the business, the entire process falters.

- *Unquestioned authority.* When business units are required to use the center, the experts there find it easy to assume the units are happy to do so. They need to monitor their customer service scores as measured by embedded HR professionals, and pay attention to the response.

- *Excess demand.* Given that centers serve multiple businesses, demand can easily exceed capacity, leaving neglected businesses to flounder on their own or reinvent the wheel on the sly.

While none of these risks are insurmountable, they indicate that centers will inevitably evolve as they refine their approach to delivering HR resources.

Line Managers

Line managers committed to using HR to reach their goals don't delegate all of HR to HR. They are the final decision makers and they make informed HR choices. They demand insight and relevance from their HR professionals but don't abdicate responsibility. They spend time making sure they have the right people in the right place with the right skills at the right time. They treat people and organization as resources that need investment to grow. They model how they expect others to behave. They demand rigorous organizational assessments, and they follow up on organization and people issues. They are the public persona of their firm's culture. They rely on HR professionals to frame important HR issues and agendas and to challenge and inform them in making decisions that lead to business results.

HR's main risk with line manager accountability is the temptation to use it as a way to delegate all HR work to line managers. This makes no sense. Line managers make choices, but it's not their responsibility to collect the data or devise the frameworks behind those choices. Line managers demonstrate their commitment to HR by being the visible, public champions for new initiatives, not by taking time from their line responsibilities to cook up those initiatives.

Steps to HR Transformation

As HR leaders become committed to a value proposition, they often realize that they must reshape their organization to deliver value. While each HR reorganization differs, the following steps generally occur over a three- to five-year period:

1. Diagnose business strategy and organization.

2. Align HR and business organization structures.

3. Differentiate transaction and transformation work.

4. Create a project team.

5. Build transaction efficiencies.

6. Develop transformational effectiveness.

7. Monitor progress.

Diagnose Strategy

Before you decide what to do, you need to know what you want. Using assessment 6-2, work with your top management team to diagnose your business strategy. Are you a single-purpose business, a diversified business, or a holding company? It may not be instantly obvious. People think of Shell as an oil company, but its worldwide HR head, John Hofmeister, points out that it consists of several related businesses: oil and gas exploration and production, oil products (fuels and lubricants), gas and power, chemicals (petrochemicals and hydrogen), and trading (about 14 million barrels of crude oil a day).

Align HR Organization

Value comes when the HR organization aligns with the business organization. Single businesses require functional HR; holding companies require dedicated HR; diversified companies require shared-services HR. Setting the overall direction of the HR reorganization shows you what elements to put into place. At Shell, John Hofmeister and his staff realized that their diversified business strategy required a new HR operating model—an HR shared-services organization able to support a "business intimate" overall HR strategy, with embedded HR generalists serving each business.

Transactions and Transformations

Adopting our two-part typology of HR work makes it easier to see what to do with different HR practices. With transaction work, the goal is efficiency through standardization, automation, and consolidation, whereas transformation work needs the flexibility to meet and exceed all stakeholders' expectations.

Project Team

Set up a project team that includes key stakeholders—line managers, HR professionals from corporate, business unit, and specialist staffs—plus external consultants if needed, and charge it with creating the business case for HR transformation. Once that is done, have the team lay out the road map for transformation, define roles and responsibilities in the new organization, implement the project, and measure success. At Shell, Bruce Culpepper (formerly in charge of U.S. oil products HR) heads a global project team to design and implement a new HR organization model for Royal Dutch/Shell. The goals are to reduce HR costs by about 40 percent while improving quality of transaction services and increasing the capacity and ability of HR professionals to add value to business decisions.

Efficiency

Options for transaction processing include service centers and call centers, technology that enables employees to do their own HR work, and outsourcing targeted or integrated HR actions to a third party. Shell is forming call centers for employees and has invested in SAP as a global technology solution. SAP, a German-based "interenterprise" software company, will standardize most of the HR transaction processes. Shell also outsourced retirement and benefits work in the United States, contracting with Fidelity.

Transformational Effectiveness

A shared-services organization needs clear roles and responsibilities: corporate sets policies and determines overall monitoring mechanisms, while centers of expertise design and consult on specific issues and share learning across businesses. Embedded HR professionals align with local business leaders, diagnose business problems, and draw on resources from the centers of expertise to create HR solutions. Line managers assume responsibility for HR and depend on their local HR professionals to create an HR organization that helps them deliver strategy. As noted, Shell is moving to centers of expertise with both design and process experts, and is expecting embedded HR professionals to concentrate on organization diagnosis, program implementation, and change management.

Monitor Progress

Measures of success should consider HR costs, which can be tracked from HR staff ratios and HR budgets. Additional measures to consider are satisfaction with HR services as tracked by employees and line managers, or perceptions of the firm by investors (as measured in intangibles) and customers (as measured by share of targeted customers).

Ideally, an HR organization aligns with the strategy of the business organization. This requires that HR professionals understand strategy and then shape their organization appropriately. As business strategies change, HR organizations will adapt as well. The ultimate test of an HR organization is the extent to which it serves customers, investors, line managers, and employees. At times this means focusing on efficiency of transactions and standard processes. At other times, this means focusing on effectiveness and delivering value through intangibles, customer share, capabilities, and abilities.

9

Roles for HR Professionals

*To what extent do our HR professionals play
employee advocate, human capital developer, functional expert,
strategic partner, and leadership roles?*

VALUE IS DEFINED by the receiver more than the giver. But the giver has to know what value is and when and how to create it. In terms of HR work, this translates to mastery of certain roles and competencies. Roles define what work must be done; competencies define how work is done. This chapter addresses the roles that allow HR professionals to add value; chapter 10 addresses the competencies those roles require.

But what is a role? A role is an identity as seen in the completion of this phrase: to deliver value as an HR professional, I must be a _____. Figure 9-1 lists some of the many terms that have been used to describe what HR professionals are and do. Sometimes more is less. The myriad of terms, concepts, and metaphors for the HR role tend to dissolve into noise and confusion.

Rather than add yet another metaphor to the list, we propose the simple framework in figure 9-2, which filters out the noise, synthesizes previous work, and reveals five major roles.

HR professionals are *employee advocates*, charged with making sure the employer-employee relationship is one of reciprocal value. Besides advocating for employees today, they build the future workforce as *human capital developers*. They are also *functional experts*, designing and delivering HR practices that ensure individual ability and create organization

FIGURE 9-1

A cacophony of HR roles

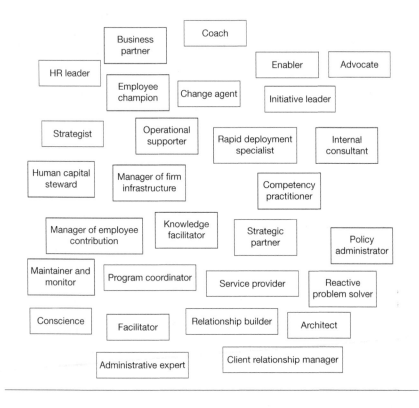

FIGURE 9-2

Synthesis of roles for HR professionals

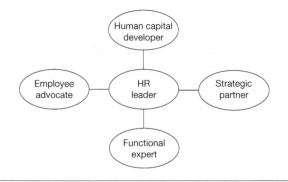

TABLE 9-1

Evolution of HR roles

Mid-1990s	Mid-2000s	Evolution of thinking
Employee champion	Employee advocate (EA), human capital (HC) developer	Employees are increasingly critical to the success of organizations. EA focuses on today's employee; HC developer focuses on how employees prepare for the future.
Administrative expert	Functional expert	HR practices are central to HR value. Some HR practices are delivered through administrative efficiency (such as technology), and others through policies, menus, and interventions, expanding the "functional expert" role.
Change agent	Strategic partner	Being a strategic partner has multiple dimensions: business expert, change agent, knowledge manager, and consultant. Being a change agent represents only part of the strategic partner role.
Strategic partner	Strategic partner	As above.
	Leader	The sum of the first four roles equals leadership, but being an HR leader also has implications for leading the HR function, collaborating with other functions, ensuring corporate governance, and monitoring the HR community.

From Dave Ulrich, *Human Resource Champions* (Boston: Harvard Business School Press, 1996).

capability. As *strategic partners*, they help line managers at all levels reach their goals. And to tie it all together, they must be genuine *leaders*—credible both within their HR functions and to those outside. In table 9-1, we show the evolution of these roles since the mid-1990s.

Employee Advocate

HR professionals spend about 19 percent of their time on employee relations issues.[1] The proportion is apt to be higher if they are working in a service center rather than in a center of expertise. Whatever the context, caring for, listening to, and responding to employees remains a centerpiece of HR work. It requires HR professionals to see the world through employees' eyes—to listen to them, understand their concerns, and empathize with them—while at the same time looking through managers' eyes and communicating to employees what is required for them to be successful. Employee advocacy involves being available and caring while also being able to assimilate and share different points of view.

Some in the field argue that HR should move exclusively to business partnering, to help business leaders define and deliver financial and customer goals. We disagree. Employee relations are not just window dressing: employees really are the primary asset of any organization. The treatment employees receive shows in the treatment of customers and, ultimately, of investors. Indirectly, caring for employees builds shareholder value. HR professionals are the natural advocates for employees—and for the very real company interests they embody.

Business, ethical, and commonsense logic run together here: loyalty comes from relationships, and relationships come from personal care. Employees are people, not chattels to be used and discarded. At the same time, these days a firm cannot promise lifetime employment, and employees often interpret that to mean lack of company care. You can build a caring yet competitive organization by knowing employees, their personal lives, their needs. Caring does not mean divesting yourself of fiscal or management responsibility. It means listening and responding to individual employee needs: resolving grievances before they turn ugly, helping find work for spouses, arranging work permits if needed. You can communicate care through special attention (ranging from birthday cards to a helping hand in a crisis), personal style (listening, reaching out, and being available by phone or e-mail), and friendly organization practices (flexibility in work hours, commitment to continual learning and growth).

Advocacy also involves systematic discussion of employee concerns. When strategy is debated among the management team about closing a plant, expanding a product line, or exploring a new geographic market, your job is to represent employees. What will this strategy do to employees? What employee abilities will help or hinder execution of this strategy? How will employees respond to this strategy? HR participation in strategy meetings should present the employees' voice—and employees should know that it does so.

Advocacy also involves managing diversity and ensuring mutual respect and inclusion so that people feel comfortable sharing and discussing various points of view. Dissent with a shared focus on outcomes generates new ideas, encourages innovation, and delivers results. Diversity can be managed through training and communication programs and statistical monitoring or tracking, but it is *created* in the culture—in how leaders make decisions, interact with people, address conflict, and share information. Your role is to root out discrimination whenever it appears. Had HR professionals countered off-color remarks with "This is just not acceptable," more than one company would have saved millions in legal fees, settlements, and lost reputations.

A corporate reputation for fairness and equity requires policies that treat employees fairly. The HR advocacy role includes proposing fair policies for health and safety, terms and conditions of work, and discipline, as well as implementing these policies corporatewide.

Advocacy isn't all sweetness and light. Sharing tough news is also part of this role. When performance is unacceptable, it's essential to act swiftly and decisively to correct the mistake or, if appropriate, to remove the employee. Good performers lose confidence in leaders who fail to act when people perform poorly. And sometimes, even competent and hardworking employees must be let go for reasons beyond the firm's control. The employee advocacy role requires HR to establish a transparent and fair process for reproving and removing employees for whatever reason, and then to help implement the process equitably throughout the organization.

Example of Employee Advocacy

Tony Rucci is one of the most successful senior HR executives in business today. He has held top HR jobs at Baxter Healthcare and Sears, and now works at Cardinal Health. In one HR department-wide meeting, he explained why he chose to go into the field. He talked about how hard it was to watch his father cope with intense physical labor in the steel mills every day, only to be treated indifferently by his employer following a workplace accident that left him severely burned and permanently disabled. His father's life-altering injuries and early death were at best due to corporate indifference, and could be interpreted as a case of his employer worrying more about its liability than about employee welfare. Then Tony talked about how he *feels* about HR's responsibility to never make an employee's child endure what happened to him. His emotions drive his commitments.

Tony is a superb and brilliant business strategist, helping shape business direction and dedicated to helping his company define and reach business goals. He has proven himself in multiple industries and companies. His framework is clearly grounded in a belief that high-performance organizations hold sacred a commitment to the individual dignity of the people they employ. No one who hears him talk about his passion for HR leaves without a clear sense of how important employee advocacy is to him, personally and professionally. When tough business decisions are made, employees know they've been heard. Tony cares, and under his influence, so do the HR professionals who report to him.

Stakeholder Summary

Employee advocacy clearly adds value for employees. At the same time, it allows HR to add value for each of the other stakeholder groups.

Investors

Shareholders worry about both tangible financial results and intangible capabilities. Nurturing employees affects both. Productivity increases output per unit of input. HR professionals should track and report productivity results so employee value-added can become part of shareholder value. Firms with higher productivity scores generally attract investor dollars. Employee advocates become productivity czars.

In addition, employees are central to every intangible. With competence and commitment, they create capabilities that deliver strategies. Investors confident in your firm's employees will rate your intangible value high. You might share employee attitude surveys with investors, particularly in tough times, to communicate your commitment to employees, your transparency in sharing good and bad news, and the importance of people in your business-value equation.

Customers

You can't treat employees badly and expect them to treat customers well. What goes on inside a firm transfers quickly to customers. Companies losing talented employees soon lose target customers; companies mistreating employees probably also mistreat customers; companies with positive and caring employee cultures tend to have enduring customer connections. They find it easy to include customers in problem solving. For example, when we encouraged one manufacturer to include its largest customer on a problem-solving team, management balked, saying, "That will let them know how badly we currently manufacture this product." We pointed out that the customer already knew the problems with the product. After reluctantly opening the problem-solving process, management found that customer input both improved the solution and built customer commitment. Employee advocates are essentially customer advocates, communicating a set of beliefs and behaviors to both groups.

Line Managers

Line managers sometimes shoot themselves in the foot by ignoring or disregarding the impact their actions have on employees. For example, at the end of a workshop designed to improve operations, a spokesperson for the participants presented some suggestions to a line manager. The manager's response was a brisk, "I've heard this all before; what *new* things do you have? Is this all you've done in the last two days?" Not surprisingly, the employees were disgruntled and hesitant to share any more information, and the workshop ended with little fanfare and no action.

After the workshop, the group's HR leader met privately with the line manager. They talked about the manager's view of the workshop and intention in challenging the presenter. It turned out that the manager had simply meant to make sure that the recommendations had been thought through carefully, and was interpreting the sudden silence as meaning the whole session had been unsuccessful.

The HR professional pointed out the consequences of the remarks for the morale of the group and the likelihood of getting reliable information from the participants in the future. At first, the manager resisted the insight, but as they discussed unintended consequences, he began to see that his style was not getting the results he wanted—and that other styles within his reach would have a better chance of doing so. This ten-minute interaction, and others like it, built a relationship of trust between the line manager and the HR professional. By advocating for employees, the HR professional served the line manager and helped him improve his effectiveness.

Human Capital Developer

Capital comes from the Latin *caput*, meaning "head." In business, it refers to the head—the chief or primary—assets of a firm (traditionally, its money). Increasingly, people are recognized as critical assets, and HR professionals manage this *human capital*: developing the workforce, emphasizing individual employees more than organization processes.[2] The term has become a catch-all for anything related to employees, from individual development to overall assessments such as Watson Wyatt's human capital index.[3] In any case, human capital focuses on wealth created through and by people in the organization.

As human capital developers, HR professionals focus on the future, often one employee at a time, developing plans that offer each employee opportunities to develop future abilities, matching desires with opportunities. The role also includes helping employees unlearn old skills and master new ones. In the rapidly changing world described in chapter 2, employee competencies need constant upgrading. You are responsible for investing resources to shape employees for the future, not the past. At times, these employee development plans may be carried out online through an employee portal where firm opportunities are listed and employees ascertain if they are prepared for the opportunity. At other times, employee development conversations occur through HR programs like performance or career management.

Human capital developers in centers of expertise set up development experiences that employees can access. They also coach leaders, acting rather like sports or music coaches. They focus on both behavior and attitudes, working from an understanding of individual differences to figure out how to motivate desired behavior. For example, in recent years many CEOs have been forced out, not because they did not understand the realities of the new economy and requirements of the organization but because they could not govern the organization appropriately. Many others have reshaped their behavior with the help of coaches who observed them in action and helped them change direction. Coaches are not always popular, but they can deliver results and they can be held accountable for the results they deliver. HR professionals coach by building trust, sharing observations, and affirming changes.

As stewards of human capital, HR professionals assume responsibility for positive team relationships.[4] This may involve formal team building, or it may involve informal dialogues with team members to disclose and resolve differences.

Example of Human Capital Development

Eli Lilly demonstrates commitment to human capital through many initiatives. The company generally recruits people right out of school, then invests in their development and reviews their skills annually. Lately, in an effort to accelerate growth, Lilly has also been recruiting experienced scientists whose worldwide reputations make them talent magnets.

Pedro Granadillo, senior vice president of human resources, meets regularly with the CEO and leaders of every major Lilly component. The group invests a day per year reviewing worldwide talent for sales and marketing, manufacturing, and research. They discuss business strategy, organization capabilities, and development plans for high-potentials—including the second and third generation of talent, people in their late twenties and early thirties, whom the business leaders are expected to know by name. The CEO meets with the board annually to review organization changes and the talent pipeline, using an early-identification tool based on learning agility.

As Pedro travels around the world, he meets with affiliates and reviews operations performance, conducts a top talent review, and sits down with top talent for lunch or coffee. He coaches the CEO to meet with top talent as well, and to speak to internship programs and at targeted schools. He says, "We don't like to lose top talent. If any of the top talent get offers, we will drop whatever we're doing to focus on the individual," and adds, "The CEO must be oriented to the talent issues. He never misses talent reviews, asks consistently about the top talent, and consistently meets with them."

Lilly measures success of talent by how outsiders comment on the talent in the organization. Informed observers note that Lilly has smart, global, and business-oriented people who get targeted by competitors, which is regarded as a compliment.

Stakeholder Summary

Human capital developers add obvious value for employees and line managers, building their individual job prospects and satisfaction and creating an environment where everyone is constantly improving and thus better able to support one another's work. But developing human capital benefits the other stakeholders as well.

Investors

Leadership coaching builds investor confidence, as does the development of relationships between current leaders (and potential future leaders) and key investors. HR can help orchestrate relationship equity by inviting investors to employee meetings or scheduling key leaders to present to investors. Human capital developers also build investor confidence by sharing the outlines of the succession-planning process and pointing out when existing relationships involve some of the probable future leaders of the company. Orchestrating both the process and the knowledge of future leaders creates value for investors.

Customers

Human capital developers help forge relationships between key employees and customers, improving the customers' commitment to the company and its service. One customer, for example, was down to two finalists for a large order when a supplier's sales team—aided by an HR professional—arranged for their CEO to meet his opposite number at the buying company. The supplier's CEO was able to propose terms and conditions on the spot that made the deal a mutual win. Similarly, HR efforts to coordinate employee-customer interfaces through joint projects, customer visits, executive account managers, customer seminars, customer research, and other mechanisms related to human capital all help customers feel more at ease with the firm.

Functional Expert

Ability to fulfill the functional expert role goes almost without saying. After all, if you clearly aren't able to do your own job, it's hard to get a hearing when it comes to anyone else's job performance. As a profession, HR possesses a body of knowledge. Access to this body of knowledge allows HR professionals to act with insight; lacking it leaves HR professionals wandering aimlessly—seeking best practices but never finding them. With the body of knowledge, HR functional experts improve decisions and deliver results. For example, as executives worry about the competencies of future leaders, they can turn to HR for advice. HR leadership development experts who know the theory and research on competencies draw on that research to create a leadership architecture for their organization.[5] Without a foundation of competency theory, HR professionals act with good intent but bad judgment.

Ed Lawler estimates that HR professionals spend about 17 percent of their time doing functional work.[6] Of course, this varies from job to job. Those in centers of expertise spend much more of their time in these areas than do those embedded in the business. Embedded HR professionals have to diagnose business needs and find experts to help them deliver HR practices.

Functional expertise operates at multiple levels. Tier 1 involves creating solutions to routine HR problems. This includes placing HR solutions online through a company intranet or secure Internet site. This first tier requires skills in simplifying complex activities and in turning them into choices that can be self-monitored. Tier 2 work is where HR specialists create menus of choices, drawing on theory, research, and best practices in other companies. The second tier relies on skill in turning knowledge about an HR domain into a program or process. Tier 3 work comes when HR specialists consult with businesses and adapt their programs to unique business needs. The third tier involves skill in diagnosing problems and in creating solutions. Tier 4 work sets overall policy and direction for HR practices within a specialty area. This calls for understanding of strategy and the ability to adapt to a strategic context. While requirements for functional experts may vary across these tiers of work, some general principles apply to all functional specialists.

Functional expertise demands specialization.[7] The range of HR work continues to increase (as discussed in chapters 5 and 6), and knowing theory and research in all areas is nearly impossible. To be an expert, you need to pick a specific domain and absorb its intellectual heritage. With respect to compensation, for example, that means knowing how it traces its roots to the motivation theorists and why people do what they do. Expertise also means keeping up with the literature of your discipline by reading journals and attending conferences. In compensation, current research might appear in *Academy of Management Journal*, the *WorldatWork Journal*, and other periodicals that carry the work of thought leaders such as George Milkovich, Dick Beatty, Jeffrey Pfeffer, Charlie Tharp, and Alfred Rappaport. Professional associations such as WorldatWork (formerly the American Compensation Association) sponsor seminars and conferences. Leading compensation consulting firms (Aon Corporation, Hay Group, Hewitt Associates, Towers Perrin, Watson Wyatt, Wilson Group) and research institutes (Cornell Center for Advanced Human Resource Studies) also produce reports and articles that a compensation expert needs to master.

No matter how much effort you put into keeping up, of course, you will never have answers to all possible questions. True expertise means knowing your limits—and where to find any information you might suddenly need. For example, a seminar participant once asked about the latest trend in base and equity compensation for account managers in European consumer-product firms. We had ideas but no direct information, so we said we would find out. We turned to the appropriate specialists and came up with trend data within twenty-four hours.

Functional expertise allows you to create menus of choices for your business: what other companies have done, what others in your company have done, what you have come up with based on your experience. These menus become the template that governs action in your area of expertise. When a menu item is chosen, you are then able to guide its implementation. You can adapt the core principles and past practices in this domain to a specific application in your company. This means you will contribute to the evolution of existing theory and practice.

Creating choices—constantly seeking ways to upgrade practices in your domain—is part of the job. Sometimes those who establish HR practices remain comfortable with them even when circumstances change, but willingness to undo work is a mark of professional maturity. To continue the compensation example, the decision to expense stock options will make it necessary to rethink this way of creating management ownership.

The choices you offer should be designed to shape processes related to your area of expertise so as to build the firm's infrastructure and improve its ability to carry out its strategies. Compensation, for example, has processes for setting standards, allocating financial rewards, and allocating nonfinancial rewards. (See chapter 5.) A functional expert should be able to map each process and apply the principles, resources, and tools to upgrade the process to meet current and impending demands.

HR professionals who serve primarily as functional experts often work in either menu design or process implementation. Designers must be HR experts who know trends and applications. Implementers offer operational support as they consult with individual businesses and apply their knowledge to specific settings.[8]

Example of Functional Expertise

Boston Scientific Corporation has been growing rapidly through acquisitions for the past decade. Bob MacLean, senior vice president of HR, says, "Every new company told us why we had to do it their way versus a unified way. This was done in silos, with each functional area doing their things." His department has emphasized the ability to apply functional expertise to business, defining the human components of a business strategy that must be addressed across the board.

He adds, "At corporate, we look for programs that are common across the company. We need frontline HR representation of HR embedded in each business who works with the functional heads who reside in centers of expertise . . . We have put functional experts into a consulting services organization so they can tailor solutions to the unique needs of the business. We want these practice leaders to have deep knowledge in their functional area of expertise, but they need to go to clients (line managers) with solutions tailored to the client."

HR at Boston Scientific measures and tracks three overriding goals: adding competitive advantage to the company's businesses, delighting internal customers with HR's products and processes, and improving quality and getting lean in everything they do. Their functional expertise is central to achieving each of these goals.

Stakeholder Summary

Functional expertise is most clearly useful to line managers, helping them turn business directions into organization processes. At the same time, it allows HR to add value for the other stakeholder groups.

Investors

Investors notice firms when they gain visibility as thought leaders—when their practices become models for rivals and firms in other industries. GE's leadership engine, 3M's innovation identity, and Southwest Airlines' "people energy" all illustrate the way thought leadership builds intangible value. HR functional experts drive thought leadership by supporting the overall reputation of the firm. And when investors understand viable HR processes, their image of the firm improves, so we encourage HR functional experts to present their ideas to and share results with targeted investors.

Customers

Customers rarely think directly about HR processes, but they know the kind of treatment they like. Customers who value service, for example, want HR processes that hire, reward, and train people to deliver great service. As noted in chapter 3, it's sometimes useful to involve key customers in the design and delivery of HR processes. Functional experts who spend time with customers or put themselves in the customers' shoes improve their ability to craft HR processes that deliver customer value.

Employees

Functional experts should ensure that employee abilities remain central to HR thinking and choices. HR practices should be designed in ways that ensure employee competence and commitment. Compensation programs, for example, should reinforce employee abilities and behaviors consistent with strategy.

Strategic Partner

HR professionals bring business, change, consulting, and learning know-how to their partnership with line managers, so that together they create value. Strategic partners are business literate and savvy.[9] They partner with line managers to help them reach their goals. Part of this business partnership involves crafting strategies based on knowledge of current and future customers and exploring how corporate resources may be aligned to those demands.[10] They help formulate winning strategies by focusing on the right decisions and by having an informed opinion about what the business needs to do. They focus on execution of strategy by aligning HR systems to help accomplish the organization vision and mission. They become systems integrators, ensuring that all the different elements of a strategy plan come together in a coordinated way. They also attend to the process of strategy development by ensuring that the right people participate in strategy decisions. In practice, they are members of the management team with a deep expertise in people and organization, but with enough business savvy to help shape future business directions.

As change agents, HR strategic partners diagnose organization problems, separate symptoms from causes, help set an agenda for the future, and create plans for making things happen. They have disciplined processes for change and implement those processes regularly in the organization, both with individual projects like those stemming from GE's Work-Out-type programs and with an overall road map for the future like GM's GoFast.

As internal consultants and facilitators, HR strategic partners advise leaders on what should be done and how, and they help manage the process for change.[11] They become rapid deployment specialists—speed mavens who are not only thought leaders but practice masters for getting things done.[12] In so doing they again resemble coaches, shaping points of view and offering feedback on progress, but doing so for groups rather than just individuals. With their expertise in the management of power and authority in teams, organizations, and alliances, HR facilitators help ensure that people are able to act when necessary without getting caught up in red tape and internecine conflicts.

Strategic partnership also involves the dissemination of learning across the organization—generating and generalizing ideas with impact.[13] In large, complex organizations, innovations often occur in subunits. Identifying and sharing knowledge becomes a source of strategic advantage. Alcoa, for example, has profited from its experience in new plant installation by documenting processes for plant start-up and then sharing that learning with new plants.

Example of Strategic Partnership

Katy Barclay, vice president of global HR for General Motors, says being a strategic partner starts with a deep understanding of the global business environment. Besides reading widely and attending the monthly, day-long strategy board meeting of GM's top fourteen leaders, she spends one-on-one time with GM's operating leaders. At least once a quarter, she sits down with each of them to discuss business issues they face, whether they are getting what they need from HR, what their future skill and capability issues will be, and whether they have made best-practice innovations that could benefit other functions or units. These discussions typically last between one and two hours.

CEO Rick Wagoner has set GM's cultural agenda—product/customer focus, acting as one company, speed/urgency, and stretch—because he regards these areas as essential to business performance. Katy, who meets monthly with Wagoner for up to two hours (plus frequent ad hoc meetings and e-mail exchanges), worked with him to select which organizational levers to pull to implement cultural priorities such as internal communication, training, talent management, compensation, and others. Rewards for performance and restructuring as a matrix management company proved to be two of the most powerful levers. For example, relative to rewards, GM had an incentive system for the top three thousand people worldwide, focused primarily on regional performance. With the shift to a one-company culture, HR changed the system so that the payout depended primarily on enterprisewide performance, with minor adjustments for regional differences. Almost immediately, regional directors began collaborating in brand-new ways.

Katy's role in cultural initiatives like this is to identify the gaps in the desired cultural state, assemble ideas, learn from other companies, find ways to move forward, and mobilize key stakeholders to develop the path. To avoid getting lost in firefighting and misalignment, she maintains a matrix that crosses the four cultural priorities with three HR priorities—

talent, transformation, and technology. If an HR initiative doesn't fit into one of the cells, she looks for an alternative that does.

Although she has prepared a strategic framework for HR that demonstrates how it could deliver value, Katy rarely mentions it outside the HR department. She has learned that it is more important to do strategic HR work than it is to talk about it, so she shows her value to the business and earns credibility by delivering strategic HR services that produce business results.

Stakeholder Summary

Strategic partnership is clearly a direct support to line management. The rest of the stakeholders also benefit.

Investors

Investors tend to be more interested in results than intentions. As strategic partners, HR professionals help deliver results, building their firms' reputations for keeping promises and thus creating intangible value for the investment community. They build the firm's capacity for execution, which has been called the key to business success.[14] Action-oriented HR professionals who make things happen help establish an accomplishment culture that resonates with investors.

Customers

By bringing the voice of the customer into management decisions—constantly asking, "What would customers think about this decision and discussion?"—strategic partners from HR add value for customers who may never know of their existence. When HR professionals screen people and organization decisions through a customer lens, they help the firm align itself with customer expectations.

Employees

Employees benefit when HR professionals carry out the strategic partner role, because that role brings employee interests to the table when strategy is shaped and implemented. HR proposals for change take into account how employees need to adapt new behaviors. This sensitivity to process and facilitation helps employees participate in appropriate ways, and the focus on learning encourages employees to focus on what can be rather than dwelling on what is.

HR Leader

Leadership begins at home, so HR leaders must lead and value their own function before anyone else will listen to them.[15] And it's easy to go wrong. For example, in one large company, HR directed a two-week leadership development program that spent a few days on each major business dimension—finance, marketing, technology, globalization, and quality—and three hours on HR on Saturday morning. The message was obvious: *even HR professionals don't think HR matters much.* When confronted with this observation, the organizer said essentially that he did not want to impose HR on business leaders. That meant he did not see HR as central to the business equation; he was not leading from an empowered HR perspective. Business leaders share the natural human tendency to learn more from what they see than from what they hear, so it's essential to set a good example.

At the top of their organization, HR leaders establish an agenda for HR within the firm, both for the way people and organization come together to drive business success and for the way the HR function itself will operate.[16] A well-led HR department earns credibility, and the reverse is also true. HR leaders who do not face up to and implement HR practices on their own turf lose credibility when they present ideas to others. This means that hiring, training, performance management, and communication within the HR function must all be top of the line.

Leadership requires both an underlying theory and a commitment. The leadership model we advocate follows a simple equation: effective leadership equals attributes times results.[17] Attributes are the things leaders know and do—setting a vision, engaging others, acting with integrity, and learning constantly. Results are the productive outcomes of the leaders' knowledge and actions. Effective HR leadership means setting clear goals, being decisive, communicating inside and out, managing change, and defining results in terms of value added for investors, customers, line managers, and employees.

HR leaders also look outward across the organization, helping all functions identify talent and develop capabilities that deliver value. In addition, HR can combine uniquely with finance to create intangible value, with marketing and sales to create customer connections, with manufacturing to ensure productivity, with service to guarantee responsiveness, with sourcing to secure quality, and with information technology to turn data into decisions. HR leaders can also be integrators of the work of other functions. Because HR leaders are rarely contestants for the top executive jobs and because their work is so central to the success of any staff function, they can often be a liaison among the staff groups, ensuring cooperation and consistency.

HR leaders can play an active role in corporate governance, serving as the conscience of the organization and raising and monitoring issues of corporate ethics.[18] They are ideally placed to ensure that legal policies (such as blackout dates for stock transactions for executives with insider information) are understood and followed. They can help the executive team craft and publish values and behavior guidelines, and then make sure that they are understood and followed. They can help with Sarbanes-Oxley compliance and other regulatory matters, and help their boards be aware of and use proper governance guidelines.

HR leaders maintain and monitor the broader HR community of the organization—both the HR function itself and everyone else who is responsible and accountable for human resource issues.[19] Some companies create separate departments for education, learning, organization design consulting, or communication, and restrict HR to traditional areas of people and performance. We believe that HR adds more value when all the elements are combined into one functional organization, but the decision to break them up need not isolate HR. It remains possible for HR leaders to build community even without direct lines of authority. The HR community also includes outside vendors who contract to do HR work and internal administrative staff who perform HR work. Bringing the HR community together is important because those who use "HR services" rarely make distinctions based on where the service comes from. As a community integrator, an HR leader sets broad themes for HR in the company, helps clarify roles, and monitors actions and results.

Although we've been discussing HR leadership mainly from the viewpoint of the top of the organization, it doesn't stop there. Every HR professional exercises personal leadership by accepting accountability for doing today's work while adapting for tomorrow's requirements. Often, HR administrative innovations come from the bottom up—for example, when an embedded HR professional identifies a business problem and generates a solution unique to that situation, then makes sure others in the function learn of it and benefit from the insight. The habit of self-reliance, reliability, and mutual support at all levels makes the HR function a more flexible and powerful instrument, enhancing its members' ability to add value at whatever level they work.

Example of HR Leadership

Paul McKinnon, senior vice president of HR for Dell Computer, describes his leadership style as committed to team decisions and more hands-off than hands-on. He believes in getting good folks and letting them do their jobs. Having spent much of his career in academia or consulting, he is now working to apply his knowledge to an HR agenda with a global perspective at Dell. He is redesigning the talent, performance management, and compensation processes to tie them to business needs and to permit the company to keep growing (at 17–20 percent, the equivalent of a new $8 billion business every year) without acquisitions.

Paul participates in Dell's management committee, the top seventeen executives who meet for a week each quarter. He also interacts personally with every one of his peers (finance, legal, IT, corporate communications) and the regional and business heads at least once a quarter. In these meetings, he reviews what the HR organization is doing and asks what it could be doing better to meet their needs. Social interactions and shared work on collaborative projects help cement his ties to these groups.

He believes that HR's credibility starts and ends with operational excellence. Without flawless basics (paying on time, training on time, hiring on time), other more strategic things don't matter. He also finds that being an HR leader means protecting the company by dealing with board issues—compliance, code of conduct, and other governance concerns. He leads the Dell HR function by being visionary yet pragmatic and by forming relationships of trust with his peers.

Stakeholder Value Summary

HR leadership is integral to the value the function provides to all stakeholders in all its roles. If leadership fails, nothing else works; it doesn't matter whether you're right, if no one will listen. It also provides specific benefits of its own to each group.

Investors

Leadership brand—the unique attributes and ability to deliver results possessed by leaders throughout an organization—can be a source of intangible value.[20] HR leaders should exemplify their firm's leadership brand through their own staffing and training, appraisal and rewards, and information-sharing practices. In the process, they help others acquire the brand and thus can help investors recognize and value it.

Customers

When HR leaders model behaviors that customers value, employees learn what to do to attract customers and connect with them. The firm's value to customers increases accordingly.

Line Managers

Effective HR leaders direct an HR organization that flawlessly and calmly delivers on expectations, freeing line managers to perform other business. As a senior executive once told an HR executive, "You do a great job because I don't have to think about what you do." In addition, HR leaders unite diverse staff points of view and ensure completed and integrated staff work, weaving together input from financial, information technology, manufacturing, marketing, HR, and Research and Development.

Employees

Credibility of HR leaders lends credibility to all HR actions. When the senior HR leaders lack standing, all HR professionals suffer. Historically, senior HR jobs were sometimes filled by leaders who had stumbled in another function. No more. Employees in HR and employees outside HR notice who holds top HR positions. In particular, the values and integrity of the top HR leader embody the firm's commitment to ethical behavior.

Playing the New Roles

The five roles we suggest synthesize the diverse thinking in the field and represent an evolution of thinking about what an HR professional must do to deliver value. In the knowledge economy and with demographic changes (see chapter 2), employees become ever more critical to a firm's success. So, instead of just being employee champions, HR professionals must serve employees both today (employee advocacy) and tomorrow (human capital development). HR functional expertise may be delivered in multiple ways and HR specialists must not only put HR online but create innovative HR solutions to business problems. Strategic partners continue to exist, but we now know with more clarity the multiple roles they play (i.e., business expert, change agent, knowledge manager, and consultant). HR leaders also become more visible and central to the roles for HR. The pattern will continue to develop, but for now these five roles capture what HR professionals do.

No one plays all five roles to the same degree. Depending on where you work in the company, different roles have primary or secondary importance. Moving from one area of HR to another (service center to embedded HR, for example) requires changing roles. This shift affects HR careers. Many people choose to stay largely in one area (such as a center of expertise) and develop increasing depth in the roles required for that work. But anyone who moves to another area of the HR department will need to recognize and learn the script for the new role. When HR professionals master these roles and play them well, they add value.

10

HR Competencies That Make a Difference

*To what extent do our HR professionals demonstrate
competence in strategic contribution, HR delivery, business knowledge,
personal credibility, and HR technology?*

H R PROFESSIONALS share the human tendency to look outward, to see and want to fix other people's problems, and to fulfill roles that deliver value. But competency building begins at home. HR has its own set of competencies that professionals need if they are to maximize the value they add for key stakeholders. Any gaps in that competency set need to be filled as quickly and effectively as possible so that HR can take its proper place as a major contributor to competitive business results.

Evaluating Competency for HR Professionals

Competency work has become the leading logic for diagnosing, framing, and improving leadership in general and human resource management in particular. Competencies have been enunciated for multiple purposes:

- To specify what people need to do to improve performance[1]

- To predict performance in complex jobs[2]

- To match individuals with jobs[3]

- To drive strategy and integrate management practices[4]

- To measure and develop the effectiveness of professionals, processes, and functions[5]

At the University of Michigan's Business School, we have performed the longest and largest ongoing study of the competencies of HR professionals. This project has been conducted in four major waves over sixteen years: 1987, 1992, 1997, and 2002.[6] Via 360-degree surveys with thousands of HR professionals and over twenty-eight thousand HR clients (line managers and peers), plus extensive reviews of academic work, we have evaluated every mainstream HR competency in companies representing a wide range of industries and sizes and from Europe, Asia, and Latin America as well as North America.

The resulting insights are qualitatively different from most others in the literature. The usual approach to developing a competency framework begins with predefined categories. Because of the size of this project, we had the luxury of collecting whatever people regarded as important to tell us. We then used a process known as "exploratory factor analysis" to identify the patterns in the data that reflect competency categories in the actual HR world. This analysis generated the model shown in figure 10-1.

We then went on to address a second issue that makes this model especially useful: How do the competencies of HR professionals in high-performing firms differ from those in low-performing firms? That is, which of the identified competencies have the most influence on firm performance? Table 10-1 summarizes results on two dimensions—how

FIGURE 10-1

Competency model for the HR value proposition

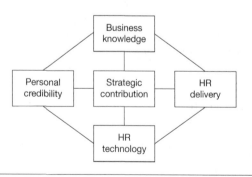

TABLE 10-1

HR effectiveness and influence on business performance

Competency category	HR effectiveness (1 = low; 5 = high)	Impact on business performance
Strategic contribution	3.65	43%
Personal credibility	4.13	23%
HR delivery	3.69	18%
Business knowledge	3.44	11%
HR technology	3.02	5%

good HR professionals tend to be at each of the five categories, and how much difference being good at that category makes to firm performance.

The key point revealed here is that what HR professionals do best (personal credibility, as shown by the top rating in column 2) has moderate influence on business performance. Meanwhile, what HR professionals do only moderately well (make a strategic contribution, as shown by the third-place rating) has almost twice the influence on the businesses where it occurs.

Impact of the Categories

The overall findings do not discount the importance of personal credibility, HR delivery, and business knowledge. Indeed, to have the knowledge and legitimacy to be involved in strategic issues, HR professionals must first exhibit these basic competencies. However, if HR professionals restrict their professional aspirations and activities to personal credibility, HR delivery, and business knowledge, they cut by almost half the total influence that they might have on business performance if they were to focus their aspirations and activities on strategic contributions.

With this in mind, it is interesting to examine each of the five competency categories in more detail.

Strategic Contribution

As noted, strategic contribution accounts for almost half of HR's total influence on business performance. Our statistical analysis turned up four subsets within this category: culture management, fast change, strategic decision making, and market-driven connectivity. Culture management and fast change each account for about a third of the impact, with the other two factors sharing the remaining third equally.

Culture Management

In high-performing firms, HR professionals exhibit the competencies of culture management as an integrated framework. They take care to define the culture as consistent with the balanced requirements of external customers, business strategy, and engaged employees. They ensure that the company's HR practices are designed and delivered to create and reinforce the desired culture by translating it into specific employee and executive behaviors.

Fast Change

In high-performing firms, HR professionals make change happen successfully and thoroughly. They are centrally involved in planning and implementing change processes. But their most critical contribution is making sure that change happens quickly. They focus on implementing decisions quickly. They involve key leaders in fast change. They ensure that human, financial, and information resources are aligned with the desired changes. They monitor progress of key change initiatives, and they capture important lessons and apply them to improve future change efforts. They not only set the broad framework for effective change management but also exercise their facilitation skills to move change initiatives forward.

Strategic Decision Making

In high-performing firms, HR professionals play two roles in key decisions. First, they know the business in enough detail to be able to set the direction of change. They walk into the strategy room with an opinion about the future of the business. They are willing to take strong stands. And they bring intellectual rigor to business decision making—that is, when HR walks into the room in a high-performing firm, the average "business IQ" in the room goes up, not down. Second, they play a reactive role relative to business decision making. They ask insightful questions; they encourage others to be strategic; they anticipate obstacles to achieving the strategy. This requires both the interpersonal skills and the intellectual capacity to look at things from all sides of an argument.

Market-Driven Connectivity

The first three competency subfactors are reasonably well known in the HR literature. This last factor, market-driven connectivity, is new—first identified in the 2002 iteration of our HR Competency Study. In high-performing firms, HR professionals play an important role in amplifying important signals (customer information) from the external environment and ensuring that these signals spread throughout the company so people act in harmony as they respond to marketplace demands. Furthermore, HR professionals prune back the relatively unimportant information that so often blocks attention to more critical matters, and thus help the organization navigate through changing customer and shareholder requirements.

Example of Strategic Contribution

Mike Tucker (senior vice president of human resources for Baxter Healthcare) has been effective at building HR agendas based on strategic contribution. As a member of the innovation leadership team (ILT), whose task it is to keep Baxter on the leading edge of pharmaceutical innovation, Tucker has helped champion several agendas:

- Align management systems with the innovation agenda, including the financial resource allocation process. Inherent in the financial resource allocation process are not only the criteria for continued investment in specific R&D efforts but also the criteria for discontinuing R&D efforts.

- Build the cultural underpinnings of successful R&D undertakings and promote knowledge transfer among various R&D silos. Mike ensures the continual balancing of long-term, creative R&D agendas with the need for short-term financial performance. He values and protects the brilliant but sometimes highly opinionated scientists who make major scientific breakthroughs.

- Track the progress and commitment of key innovative talent. He engages key employees in the acquisition of future talent and works to provide an environment in which the capabilities of these talent leaders are optimally applied.

- Build internal ILT discipline to focus on a limited number of agendas. He helps ensure that the company's innovative agendas do not disintegrate into chaos while concurrently encouraging the ongoing examination of innovative R&D alternatives.

- Keep the research agendas relevant to specific market applications. Having a culture of innovation is good; having a culture of customer-focused innovation is better.

Because Mike Tucker and his HR team have possessed and applied strategic contribution competencies, they have been able to play a higher value-added role at Baxter.

Personal Credibility

Personal credibility accounts for just under a quarter of HR's impact on business performance. That makes it important on its own, in addition to serving as the table stakes for the strategic contribution game. About half of the personal credibility category can be explained by the track record for results, a third by interpersonal skills, and the remainder by communications skills.

Achieving Results

Credible HR professionals have a track record—a reputation for meeting their commitments, for doing what they say and saying what they will do, and for getting error-free results. They improve others' results by asking questions that help them frame complex ideas in useful ways. And they do all this with personal integrity. In the HR Competency Study, the factor analysis showed the integrity variables grouped with the achieving-results variables. That is, according to line executives, *how* results are achieved is as important as the results themselves. HR professionals must achieve results in a way that meets the highest standards of integrity.

Effective Relationships

Given that HR professionals focus on the human side of business, it is reasonable to expect them to be able to foster and maintain effective interpersonal skills. These skills enable them to work well with HR colleagues, individual line executives, and the management team as a whole.

They must be able to diagnose and deal with intrapersonal challenges with their colleagues as well as interpersonal problems. They must also be able to create an atmosphere of trust within the team and with individuals with whom they work. In working with teams and individuals, they personally follow agreed-upon behavioral and achievement standards and encourage others to do likewise. They develop "good chemistry" with their colleagues, highlighting whatever core values they share and building on elements of common interest that frequently go beyond work boundaries. Effective HR professionals are helpful and empathetic in addressing concerns whether or not directly work-related, and they can decompress tense interpersonal issues.

Communication Skills

HR professionals must communicate well, both on paper and face-to-face. As organizations have flattened out over the past twenty years, the average span of control has more than doubled. As is noted in chapter 2, the speed of information processing and transfer has increased dramatically within this same period, so the mandate to communicate quickly, clearly, and effectively is obvious.

Multiple messages compete for the mental space of virtually all organizations. To have personal credibility, HR professionals must be able to accurately select and then clearly present the messages most critical for organizational success. (See chapter 6.) And they can't restrict themselves to formal communication channels; virtually all HR activities have an important communication component. When HR professionals hire, promote, and fire certain people, when they design and implement measurement and reward systems, and when they offer specific training programs, they are sending powerful messages about what is important to the organization and to its success.

Example of Personal Credibility

Chuck Nielson, who is now retired as senior HR executive at Texas Instruments (TI), has an outstanding ability to build effective relationships. His remarkable breadth of business and general knowledge enables him to connect with a broad range of people, and he is extraordinarily clear and concise in his verbal and written communications. During his career at TI, his personal credibility often made a difference to the success of the company:

- Under Chuck's leadership, TI was one of the first companies to have a direct line of sight between HR practices and central and critical business issues and to build efficient and accurate HR processes housed in a service center.

- He successfully established a top-down competency-based evaluation process for the top three thousand TI executives.

- When TI's highly regarded chairman and CEO died of a sudden heart attack, Chuck helped the board and the senior leadership keep the company on an even keel as a new CEO was selected—a CEO who became equally highly regarded.

- Chuck established himself with individuals throughout the company as a sounding board for difficult business and personal issues.

Not a bad record for anyone, let alone a person who is 99 percent blind as a result of retinitis pigmentosa.

HR Delivery

The traditional tools of the HR trade include staffing, training and development, organization design, performance management, HR measurement, and legal compliance. This domain of HR involvement is akin to one of the dominant HR frameworks of the 1980s and early 1990s: "Right person, right people, right place, doing right things."

Applying these tools—delivering traditional HR services—accounts for 18 percent of HR's influence on business performance. This is true even when the tools are designed to reflect "state of the art" practices. That is, HR delivery is not a key differentiating factor; HR professionals in low-performing firms generally design and deliver basic HR tools as well as HR professionals in high-performing firms.

This does not suggest that HR practices do not need to be done well. In fact, when the HR tools are applied as part of a powerful culture-based HR strategy, their impact on business performance moves from 18 percent to 43 percent. (See chapter 7.) When used in the context of cultural or change agendas, these tools strongly contribute to business performance, whereas without such agendas, their differentiating impact is relatively weak.

HR professionals must be able to design and deliver basic and innovative HR practices. If they cannot do so, they may create competitive disadvantage. Furthermore, if they cannot design and deliver strong HR basics, they will probably not be allowed to make the strategic contributions that strongly differentiate performance. However, if HR professionals limit their involvement to designing and delivering the HR basics without an overarching cultural or change agenda, they severely limit their eventual influence on business performance.

The HR Competency Study revealed the following relative impact of the HR delivery subfactors: staffing, 29 percent; training and development, 28 percent; organization design (including legal compliance and HR measurement, which were too closely entwined to report separately), 26 percent; and performance management, 17 percent.

Staffing

From the point of view of many line managers, HR is first and foremost about the staffing process. HR professionals must know how to hire, promote, transfer, and fire people—both as individual and discrete decisions and as part of an overall staffing agenda. They must integrate the full breadth of staffing practices into a comprehensive system. (See chapter 5 for choices in this area.)

In a world of change, the individual competencies and organizational capabilities in each company need to be continually defined and created. Some individual competencies will be kept by aggressive programs that retain the key talent. Other competencies may need to be developed. Still others may no longer be relevant as the competitive environment changes, necessitating divestitures or outplacement. Staffing thus plays a central role in updating individual competencies that contribute to overall organizational capabilities. Of the HR basics, staffing practices have greatest influence on financial performance.

Training and Development

In high-performing firms, individual training and overall organization development activities are integrated into a cooperative whole. Conceptually and practically, they are linked as a single comprehensive agenda. Elsewhere, they often turn into a tug-of-war between psychologists who emphasize individual training (classroom and on the job) and organizational development (OD) specialists who focus on team or organizational interventions and tend to ignore individuals. One-upmanship between the two groups—each trying to outdo the other in importance, impact, and image—can become so dysfunctional as to undercut performance.

Training programs may consist of five major sets of activities:

- Training in basic skills (reading, writing, arithmetic), technical skills (activity-based costing, inventory management), or leadership skills (strategy, organizing, coaching).

- Pursuit of overall culture and strategy agendas.

- Individual career development.

- Filling cultural and technical performance gaps.

- Providing experience in high-value-added and challenging work assignments. Cognitive training must include an application component in which the individual is able to synthesize and practice lessons before applying them on the job.

Organization development is also a key component of an overall developmental agenda. OD probably has as many different definitions as there are companies employing OD specialists. At a minimum, OD generally refers to change interventions at the organization and team levels. In the HR Competency Study, we identified two key OD activities:

- Designing developmental intervention programs that facilitate change

- Orchestrating large-scale communication initiatives that help people know where the organization is headed and how it will get there

Organization Design

Organization design itself has two aspects: overall structure and process design. (See chapter 6 for review of these choices.) It also is very closely related to two other categories of HR competencies—measurement and legal compliance.

STRUCTURE

Given that structure is an important driver of human behavior in formal organizations, HR professionals should be able to apply these four key principles:

- Bring together those people who are mostly likely to create wealth within the company (differentiation).

- Create alternative coordinating mechanisms—meetings, task forces and committees, common goals, measures and rewards, lateral and diagonal transfers, and work process integration—for people who are not brought together via the organization structure (integration).

- Create more efficient and productive organization structures through reduction in managerial and support staff layers (configuration).

- Design and implement alternative control mechanisms to make up for the reduction in hierarchy (rationalization).

When designing organizational structures, HR professionals should work with the design teams to minimize political considerations and maximize attention to business logic. They should defend the strategic objectives of the restructuring and shepherd its integrity. They should make sure that the right people are placed on the design team and given the correct instructions, along with free access to information and instructions from key stakeholders. Finally, HR professionals should ensure that measures are in place to evaluate the effectiveness of the new structure within specified time frames.

PROCESS DESIGN

The current trend in organizational structure is to redesign organizations around processes. This effort begins with a target customer or group of target customers in mind. Work processes then trace information and activities as they flow from the customer into the organization through market research, R&D, product or service design, manufacturing (or its service-based company equivalent—logistics, delivery, sales and service). The key issue at each stage is maintaining consistency of customer focus.

The resulting processes must be concurrent and integrated. The idea is that heretofore sequential steps will be planned and executed so that they happen at the same time whenever possible. Simultaneous processes take advantage of team-based work flows rather than individual assembly lines, allowing integration to improve time, quality, and cost controls across the board.

HR Measurement

HR professionals must have a concept of the full HR value proposition and be able to measure their specific value-added element. That effort requires measures for each component of the HR value proposition that validate and verify statistical relationships between HR activities and the actual well-being of the firm and its stakeholders. Two categories of HR measurement may be distinguished: efficiency and effectiveness.

The HR measurement literature has traditionally been dominated by measures of efficiency. These measures tend to focus on how well HR does specific things:

- Costs per hire

- Retention time per hire

- Time to fill a job

- Percentage of nontraditional hires

- Employee satisfaction with pay, benefits, and so on

- Training hours per year per employee

While these measures do serve useful purposes, they have no direct relationship to outcomes—to what HR delivers to the organization or its customers and shareholders. In recent years, substantial progress has been made in measuring the contributions of HR. It turns out that measuring HR is easy; the hard part is not the measurement but rather knowing what to measure.

Before you can take measurements, you have to identify HR's dominant and focal contribution to your firm. For example, HR's strategic contribution as described in chapters 3, 4, and 7 suggests that HR creates great value as it creates and sustains powerful organizational capabilities and a market- and strategy-focused corporate culture. This results in a clear formulation of the HR value chain: results in the marketplace for products or services and capital are driven by results in executing the business strategy, which are driven by the identification of key organization capabilities and a competitive corporate culture, which are driven by HR practices that create and maintain the required culture.

This formulation of HR's value proposition readily suggests an HR measurement logic, shown in table 10-2.

The measures for each portion of the HR value proposition must be customized for specific companies. With each of the measurements taken, you may then examine the relationship among the measures. This will establish that increasing HR practices increases the presence of the desired culture; and that increasing the desired culture increases the level of strategy execution; and that increasing the level of strategy execution increases marketplace results. By performing this array of measurements, companies can establish which HR practices are delivering the desired results and which are not, so that they can initiate appropriate improvements.

Legal Compliance

To be effective in working with the human side of business, HR professionals must know the legal issues that influence and safeguard people at work and the organizations they work for.[7] They need to understand peo-

TABLE 10-2

HR measurement logic: what to measure and sample measures

What to measure	Sample measurements
Marketplace results: What results does your company want most to achieve in its markets for capital, products, services?	ROI, share price, market share, profitability
Strategy execution: What are the key strategies and how do we know if they are being achieved?	Percentage of revenues that come from products less than three years old, time to market, Six Sigma quality indicators
Cultural design and creation: What culture do we need to have to execute the strategy and win in our markets?	Conduct a customized cultural audit, an employee survey that is designed to measure the desired culture
HR practices: What HR practices do we need to focus on to create the desired culture?	Include on the cultural audit questions about the extent employees and managers see HR practices as consistent with the desired culture

ple's rights to work free from discrimination based on gender, race, religion, sexual orientation, ethnicity, age, or disability, and to work in a safe environment that is free from physical threat or psychological harassment. They should understand the legal rights of people at work relative to testing, evaluation, discipline, compensation, and privacy. They must be familiar with legal issues that have direct influence on union relations and other components of the workforce. And increasingly, HR will also play a role in helping to address legal issues that have ethical overtones, including honesty in financial and other kinds of reporting.

Performance Management

Performance management is a foundational element of HR, and needs attention even though it is the element of HR delivery that is the weakest differentiator of business financial performance. (See chapter 5 for a review of performance management choices.) In part, this loose coupling is due to the many other influences on pay and incentives besides performance—seniority, guaranteed base pay, hierarchical level, and functional category—plus the tendency to set large compensation packages as part of preemployment agreements rather than solely on the basis of performance. In addition, most companies link compensation to performance when business is good and cash flow is strong, but revert to base pay entitlements when business is bad and cash flow is weak.

Performance management systems consist of two basic elements: measurements and rewards.[8] Effective measurement systems have four important features:

- They differentiate high-performing teams and individuals from low-performing teams and individuals.

- They are simple but complete, measuring both results and behaviors—including ethical integrity. This both captures past performance and provides important predictors of future performance.

- They draw data from several sources so as to be credible to the people being evaluated and to capture the richness of multiple perspectives.

- They provide comparable measurements for key benchmarks such as previous year-to-date performance, other individuals doing the same tasks, and preset targets or goals.

Reward systems include many elements required to encourage and reinforce performance. And of course, without some form of compensation and probably some benefits, you won't have a workforce at all. However, these baseline offerings are insufficient to drive performance. Effective rewards systems have six important characteristics:[9]

- They are linked to performance.

- They offer rewards of value to the receiver, not just to the giver.

- They are visible both to the receiver and to those whose opinions the receiver values.

- They provide feedback soon after the achievement of the desired results or the expression of the desired behaviors.

- They include rewards that can be taken away if performance is not sustained.

- They include nonfinancial rewards valued by the recipient.

Nonfinancial rewards need not be limited to physical and social perks—office size, titles, public acknowledgment, and the like. For many employees, the greatest motivation comes from the option to do challenging and high-value-added work in an area outside the formal job description. HR professionals need to be alert for ways to provide such opportunities, to the mutual benefit of the firm and the employee.

Example of HR Delivery

Steve Kerr worked at General Electric as VP of leadership development and chief learning officer from 1994 to 2001. During this time, he worked closely with other HR professionals and senior line executives to build GE's success. Here are the highlights of effective HR delivery at GE, as Kerr sees them:

- The John W. Welch Corporate Training Center (best known as "Crotonville"), where courses are built on a foundation of leading concepts and application projects that are framed as part of the training experience. Within the context of a feedback-rich environment, participants are encouraged to take responsibility for their individual careers.

- A series of large-scale change programs—Work-Out, Change Acceleration Program, and Six Sigma—that support aggressive productivity, quality and debureaucratization initiatives in the context of ongoing restructuring and work process design.

- Performance management systems that drive company performance by monitoring and responding to clear indicators of achievement of results and expression of behaviors. Results targets are negotiated at the beginning of each time period and updated as conditions change for better or worse. Behavioral criteria are communicated through competency models and through company value statements.

- Measurement information provided by multiple sources, including a rigorous 360-degree interview process.

- Forced ranking requires management to distinguish among "A players" (most productive), "B players" (solid midlevel productivity), and "C players" (must improve).

Business Knowledge

The 12 percent proportion of HR's total influence on business performance made up by business knowledge may seem low, but all that result means is that HR professionals invariably assume the need for such knowledge. Thus HR professionals in low-performing firms know as much about business as do those in high-performing firms—but knowledge by itself is not a differentiator of performance. What does matter is not what you know but rather what you do with that knowledge.

To be partners in the business, HR professionals must understand the company they serve and the industry in which it functions.[10] Making a strategic contribution—building a culture linked to external customers and to the business strategy—requires substantial knowledge of customers and strategy. Success at managing fast change requires knowledge of the business in order to set the direction of change. Asking insightful questions about business strategy, raising the level of intellectual rigor in strategy formulation, and having a vision of the future of the business all presume extensive knowledge. Finally, connecting the organization to key trends in the marketplace requires knowledge of what information to focus on for business success.

This category breaks down into three subfactors: *value chain* knowledge accounts for 56 percent of its overall impact, knowledge of the company's *value proposition* for 28 percent, and *labor knowledge* for the remaining 16 percent.

Knowledge of the Value Chain

The value chain is what links market demand with internal supply. HR professionals need to understand the firm's external customers, suppliers, and competitors well enough to see how the dynamics and requirements of the competitive environment translate into internal financial and production requirements, and how the firm's products and services are distributed to the marketplace. This knowledge allows HR to make a major contribution toward enhancing the value chain—to make the value chain whole greater than the sum of the parts. By finding ways to build the capabilities of suppliers, to design and deliver organizational capabilities for their own firms, and to improve the performance of customers, HR professionals can increase the size of the pie that all share.

Knowledge of the Firm's Value Proposition

Three key categories of wealth creation determine the context within which other value-creating activities occur. HR professionals should be familiar with each aspect of the firm's value proposition:

1. Companies create wealth by developing a portfolio of businesses that maximize returns while mitigating risks. Company leaders

determine which businesses to buy, which to keep, and which to close or divest. This must be done with focused consideration of the risk tolerance of the investment community. HR professionals play a role in determining which activities to conduct through which internal channels (within business units, within corporate headquarters, and within shared services) and which to outsource.

2. In harmony with determining which businesses to emphasize, companies must also determine which markets to pursue and which marketing activities to use to approach their selected markets.

3. They must know the basic processes through which products and services will be provided and the quality standards to which these processes will be held accountable.

Labor Knowledge

Knowledge of labor issues is essential to HR's key staffing functions. Labor issues may be divided into four categories that HR professionals need to understand:

1. Both the infrastructure and logic of unions in general and of the local unions they deal with, along with the personalities of key local and national labor leaders. In unionized companies, HR professionals must know how to make use of the positive aspects of an organized workforce. (Example: Ford Motor Company.)

2. How to avoid unionization by being aware of which issues matter most to the workforce, maintaining accurate mechanisms to track employee satisfaction relative to these key issues, ensuring that their company is meeting the key needs of employees, and maintaining ongoing two-way communications with the workforce. They also need to be able to advise management on plant and office locations on the strength of local organized labor. (Example: Wal-Mart.)

3. The key issues of collective bargaining. What are the legal requirements of collective bargaining? How do you work smoothly with the National Labor Relations Board? How do you make your business case to union leadership and to union members? What personality issues need to be managed during bargaining sessions?

How do you maintain an atmosphere of trust before, during, and after bargaining? (Example: Dow Corning.)

4. How to work within the provisions of the labor contract and within the spirit as well as the letter of the law. For example, they need to know how to handle grievances and, what is more important, how to create an atmosphere where grievances are less likely to occur. (Example: General Motors.)

Example of Business Knowledge

In the wake of the Enron upheaval, Michael Johnson of The Williams Companies has played a centrally active role—as senior HR executive and later as senior vice president of strategic services and administration—in an ongoing, high-pressure effort to identify the energy firm's key wealth-creating propositions and to emphasize them to the satisfaction of the financial markets. He has helped Williams answer the following questions:

• Which businesses will we keep and which will we sell?

• How do we identify and respond to requirements from the investment community?

• What are our target markets and how do we best serve them?

• What core processes will we establish to create value for customers and shareholders?

• How do we identify the quality and ethical standards to which our products, services, and processes will be held accountable?

Addressing such complex issues requires a considerable knowledge of the company, its value chain, and its value proposition. From the edge of bankruptcy in 2000, Williams is now ranked in Standard & Poor's top fifty companies in terms of shareholder value—a remarkable achievement. Williams's executives are realizing that it is valuable to have HR professionals such as Michael Johnson at the heart of the dialogues and decisions.

HR Technology

HR departments regularly find new applications of technology to improve their efficiency and their effectiveness. Nonetheless, technology accounts for just 5 percent of HR's total influence on business performance, making this the only HR competency domain that is not significantly related to financial performance.

This is hardly surprising. Overall, only about 10 percent of business information technology (IT) projects come in on time and on budget, and HR-specific projects probably fit the general pattern. The financial promise of technology has largely yet to be realized, and most firms have spent more than they have saved. And even where projected cost savings have been realized, they are apt to be relatively insignificant in the firm's total cost structure. Thus the application of technology to HR has small impact on the total variability in a firm's performance.

In addition, in most firms the primary application of HR technology to date is in transactional HR work, which has a relatively low impact on performance. No matter how much HR technology improves benefits administration, for example, at the end of the day what the company has is more efficient benefits processing—and that is a long way from major impact on the bottom line.

None of this means that companies should not invest in HR technology. The direct influence of HR technology on the company's financial performance will probably never be very high, but its indirect influence is still important. What it will do is free up the time, focus, and energy of HR professionals so they can make the important strategic contributions that do allow them to influence overall performance.

Examples of HR Technology

A variety of firms have found ways to improve their HR operations via technology:

- Boeing uses HR technology for basic administrative transactions and to track individuals through the employment cycle. Employees can update their own employee records and files, and enroll in and modify benefit preferences. Managers can enter and track individual performance indictors and compensation numbers. Boeing also applies HR technology to communicate static information such as policy manuals, new-employee orientation materials, technical data, and key announcements.

- Unilever uses HR technology to assist in identifying key individual and team capabilities, in disseminating job expectations, in conducting online employee surveys, and in facilitating 360-degree online evaluations and feedback.

- Hewlett-Packard uses HR technology to help build and sustain key capabilities in the workforce through online training programs, through interactive learning modules, or through online career planning.

- Microsoft uses HR technology to allocate key capabilities accurately and quickly by tracking individual talent profiles, by communicating job openings and requirements, and by matching talent needs with talent profiles.

- British Petroleum uses HR technology to facilitate greater clarity and effectiveness of project management through virtual project management tools and through chat rooms and other 24/7 communication tools.

Assessment Tool

Assessment 10-1 is a self-evaluation of the knowledge that an HR professional might need to have about the competencies discussed in this chapter.[11] This test allows you to evaluate yourself on two criteria:

- To what extent do I have this competency?

- To what extent do I need this competency?

The scores on assessment 10-1 occur at two levels: personal and departmental interpretation. Personal interpretation: based on these scores, you have identified those competencies in which you have the greatest need for improvement. Since each competency has relevance under different conditions, calculating an overall developmental need score may not be useful. For those competencies for which you have given yourself a 4 or 5, you can construct a developmental action agenda. The last half of chapter 11 provides suggestions for personal developmental actions.

Departmental interpretation: if you are responsible for the effectiveness of an entire HR department or a group of HR professionals, you may modify this scale and apply it to your HR unit. For those competencies where improvement is needed, the developmental initiatives as outlined in chapter 11 will serve as a starting point.

ASSESSMENT 10-1

Self-evaluation of HR competencies

	To what extent do I need improvement in this category?
	Low High
1. Design and deliver a culture-based HR strategy that links the internal culture to the requirements of external customers and the business strategy and focuses HR activities to create and sustain the required culture.	1 2 3 4 5
2. Plan and implement large-scale interventions that make change happen quickly.	1 2 3 4 5
3. Contribute to business decision making by critiquing the existing strategy, by having a personal vision for the future of the business, and by raising the standard of strategic thinking in the management team.	1 2 3 4 5
4. Facilitate the dissemination of customer information throughout the firm to create organizational unity and responsiveness.	1 2 3 4 5
5. Meet my commitment in performing accurate work and achieving results with complete integrity.	1 2 3 4 5
6. Have good relationships with internal clients based on respect and confidence.	1 2 3 4 5
7. Effectively communicate with others in writing and in speaking.	1 2 3 4 5
8. Design and deliver staffing cycles that include hiring, promoting, transferring, retaining, and firing.	1 2 3 4 5
9. Design and deliver developmental agendas that integrate individual and organizational learning and development.	1 2 3 4 5
10. Design organizational structures and work processes.	1 2 3 4 5
11. Design and deliver measurement and reward systems that motivate greater performance.	1 2 3 4 5
12. Measure results at each stage of the HR value proposition.	1 2 3 4 5
13. Understand the legal requirements that are relevant to employees.	1 2 3 4 5
14. Have knowledge of each component of the business value chain and its integration that makes the value chain whole greater than the sum of its parts.	1 2 3 4 5
15. Have knowledge of how the company creates value through portfolio management and meeting requirements of the competitive marketplace.	1 2 3 4 5
16. Have knowledge of labor law, collective bargaining, and effective labor relations.	1 2 3 4 5
17. Apply information systems technology to HR processes.	1 2 3 4 5

Competencies Matter

Many wonder what the "new" HR means for them. Can they do it? What must they know to do it? What can they do to prepare to do it? We believe that when personal competencies are grounded in the logic of creating value, we can specify what HR professionals must know and do to have impact. Most efforts to define desired competencies draw on a limited sample of a few people and a few companies. Over the last fifteen-plus years, we have surveyed over twenty-five thousand people worldwide and determined what matters most to HR professionals. When HR professionals demonstrate the five competence domains suggested in this chapter, they make a difference. Few master all the competencies at once, but all of the competencies can be defined and developed.

11

Developing HR Professionals

To what extent do we invest in our HR professionals through training and development?

Ultimately, all change is personal. Faced with changing realities and increasing stakeholder demands, HR professionals need new roles and competencies. Roles define what we do and who we are, and competencies define how we do our work. But knowing what to do and even how to do it does not ensure that it will be done well. Personalizing change and making it real requires learning and development. In this chapter, we describe some of the underlying principles of learning, then review how training and experience can sustain or build better HR professionals.

Principles of Professional Development

Unlike adolescent learning, which focuses on mastering facts and assimilating information, adult learning focuses on applying facts and turning information into action.[1] Adults have already developed cognitive frameworks through life experiences, and they are interested in learning how new ideas will help them get what they want rather than in simply accumulating more knowledge. Here are the key principles of adult learning applied to HR professional development:[2]

- *Base new ideas on business reality.* When adults understand why they should learn, they more readily accept what they should learn. For example, HR professionals who have spent their careers doing administrative work (say, compensation or benefits) become more open to learning new tasks when they recognize and accept the reality of outsourcing and technology as replacements for their traditional work and of the emerging mandate for strategic contributions.

- *Focus on application.* Working adults are less interested in theory than in how theory can help them. Thus HR professionals are apt to find the underlying theory of human nature and motivation less interesting than its implications for building a compensation practice that focuses employees on high-value-added performance and behaviors. They need to know theory as an anchor against the winds of management fads, but they absorb it best when it is presented along with the action it generates.

- *Accept multiple learning styles.* Most adults have a learning style, or preferred way to learn. The Center for Creative Leadership has classified four such styles—active, reflective, advice seeking, and emotional—and found that people learn best when presented with material tailored to their own style.[3] HR professional development programs thus need the flexibility to appeal to the diversity of learning styles among participants, and they need to be able to match individuals to developmental approaches.

- *Present information via multiple channels.* Adults adapt and learn through reading, listening, observing, watching videos, analyzing case studies or live cases, role-playing, discussion, and so forth. Participants may be face-to-face or remote, working alone or in groups. HR professional development programs need to employ a variety of learning technologies so all participants can gain insights from them.

- *Ground the program in personal reality.* Adults develop when they recognize their strengths and weaknesses and make realistic plans for personal improvement—but honest assessments are difficult to come by. Candid and open feedback is rare, as people withhold information under the guise of sensitivity. Helpful assessments are also hard to give, as few people can accurately see just what information someone else needs. And information is difficult to interpret; most recipients tend to overreact to anecdotes and underreact to patterns of behavior. Moreover, few people really want to know their own weaknesses. An HR professional development program should begin with honest self-assessment and seriously consider whatever feedback is available.

- *Articulate a clear goal.* Adults who know what they want find it easy to focus their attention. In shaping your professional development, you can compare yourself to others, to the competencies that the strategy of the business requires of you, to what your boss and other clients expect of you, and to where you think the HR profession is headed. These sources for defining your future enable you to figure out where to focus your energies. A clear and precise vision of the future becomes a true magnetic north, guiding efforts at three levels: What HR strategy will enable the department to contribute most value to the organization? What HR practices will bring the HR value proposition to life? What roles and competencies do HR professionals need to make it all happen? HR professional development plans that incorporate these elements will provide solid guidance.

- *Earn and build on respect.* Adults learn best from those they respect, and a faculty that lacks credibility will ultimately lack impact. HR professionals can learn as much from peers as from experts if the learning process is set up to share experience and insight. An effective HR development program includes forums for peer sharing as well as faculty members with real-world experience.

- *Create a friendly learning environment.* Adult learners commit to action when they draw their own conclusions from the material presented. They often chafe at the traditional schoolroom where teachers teach and students study. HR professionals need a setting that is informal, two-way, nondictatorial, and more inquisitive than directive.

These eight principles may be used to assess and guide investments in developing HR professionals (or others) or in selecting professional development experiences. They can be applied to the two major options for improving HR professional performance: training and development. Training focuses on formal education—events where participants learn specific skills and information. Development includes the array of guided activities that help people learn by experience.

Training for HR Professionals

The principles of adult learning have a number of implications for the design of HR training programs. First and foremost, the program needs to have roots in a clear and integrated theory of HR—one that offers a rationale for why HR exists, what goals HR should deliver, and how HR professionals should act. Presentations should all build on the same key themes, two to four basic ideas woven into a consistent structure, rather than presenting a potpourri of ideas, tools, and stories. We have seen some programs so constructed around the process of training and innovative training techniques that they minimize the content, or the theory of what is taught, and participants leave with a positive experience, but no sustainable improvement in performance.

Essential Elements

At every opportunity, the program should share best practices—innovative approaches to HR that have been applied successfully—and tie them back to the key themes. For example, a presentation on HR strategy might include the way Motorola applied the steps of linking strategy to HR (as discussed in chapter 7). Or the group might be exposed to written or live case studies on the topic, so they can read about what others have done or listen to veterans share their firsthand experience.

Best practices anchor ideas in reality and enable participants to see how they are doing, but the program should emphasize that such practices must be *adapted* rather than adopted. That is, participants need to understand that they can't simply copy best practices intact. They must understand why the practices worked and how, so that they can get similar results in their own organization.

A successful HR development program needs credible, proficient faculty—people with both the right knowledge and the ability to deliver it. Good teaching is less about what the faculty knows than about how faculty knowledge increases participants' performance. Participants always start by asking themselves, "Why am I listening to this person?" If the answer isn't satisfactory, they're apt to tune out. We have found that participants judge faculty by watching for some or all of the following:

- Framing problems so as to organize thinking in different and better ways.

- Having something useful to say that can help improve current work: an insight, a tool, an approach, a set of useful questions . . .

- Being funny, witty, entertaining. (This makes a valuable short-term impression, but maintaining respect in the long term requires real substance.)

- Recounting interesting stories, examples, and cases or otherwise being clever with words, images, humor, and mental models.

- Being smart and intellectual.

- Having earned respect as a thought leader and researcher who defines the future of the profession because of publications, experiences, or affiliations.

- Being kind and caring about the participants.

- Having experiences that can be drawn on to help participants do what they need to do.

- Helping participants feel good about themselves and confident that they can achieve what they desire.

The idea is to select faculty who can earn participants' trust by what and how they teach, and who can work together as an integrated staff instead of as a parade of stars. Ideally, faculty will respect one another, understand their own and one another's teaching styles, and meld teaching and consulting by responding to participants' questions. Effective facilitators know what others on the staff are presenting and build upon their colleagues' work. Before a major training initiative, it can be useful to invest in a faculty-only day, bringing the presenters together so they can go over their plans and offer an integrated message to participants.

Pay attention to physical settings, social dynamics, and personal issues. We worked with one company that staged a weeklong development workshop for senior HR executives—in the cheap, cramped, and windowless basement of a community center. This turned out to be a false economy, as discomfort soon dominated participants' attention and overwhelmed their desire to learn. If a program is worth the cost in salary and delayed output to bring the participants together, it's worth making sure the conditions don't inspire mutiny.

Likewise, social dynamics can make or break a workshop: include no more than three levels of management, seat participants at round tables rather than in rows whenever feasible, and leave adequate time for informal conversation. Make sure all the participants receive advance materials so they arrive knowing what to expect. Ask them to read and answer e-mail at night (not during the day), turn off their cell phones, and limit other distractions. Pay attention to personal issues such as fitness, health maintenance, food, breakouts, chairs, and the like. When you get the logistics right, you enhance the quality of the educational experience—but don't expect anyone to notice or comment on these physical accoutrements unless you get them wrong.

Encourage a variety of pedagogical styles. Cases, small-group discussions, videos, role plays, assessments, and the like adapt ideas to different types of learners. Faculty should speak only about 60–70 percent of the time. We find that when presentation occupies a much smaller segment of the program, participants tend to view faculty as irrelevant and inadequate, but much more makes participants feel their own knowledge is undervalued.

Summarize and integrate lessons learned. Resist the temptation to present more than can possibly be applied, and pause after each module to give participants time to apply their new knowledge to their work setting. One tool we have used is the two-minute teaching drill.[4] After a content module (one or two hours), stop and pair up participants. The first partner has two minutes to teach the second what the module contained; then they switch roles and the other partner teaches. This brief interlude grounds the module and surfaces questions if its ideas were not clear. Pause again after a longer interval (say, at the end of the first week of a two-week program) and give participants time to assimilate, translate, and transfer what they have learned.

Apply, apply, apply. Encourage application in various ways—a case study where participants can see how others used the insights, a team presentation where the participants apply the knowledge to their work setting, or simulation exercises, application workshops, or personal case studies. Participants should come away with a personal agenda: an expanded vision of an HR professional and what they will do in the near and long term to make it real.

Follow up. Listening to a new idea, or even memorizing it, is far different from applying it. An educational experience needs provisions to follow up with participants and encourage them to apply what they have learned. Marshall Goldsmith, a master leadership coach and developer, says, "Follow-up works. Many leadership development efforts focus exclusively on the 'front-side' of the development process (impressive training, well-designed forms, clever slogans, and lots of 'flash'). They do not focus on the 'back-side' of the development process—the ongo-

ing application of what is being learned."[5] Follow-up may involve formal presentations and accountabilities or informal phone calls, but it
needs to occur for education to have impact.

A Complete HR Educational Experience

We have worked with hundreds of companies on HR professional training sessions—ranging from one-hour speeches (for example, noontime
or after-dinner talks) to integrated programs taking months to deliver.
Our complete HR development program contains nine discrete learning
events (see figure 11-1), but it can be divided and delivered in modular
form, depending on the resources and setting. The following sections
review each event and offer suggestions for shaping it to create value.

Event 1: Organization and Individual Assessments

Learning begins by understanding *what is*, or the current state. This
understanding comes from conducting two levels of assessment:

- *Organization audit.* The intangibles audit we proposed in chapter 3
  helps identify specific needs that participants must address in their
  work setting to have impact. This data helps define what value the
  HR function (practices, organization, and professionals) should
  deliver to the company. It also highlights the business relevance of
  HR for the particular organization.

- *Individual assessment.* Put all prospective participants through a 360-
  degree evaluation to provide a starting point for personal development.

FIGURE 11-1

A fully integrated HR educational experience

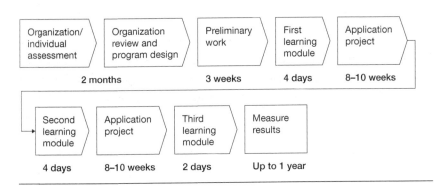

The HR competency survey discussed in chapter 10 may be used with participants' HR and line bosses, direct reports, peers, and internal clients. During the program, each participant receives a detailed individual feedback report that compares individual scores with the company averages and the averages from the total global data set. The feedback reports also include a professional development summary.

These two assessments, conducted jointly by the faculty and internal HR staff, inform faculty about the company and the new direction for HR within the company. For example, the questions about intangibles lead HR professionals to reflect on the value they must deliver. It normally takes about two months to complete these assessments in the required detail.

Event 2: Organization Review and Program Design Session

Senior HR and training executives spend a day working closely together, tailoring the program to the organization's business strategy, the HR strategy, and the competency gaps of the HR professionals scheduled for the program. Based on the organization and individual assessments, senior HR executives define the key deliverables or outcomes (organizational capabilities or individual competencies) they would like to focus on during the learning program.

Event 3: Preliminary Work

Prior to the first learning module, participants engage in a dialogue with senior internal clients to gather information concerning the following issues:

- What changes do you see happening in our competitive marketplace over the next three to five years, including major trends among customers and competitors?

- What major changes do you see happening with your part of the business in the next three to five years?

- What are the key capabilities that our organization needs to have to be successful?

- In what areas does our organization need greatest improvement?

- How can HR professionals and the HR function add greater value to our business?

- What would you like more of and less of from your HR professionals?

Discussing these questions with senior line managers sensitizes both sides to new aspirations and standards for HR professionals and sets expectations for the educational experience. Besides conducting these interviews, participants familiarize themselves with the business strategy, financial picture, and HR theory by reading articles and the organization's latest financial reports.

Event 4: First Learning Module: Linking HR to Business Strategy

Participating in the first three events changes the focus of the experience from spending time in a classroom to intervening in how HR is done. The assessments, design day, and preliminary exercises signal what matters and that a significant change is under way.

Next, HR professionals attend a four-day classroom session that links their HR strategy with their business strategies. As noted in chapter 10, strategic contribution is the most critical HR competence for business success. On the first day, participants take off their "HR hat" and review the business strategy of the company, together with an overview of state-of-the-art strategic thinking and strategy formulation. The next two days begin with a review of the increasing demands on HR. Faculty then provide an in-depth examination of the six-step process described in chapter 7 for linking HR to business strategy. Concepts, logic, and best practices are translated into specific tools. The fourth day is devoted to a review of HR roles (chapter 9) and competency research (chapter 10). Participants then break up into learning teams in a work-planning exercise to generate the list of activities, deliverables, and milestones for building the HR strategy in their business unit. Exhibit 11-1 presents the fourteen modules for this learning event.

Faculty members interact with one another and use extensive small-group discussions, personal application, case studies, best-practice sharing, and mini-lectures. The participants all emerge knowing how to define value, how to build an HR strategy for creating value, and how to adjust their own roles and competencies to deliver value.

Event 5: Application Project: Culture-Based HR Strategy

Over the next eight to ten weeks, participants apply the materials from event 4. They split up into teams and work together to develop HR strategy for their assigned business. For support, each team participates in at least one conference call with the program faculty around the midpoint of

EXHIBIT 11-1

Event 4: linking HR to business strategy

	Day 1	Day 2	Day 3	Day 4
A.M.	1. Introduction 2. Trends in business strategy 3. Value creation for investor, customer, line manager, and employee	6. Step 1: identify organization unit for HR strategy 7. Step 2: prioritize trends in business environment	10. Step 5: identify HR practices that will have greatest impact on creating and sustaining desired culture	12. Roles: define the roles required for successful HR and the organization of the HR function to deliver these roles
P.M.	4. Business case for strategic HR with video case study 5. Overview of 7-step HR strategy process	8. Step 3: specify and measure key sources of competitive advantage 9. Step 4: define desired cultural capabilities and their behavioral expressions	11. Step 6: develop an overall implementation plan	13. Competencies: define the required competencies for effective HR; receive feedback on personal competencies 14. Team: prepare teams for project application

the project, and the faculty or other support staff also make themselves available for additional contact as needed. These phone calls provide additional momentum for the projects and the opportunity for midcourse encouragement and corrections as needed.

This application project grounds concepts from the first learning module in reality and helps participants learn how to translate ideas into action. As a wrap-up, the teams prepare twenty-five-minute presentations on what they've learned, covering the following points:

- *Review of what happened.* What did we do and when?

- *Review of final or interim results of HR strategy.* What did we accomplish?

- *Review of difficulties or challenges.* What trouble did we run into, and what did we do or plan to do about it?

- *Review of learning.* What are the major "takeaways" from the experience?

Event 6: Second Learning Module: Developing Key Organizational Capabilities

The second learning module looks to the future. It focuses on building organizational capabilities and organizing the HR function to deliver value. As a review, the first day begins with the team presentations on their organization HR strategy experience.

The rest of the four-day program covers the key organizational capabilities on which the organization is focusing. The faculty starts with an overview and diagnosis of organizational capabilities and managing intangibles. A series of two- to three-hour learning modules follows, focusing on specific organization capabilities, such as talent, speed, innovation, and leadership (see exhibit 11-2). At the end of these modules,

EXHIBIT 11-2

Event 6: developing key organizational capabilities

	Day 1	Day 2	Day 3	Day 4
A.M.	1. Introduction 2. Team reports from first project 3. Presentation on the value proposition of HR and how HR affects investors, customers, line managers, and employees	7. Culture: building a shared mindset 8. External sensing and customer relations: linking to external stakeholders 9. Innovation: finding new and better ways to get things done	12. Learning and knowledge management: being able to generate and generalize ideas with impact 13. Collaboration: making the whole more than the sum of the parts 14. Alliance: building relationships across boundaries	18. Capability plan: how to facilitate a half-day session to build capabilities 19. Channel: how to organize and govern HR work
P.M.	4. Presentation on organization diagnosis 5. HR measures 6. Talent: gaining competence and commitment from employees	10. Delivery and accountability: making sure that we do what we say 11. Speed: making change happen fast	15. Leverage technology: investing in new and ongoing technology 16. Profitable growth: growing and reducing costs at the same time 17. Leadership: building a leadership brand	20. Application team project • Introduction, assignments, and descriptions • Meeting with sponsors, definition and outcome expectations • Planning session • Virtual learning space • Next steps

each participant should be prepared to conduct an organizational diagnosis and facilitate a half-day meeting to deliver the prioritized capabilities. On the final day, participants discuss how to organize the HR function and to prepare for the second project, which will incorporate the tools and frameworks presented thus far. Participants can choose their own projects, but whatever they choose must promise a substantial financial return. The teaching style continues the highly interactive mode and techniques of the first module.

Event 7: Application Project: HR Organization Improvement Project

The projects designed in event 6 and carried out in event 7 promise an immediate and quantifiable financial return if they succeed. Such projects normally cost $100,000 to $300,000 when purchased from outside vendors, so they would guarantee a high return on investment even if the program had no other result.

Participants divide into teams that meet for 8 to 10 weeks to develop an action plan and produce key project deliverables. Sample topics:

- How can HR influence organizational change to develop a high-performing culture?

- How do we design and implement the strategies, processes, and practices that allow disparate business units to share intellectual capital?

- What impact should or will globalization have on our HR practices in the future?

- How do we create a customer service cultural brand in the marketplace that is supported by an internal customer service culture?

- How can the HR organization add maximum value for each element in the company value chain?

To ensure the effectiveness of the overall experience, faculty members are available to coach individuals and teams through the design and implementation of their application projects. Teams will participate in at least one conference call with the program faculty around the midpoint of the project. In addition to the faculty coaching, each project team has a sponsor from the HR leadership team. This sponsor will provide a reality check on the team's progress and help with implementation planning and execution.

As before, the teams wrap up their work by preparing brief presentations for the rest of the group.

Event 8: Third Learning Module: Program Reflection
and HR in the Leadership Role

This two-day session begins with a morning devoted to finalizing the HR application project. Teams meet with faculty to review the materials and prepare for reporting out. The afternoon is devoted to a report-out of all team projects to sponsors. If participants have successfully selected and completed the projects, they will have immediate application for the business. In our experience, about half are immediately applicable, while many of the rest prove to be feasible but require some additional work.

The second day summarizes the experience and focuses on establishing the leadership role of HR professionals. Participants emerge with a personal agenda for how they can accomplish their leadership role. The interactive teaching style continues with the same techniques used in earlier sessions. The modules are reviewed in exhibit 11-3.

Event 9: Measure Results

Over the following year, four measurement processes track the results of the program:

- *Immediate.* Participants complete a standard written program evaluation that is both quantitative ("Rate the module on a value scale of 1 to 5") and qualitative ("Describe how the module helped you").

- *Three months out.* An informal "buzz" should have developed among the participants. This is not a formal measurement, but it provides real insight. In conversation, participants should be reporting spontaneously that they learned ideas they can use, that their projects are having real impact, and that "things are different" around here.

- *Six months out.* The application projects' results will reveal whether they have accomplished their goals and enhanced business performance.

EXHIBIT 11-3

Event 8: program reflection and HR in the leadership role

	Day 1	Day 2
A.M.	1. Finalize application project (receive coaching from faculty, share projects with other teams)	3. Leadership role of HR professionals 4. The future of HR
P.M.	2. Report out application project to sponsors	5. Creating a personal leadership agenda

Since the projects are designed to either save specific costs or increase the top line in clearly measurable ways, their outcomes will provide a quantifiable index of the program's success.

- *One year out.* The following HR measurement process will assess final results:

  1. To what extent are HR practices being implemented according to plan?

  2. To what extent are the human and organizational capabilities required for success being created?

  3. To what extent are the business metrics improving?

  4. What statistical linkages emerge among data from the first three steps?

Application

BAE Systems, a British-based defense aerospace firm, implemented these nine events, sponsored by HR head Alastair Imrie and resourcing and development director John Whelan. The firm had outsourced much of its HR transaction work, and now felt the need to develop the strategic role of the remaining HR professionals. About ninety people participated in one of the three iterations of the program. These were the results:

- Participants acquired greater aspirations for their HR careers and departments.

- Participants developed a way of thinking and a line of sight between their activities and business requirements.

- Participants acquired specific tool kits to act on these ways of thinking.

- The firm built a specific HR strategy process for use in new or existing business units.

- Participants learned how to lead executives through half-day planning sessions designed to address new capability requirements.

- Participants emerged with the self-confidence and mutual trust to apply their knowledge.

In one case, an HR professional from BAE Systems moved to a new business, where she was at once challenged to provide a more powerful HR strategy. She led her new leadership team through a two-day workshop on building an HR strategy (using ideas from event 4 of the training). This work helped the business clarify its goals, and it ensured that HR was part of the business agenda. She knew what to and how to do it.

Program Options

As presented, the nine events offer a complete and integrated educational and development experience. With 30–40 participants occupied for six to eight months per cycle, however, the program represents a large commitment of HR professional time and resources. When that is not feasible, the program can be modified and compressed. For example, within three to four months you can stage two learning modules and one application project, based either on building an HR strategy or on HR organization improvement. The second learning module incorporates the reflective exercise and the leadership input from the third content module. Alternatively, the program could focus on only one of the learning modules, with no project application. The modules would cover either linking HR to business strategy or developing key organization capabilities. The preliminary work would be customized to prepare HR participants for the learning module.

British Petroleum (BP) outsourced its transaction work to Exult (now Hewitt Associates). BP's HR leaders—first Nick Staritt, then Chris Moorhouse—realized that the remaining transformational work for HR professionals would need to be done differently. They designed a learning experience in which their top 120 HR professionals could learn to be business partners. Many of these HR professionals were embedded in businesses and needed to learn skills in organization diagnosis, consulting, and action planning. Others were in centers of expertise and needed to learn how to adapt their knowledge to business conditions. This learning event focused on mastering capabilities required to accomplish business results. Participants learned how to conduct an organizational audit, construct an action plan for key capabilities, and build relationships of trust with business leaders. Each participant left the workshop with a personal agenda for application.

Development Experiences for HR Staff

Training has its place. But even with the best use of adult learning principles and the most carefully chosen preliminary work and projects, organized educational experiences can be enhanced by development *in place*—that is, by reading, listening, observing, and practicing.[6]

Reading

To maximize the value of your reading time, choose authors, not titles. That is, avoid browsing bookstore shelves crowded with appealing titles and dramatic covers. Instead, visit with colleagues whose opinions you trust to develop your list of "should read" thinkers in the fields of general business, management, organization strategy, culture, change, and HR. In addition to being author-oriented, your reading should also be current. As obvious as this sounds, it is difficult to achieve. Even the most recent book is probably three or four years behind in state-of-the-art concepts and practices. As useful as a text may be, it won't be the latest word. Journal articles and magazines are more timely, because their cycle for writing, reviewing, and publication is measured in months instead of years. Among the journals worth perusing are *Human Resource Management*, *Human Resource Planning*, *Harvard Business Review*, and (for the more adventuresome) *Personnel Psychology*.[7]

As you read, think about application. Before starting a book or an article, ask yourself, "What do I need from this?" If you are clear about the problem or situation you want help with, you can more immediately apply what you read to your personal situation. Reading with a purpose is more useful than general reading. Obviously, it is helpful at times to read for the general accumulation of knowledge, but focused and purposeful reading helps turn ideas into action.

Listening

Learning through listening can be accomplished in three ways. First, attending conferences often provides quick access to current concepts and practices. The annual meetings of the Society for Human Resource Management (SHRM), the Human Resource Planning Society (HRPS), the National HRD Network (India), or Chartered Institute of Personnel and Development (CIPD) can be important sources of information. This is true at the national level as well as at the local affiliate level. The SHRM certification process is an excellent example of learning by listening. Topic-specific mini-conferences also provide state-of-the-art thinking that is linked to application projects. Such mini-conferences may be public offerings or scheduled, in-house programs. The most intense listening experiences are probably found at the one- or two-week immersion programs offered by a number of leading universities.

Observing

Learning by observing and experiencing goes on constantly for those who are inquisitive and seek new ideas.[8] You can compare yourself to others you admire, seeing what they do and looking for ways to adapt it. You can experiment with new behavior, then observe how others respond and how you feel. If you are predisposed to be quiet, speak up. If you tend to analyze numbers before making decisions, try making spot decisions first. Be willing to take risks—to look stupid and not get something right the first time. Insistence on being correct at the beginning is often the main barrier to learning. When you try something new, you may not succeed at first, but if you don't try new behaviors, you will atrophy.

Volunteer for tough assignments and projects, especially those outside your comfort zone. Putting yourself on teams and projects that stretch you will force you to learn and grow and help you build relationships with new people. Keep a learning journal to help you see how you are progressing and what you are learning. Be in a constant inquisitive mode to see what could be done better. When you visit a restaurant, grocery store, shopping mall, or government agency, ask yourself, "What could be done better here?" These personal learning strategies help you develop a learning attitude and mindset.

Practicing and Reflecting

Learning-by-doing-and-reflecting has long been recognized as a powerful way to enhance personal skill development. Developmental projects are a key element of both in-house and publicly available programs. For maximum benefit, such projects need to focus on application, not just on learning. They should push participants to use skills and knowledge substantially beyond their current levels, and should hold participants clearly accountable for success or failure. These principles can be applied to projects directly related to HR (implementing a new service center, designing a major leadership development intervention) or to business results (how to enter the China market, how to enhance the rate of new product innovation).

For each of the five competency domains proposed in chapter 10, we can identify specific learning activities. These are summarized in table 11-1, along with the names of some noted authors who write in each area.

TABLE 11-1

Learning activities for five competency domains

Competency domain	Development activity	Selected authors
Strategic contribution	• Identify new ways your managers and employees need to behave in the future if they are to achieve their goals and outperform their business competitors. • Build a more effective culture by sharing information, experience, and knowledge across organizational boundaries. • Develop and implement guidelines that will help meetings reach decisions more quickly, with greater commitment, better follow-through, and consistently measurable results. • Prior to facilitating a decision-making process, develop your own recommendations for each issue likely to be raised. • Develop an internal communication plan that disseminates customer or shareholder information in a high-impact manner. • Visit customers to elicit direct feedback about company performance. • Serve on a cross-functional team to identify customer buying habits and recommend action steps to improve market share. • Apply Six Sigma quality standards and processes to improve the accuracy of all HR activities and practices.	Jim Collins Lee Dyer Paul Evans Jac Fitz-enz Charles Handy John Kotter Edward Lawler Dave Nadler Jeffrey Pfeffer Vladimir Pucik Edgar Schein Arthur Yeung
Personal credibility	• Avoid using the word *I* for an entire day. • Practice nonjudgmental empathizing with family members or close friends. • Practice drawing visual images of complex problems that clarify the key issues so that they can be specifically addressed. • Lead an HR or management team in a discussion of ethics and business issues to clarify the company's ethical parameters and define processes that will help ensure compliance. • Elicit feedback from colleagues on a key dimension of your interpersonal skills. Act on the feedback. Don't be defensive. Translate the feedback into simple and focused action.	Peter Block Dale Carnegie Steven Covey Marshall Goldsmith Daniel Goleman Dale Lake Brian Tracy

continued

TABLE 11-1

Learning activities for five competency domains *(continued)*

Competency domain	Development activity	Selected authors
	• Make a presentation to a major conference on an HR activity in your company. Arrange to repeat the presentation for an internal audience.	
	• Have some of your written materials critiqued by a writing coach from a local college or university.	
	• When listening to effective speakers in any forum, take notes about the content of the message and also about the speaking techniques they use to get their messages across.	
HR delivery	• Work for a local voluntary association in a position that involves evaluating association members for promotion.	Dick Beatty John Boudreau Robert Eichinger Fred Foulkes
	• Work with a line manager to identify the technical and cultural competencies that organization may need in the future, which of these competencies have a shortage or surplus, and what needs to be done to bridge the gap.	Jay Galbraith Lynda Gratton Mark Huselid William Joyce Robert Kaplan Steve Kerr
	• Help a colleague design an individual developmental plan for becoming a relatively more effective player in a major company change initiative.	Mike Lombardo Henry Mintzberg Robert Quinn Craig Schneier
	• Engage a coach to observe you and give you feedback on your behavior and performance.	
	• Become involved in an organization restructuring task force.	
	• Critique a recent organization restructuring. What problems were solved? What problems were created? How might the new problems be resolved?	
	• Interview five line executives on what characteristics they need from the human side of the business and configure a measurement process that will identify and track those characteristics.	
	• Interview two on-staff attorneys about legal threats that your company might face. What are the major issues? What is the likely outcome?	

continued

TABLE 11-1

Learning activities for five competency domains (continued)

Competency domain	Development activity	Selected authors
	• Identify what percentage of employees create 90 percent of your company's wealth. Interview employees in that group concerning what they desire by way of both financial and non-financial reward. Design customized rewards for those individuals.	
	• Determine what percentage of your reward system is at risk and what percentage is entitled. Determine what might be done to make the system more responsive to performance.	
Business knowledge	• Interview leading thinkers from each component of the value chain. • Develop a process for identifying and transferring internal best practice across departments or businesses within your company. • Conduct a value chain analysis. Where in the value chain does your company outperform your competitors and vice versa? Where in the value chain is it most important for your company to outperform the competition? • Work with the your company's investment officer to identify the buy, hold, or sell criteria of some of your dominant shareholders. • Study five recent speeches by national union leaders and identify the major themes and their implications for your future contract negotiations.	Ram Charan Gary Hamel Gordon Hewitt Michael Porter C. K. Prahalad Adrian Slywotsky
HR technology	• Chart the flow of major HR information in your HR department and identify the points at which HR technology might be applied more effectively. • Determine how your employee recruitment process might be redesigned to use less paper, replacing it with electronic tools. • Experiment on employee portals from other companies.	Naomi Bloom Elliot Massie Al Walker

Outcome of HR Development: Professionalism and Learning Agility

The experiences we propose apply principles of adult learning to HR professional development. The most important lesson we have learned about such initiatives is simply to do them. HR often advocates development for others but too often fails to invest in its own development.

Investing in rigorous and thoughtful development will pay off, encouraging HR professionals to act professionally and learn readily. Mike Lombardo and Bob Eichinger have found that learning agility is one of the key predictors of leadership success.[9] Investing in HR development produces leaders who are "learning agile." Learning-agile people share several common traits:

- They are critical thinkers who examine problems carefully and make fresh connections with relative ease.

- They know themselves well, apply their strengths effectively, and know how to compensate for their weaknesses.

- They like to experiment and are at ease with the discomfort that comes from change.

- They deliver results in first-time situations through team building and personal drive.

Learning agility manifests itself in several ways. Learning-agile people have mental agility—they have more "tools" in their problem-solving kit. They can use the analytical-systemic side of their brain as easily as the creative-emotional side. They can sort out what needs immediate action from what needs long-term consideration. HR professionals with mental agility can shift from business strategy to HR action, assess and improvise new HR practices, and reshape their resources to deliver value.

Flexibility in learning also shows up as *results* agility. Learners can both build teams and apply personal drive and presence. They are comfortable with themselves as well as with diverse populations. They are open-minded and flexible in thinking and behavior. They are nonjudgmental, able to recognize people as peers. They think in terms of not only designing and delivering HR programs but also achieving results for shareholders, customers, managers, and employees. They focus on general business issues as well as on HR functional contributions. In short, they contribute to the firm's whole value proposition as they act in the full range of HR professional roles.

Another valuable skill of motivated learners is *conflict* agility—that is, sensing when to avoid, accommodate, compete, compromise, and collaborate. Learning-agile professionals know how to build relationships with their bosses, clients, peers, and subordinates to deliver value. They know when to push their own agenda and when to serve someone else's agenda, and they know how to frame problems while giving someone else visibility and credit for solving them.

Becoming Competent

When HR professionals engage in learning, either through formal training or through development experiences, they become learning-agile. As business conditions change, as expectations on HR increase, and as the bar is raised for HR professionals, the ability to learn becomes critical.

This chapter lays out principles of adult learning and tenets for HR professional growth. It also outlines specific ways to build both training and development experiences for HR professionals. For those charged with developing HR professionals, this chapter serves as a road map for the journey, suggesting both programs and experiences that might enhance HR professionalism. For individual HR professionals, this chapter offers insights on what to seek in HR learning events and what you might be doing to develop those skills yourself.

12

Implications for the Transformation of HR

Picture this: You have just been appointed to head the HR function in your company. You want to deliver value, but how will you go about doing it? Or this: Your senior line manager has just challenged every staff group (finance, legal, human resources, information technology, and research and development) to conduct a functional review. You have been asked to create a template and process for guiding the process. Where do you start? Or this: You have heard and read about the transformation of HR and you suspect your HR function lags. You sense that things could be improved. What are your options?

In each of these scenarios, you sense either intuitively or by directive the need to upgrade and update the HR *function* (i.e., the department HR practices and HR professionals). Effectiveness begins at home, after all, and the HR function needs to embody the improvement ethic it recommends for others. This chapter pulls together the themes and tools we have described and applies them in transforming HR.

We believe that fundamental transformation of HR requires addressing the entire logic stream suggested in this book. This chapter lays out a four-phase process—theory, assessment, investment, and follow-up—that will enable you to transform your HR function by adding greater value. *Theory* gives you a blueprint for the overall HR system in your organization and criteria for effectiveness. *Assessment* enables you to determine how you are performing against your effectiveness criteria. *Investment* suggests what you can do to improve your function. *Follow-up* ensures that things get done.

Phase 1: Theory

Theory provides a conceptual framework of all the elements of HR and how they fit together. It lays out the key components of the entire HR process and offers a visual and verbal image of what makes an effective HR department. Theory also suggests criteria to evaluate as you build your HR department.

The value proposition that drives the theory of HR has five elements that form an integrated HR blueprint. As we suggested in figure 1-1 (repeated here as figure 12-1), we offer a framework for an HR value proposition with five elements: external realities, stakeholders, HR practices, HR resources, and HR professionals. Each element represents a section of this book. External realities and stakeholder interests determine why HR matters to an organization and why HR needs to focus on *what it delivers* more than on what it *does*. HR practices, HR resources, and HR professionals are the elements that represent the HR function within your organization.

FIGURE 12-1

The HR value proposition

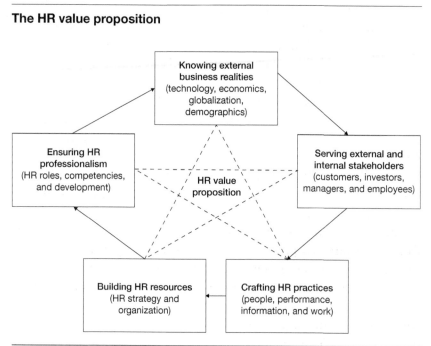

Each of the five basic elements incorporates criteria for what makes an effective HR function. The resulting fourteen criteria form the backbone for our book and introduce each chapter. In initiating your HR transformation, these criteria should be discussed in presentations and team meetings as a way to envision the future. Ideally, every HR professional will be able to recite what HR value means, how it is created, and why it matters. In talks with the HR team, line managers, and employees throughout your organization, ground your transformation presentations in the vision, goals, and actions prompted by these guidelines. (Note that this logic can be applied to other staff groups by changing "HR" to IT, marketing, finance, legal, and so forth. Each of the five elements can be used to create a template for transforming any staff function.)

Phase 2: Assessment

An assessment defines where you are now and where you need to focus in order to improve. An assessment helps you determine which elements of the HR value framework are in place in your organization and which are not.

Assessments, like audits, rely on assembling data, a task that involves two issues: content and process. *Content* deals with what information you collect, *process* with how you collect it. The blueprint in figure 12-1 suggests a framework for assessing your overall HR function. Based on the fourteen criteria, you can create an interview protocol like the sample in assessment 12-1. Responses to these questions indicate the strengths and weaknesses of your HR function.

Kinds of Assessment

Process deals with techniques, including the means of collecting data (through interviews, surveys, or observations), and the source of the data (choice of respondents). Interviews generally allow for a smaller sample size and the opportunity for in-depth research; you collect data from fewer targeted people and can explore what people think about the questions you raise. Surveys, on the other hand, benefit from a larger sample size (meaning that the data is statistically more accurate) but follow a more structured and inflexible format. These extremes are true of the assessment process, as well, which can be more or less comprehensive depending on the process. As we discussed in chapter 3 with

Sample interview protocol

1. To what extent do the HR professionals in my department understand how external realities of technology, economics, and demographics in the global context affect our industry and business?

2. To what extent does our HR work link to the intangibles that investors value?

3. To what extent do we use HR practices to build long-term connections with target customers?

4. To what extent do we audit and create organization capabilities that will turn strategy into action?

5. To what extent do we have a clear employee value proposition that lays out what is expected of employees and what they get in return?

6. To what extent do our HR practices that focus on people (staffing, training, development) add value?

7. To what extent do our HR practices that focus on performance (setting standards, allocating rewards, providing feedback) add value?

8. To what extent do our HR practices that focus on work flow (who does the work, how is the work done, and where is the work done) add value?

9. To what extent do our HR practices that focus on information (outside-in and inside-out) add value?

10. To what extent does our HR strategy process turn business goals into HR priorities?

11. To what extent is our HR organization (e-HR, service centers, centers of expertise, embedded HR, and outsourcing contracts) aligned with the business strategy?

12. To what extent do our HR professionals play employee advocate, human capital developer, functional expert, strategic partner, and leadership roles?

13. To what extent do our HR professionals demonstrate competence in strategic contribution, HR delivery, business knowledge, personal credibility, and HR technology?

14. To what extent do we invest in our HR professionals through training and development?

intangibles audits, assessments may fall into three general categories: 90-degree, 180-degree or 360-degree, or 720-degree.

The basic 90-degree reviews are like pulse checks that monitor vital signs (heart rate, blood pressure, weight) to check on the health of an individual. Organizational pulse checks monitor vital signs of your HR function. Through interviews with your HR executive team or surveys of targeted people, you can determine the extent to which your HR function meets the criteria we suggest for effective HR. Collecting data quickly from a targeted group of respondents will offer insights on the general strengths or weaknesses of your HR function. For example, you might have your HR team respond to the questions in assessment 12-1 and then share the results at a team meeting, using the data as a springboard for a discussion rather than a definitive statement of performance.

Comprehensive 180-degree or 360-degree reviews are more like the physical exams that evaluate a range of individual health measures, including blood work, treadmill tests, cardiograms, and the like. Here, you collect data from multiple constituents of your HR function, including clients (line managers), peers (other functional heads), and employees both inside and outside HR. Using interviews, surveys, or reports, you can determine how others see the strengths and weaknesses of your IIR function.

The 720-degree review resembles the total life management study, which looks at the entire context of an individual's well-being, including exercise, driving habits, stress levels, social supports, and so forth. As applied to HR, this means consulting stakeholders both inside and outside your company—investors, customers, suppliers, regulators, and competitors—about the quality of the work you are doing. At times, those inside the company will have different perceptions from those outside it. In one 720-degree review we conducted, for example, we found that insiders uniformly saw their HR vision and focus as appropriate, but customers did not regard HR's efforts as aligned to their needs. In the end, the department adjusted its investments to ensure that HR resulted in value for the external customers.

Putting It All Together

In interpreting information from the assessment, look for themes—that is, the story lines that emerge from the data. The various stakeholder groups you consult in the data-gathering phase will generally have similar perceptions of what you do well and poorly. When your HR professionals identify the common themes for themselves, they are more likely to accept them.

One method we have used is to turn quotations from interviews into a deck of cards.[1] We give each member of the HR team a deck of forty to sixty card quotes (including some of their own comments) and ask them to spend two or three hours personally reading, sorting, and summarizing and then return to the group with three to five themes, stories, or messages they have distilled from the interview data. When the HR team members share their individual observations, they invariably come up with similar themes. The discussion from this exercise highlights both strengths and weaknesses of the HR function and helps point toward areas where improvement is necessary.

When examining survey data, it is useful to look for low or high scores or differences in ratings between groups of raters (as with the company whose HR employees consistently rated it higher than its customers did). With larger survey samples, your data analysis can become more statistically accurate, and you can identify specific items that most predict overall HR effectiveness.

Whether you use surveys or interviews, it might be helpful to think of assessment as a funnel: you put data in at the top, sift and filter it, and at the bottom withdraw a few key themes or messages that indicate what you should focus on. These themes become your priorities, generating high-impact initiatives—ideally, things you can implement relatively easily. This is where you want to focus to make your transformation a success.

Phase 3: Investment

With the assessment complete, you can begin to make investments to upgrade your HR function and ensure that it adds value. In helping dozens of HR organizations through this process, we have identified some keys for ensuring that the transformation goes well.

Form a Transformation Team

To effect transformation as well as gain acceptance for it, you need to enlist a team that includes HR professionals representing the different areas in your organization (corporate, embedded HR, centers of expertise) and line managers who are clients of HR. The transformation team should be visibly and publicly accountable for delivering a transformation plan and results. Key members of the team will probably spend 15–20 percent of their time for six to nine months on this transformation. By investing their time and resources, they demonstrate their commitment to the process.

Announce What You Are Trying to Do

Inevitably, HR transformations are complex—changing *how* work is done, *what* work is done, *who* does the work, and *when* the work is finished. Transformations revolve around a fixed center point: the rationale for the transformation and the criteria for success. This center point should be presented repeatedly, until your entire HR staff grasps why you are doing what you are doing.

Our rule of thumb is 10:1; things have to be explained 10 times for every unit of understanding. This means keeping your overall message simple and focused on what you hope to do. One successful HR transformation leader prepared overheads to describe the transformation and then asked everyone on the team to share these materials with their staff so that the message of the transformation would be clearly disseminated throughout the organization.

Your simple goal statement should focus not just on the activities of the transformation but on its outcome: the value it will create for stakeholders. Remember, intangibles for investors, connection with targeted customers, organization capabilities for line managers, and abilities for individual employees are the deliverables for HR. The transformation becomes the means of providing these deliverables.

Start with Simple, Visible Actions

HR transformation is more likely to gain support when people see early results and visible successes, so it's useful to have a portfolio of possible activities. Table 12-1 lists activities that support each of the fourteen criteria for an HR value proposition. From this menu, select one or two actions and get started. While these actions don't occur in isolation, they ensure early successes that show that the transformation is under way. Often, taking lots of little actions creates a large and sustained transformation. Starting in an area where you can get visible results will help you build momentum for the change effort.

Have an Integrated Transformation Plan

While you begin with some specific and simple actions, you need a blueprint for the entire transformation. For example, if you begin with training your HR professionals, you should know when you will interject the other elements of HR: aligning with external realities, serving external and internal stakeholders, crafting HR practices, building HR resources, ensuring HR professionalism. With a direction in mind (your vision to add value), goals that express what you will accomplish (the elements of value creation), and criteria in place (the criteria for effective HR), you can start immediately. Transformation entails both a vision of the future and a commitment to action today.

TABLE 12-1

Portfolio of HR investments

Elements of the HR value proposition	Criteria for the new HR (An effective HR function . . .)	Portfolio of potential actions
Knowing external business realities	1. Recognizes external business realities and adapts its practices and allocates resources accordingly	• Present seminars or other learning tools (online or disc-based) on new competitive realities. • Have HR professionals attend business seminars. • Include new business realities in existing training programs. • Test your HR professionals on their knowledge of technology, economic trends, and demographic changes in global context (use tools in chapter 2).
Serving external and internal stakeholders	2. Creates market value for investors by increasing intangibles	• Invite CFO, investment relations manager, or investors to meet with HR team and review investor criteria for your firm. • Report intangibles on your firm and its competitors. • Create and design an intangibles audit (see chapter 3). • Align HR practices with investor expectations. • Participate in investor calls and presentations.
	3. Increases customer share by connecting with target customers	• Ensure that your HR professionals can pass the customer literacy test (chapter 3). • Track share of targeted customers. • Align HR practices with targeted customers. • Involve targeted customers in HR practices. • Think and act like a customer.
	4. Helps line managers deliver strategy by building organization capabilities	• Build relationships of trust with line managers by setting and exceeding expectations. • Focus on deliverables of HR (capabilities) and create action plans for delivering them (as described in chapter 4). • Measure your results in terms that matter to line managers.
	5. Clarifies and establishes an employee value proposition and ensures that employees have abilities to do their work	• Create and publicize an employee value proposition (see chapter 4). • Ensure that employee interests are shared with line managers. • Take care of employee administrative needs flawlessly. • Help employees acquire abilities to do their work.
Crafting HR practices	6. Manages people processes in ways that add value	• Reengineer how your organization buys, builds, borrows, bounces, binds, and boosts talent (from chapter 5). • Prioritize ways to ensure that your organization has the best talent.

continued

TABLE 12-1

Portfolio of HR investments *(continued)*

Elements of the HR value proposition	Criteria for the new HR *(An effective HR function . . .)*	Portfolio of potential actions
	7. Manages performance management processes and practices in ways that add value	• Reengineer how your organization manages performance by setting standards (determining what is measured, building measurement systems, and establishing an appraisal system), allocating financial and nonfinancial rewards, and following up on employee performance (review chapter 5). • Prioritize ways to ensure that your organization has a performance culture.
	8. Manages information processes and practices in ways that add value	• Reengineer how you share information and communicate with those inside and outside your organization (see chapter 6). • Prioritize ways to ensure that you communicate effectively.
	9. Manages work flow processes and practices in ways that add value	• Decide who will do work and figure out coordinating mechanisms across organization units (as discussed in chapter 6). • Figure out how to do work by reengineering key processes. • Focus on where work is done by investing in work space and place.
Building HR resources	10. Has a clear strategic planning process for aligning HR investments with business goals	• Develop a disciplined process for creating an HR strategy that begins with the business environment, focuses on cultural priorities, and ends with HR practices (as described in chapter 7). • Prepare an annual HR strategy that aligns with business priorities. • Develop an HR strategy workshop that lays out perspectives and aspirations through the logic of the HR value proposition. • Communicate the total HR value added throughout the HR department and organization.
	11. Aligns its organization to the strategy of the business	• Invest in service centers, e-HR, and outsourcing to deliver HR administrative work more efficiently (as discussed in chapter 8). • Create centers of expertise that can both design and deliver HR services. • Upgrade embedded HR professionals to diagnose how HR can add value to business strategy and to implement an HR agenda. • Revise incentives for HR professionals to align with the value they create.

continued

TABLE 12-1

Portfolio of HR investments *(continued)*

Elements of the HR value proposition	Criteria for the new HR *(An effective HR function . . .)*	Portfolio of potential actions
Ensuring HR professionalism	12. Has staff who play clear and appropriate roles	• Define and delineate roles that HR professionals play in your organization: employee advocate, human capital developer, functional expert, strategic partner, and leader (as reviewed in chapter 9). • Ensure that HR professionals all know their role and how to perform it. • Redesign HR jobs to ensure that HR professionals play the right roles. • Promote HR professionals based on the extent to which they add value by playing roles and demonstrating competencies.
	13. Builds staff ability to demonstrate HR competencies	• Identify the competencies that HR professionals must master to be successful (see chapter 10). • Assess the competencies of your HR professionals. • Create an HR professional development program. • Provide career assignments and action learning development experiences to build HR professionals' skills.
	14. Invests in HR professionals through training and development experiences	• Design and deliver training programs that increase the competencies of HR professionals (as described in chapter 11). • Tailor a training program to your specific organization requirements. • Offer development experiences to help HR professionals learn through reading, listening, observing, and practicing.

Make Hard Decisions Quickly

Inevitably, an HR transformation will require hard decisions about what programs or staffs to cut or expand. Generally, the transformation will reduce overall HR head count. Clarifying options about which people to remove and then making tough decisions fairly and quickly helps people see the intensity of the transformation and creates commitment to it. At times, programs or practices need to be changed. Again, decisive action builds momentum. When organization changes are established (e-HR, service centers, centers of expertise), moving quickly with the changes helps create impetus for longer-term change.

Weave the Changes into Ongoing Business

A workshop kick-starts the transformation process, but it won't generate continued success. For sustained transformation, new patterns must become institutionalized. For example, a new HR organization needs new people practices. As expectations of what makes an effective HR professional increase, standards rise. Newly hired employees come into HR with more know-how. Training focuses on ways to deliver value, not just do projects. Moving poorer-performing HR professionals out of the organization sends a message to those who are performing well.

A transformed HR organization:

- *Generates new performance management practices.* Standards and appraisals for transformed HR professionals focus more on value created than on activities performed. Financial and nonfinancial rewards follow those who deliver value.

- *Shares information smoothly.* HR professionals throughout the organization know external business realities and have information about how their work affects those realities.

- *Allocates work in ways that get the job done effectively and efficiently.* These HR practices in people, performance management, information, and work flow enable the new HR organization to endure beyond any one HR leader. Solid HR practices make HR transformation a new way of doing HR.

Learn and Adapt

The transformation team should continually monitor how the transformation is progressing. This means seeing what works and what does not, and adapting accordingly. One company started with a pilot program to train HR professionals. After the first program cycle, the company made improvements to the next four sessions. Another company invested heavily in e-HR, but continually monitored the effort and kept enhancing the portal and HR interfaces. Successive adaptation ensures that a program or process keeps improving (as measured against each of the fourteen criteria).

Phase 4: Follow-Up

Often, the difference between strong and weak efforts at transformation is in follow-up rather than design. Successful programs use indicators such as the investment impact measures in table 12-2. These measures create an "HR dashboard" that can be monitored and tracked to ensure that the transformation occurs.

TABLE 12-2

Measures of HR investment impact

Elements of the HR value proposition	Criteria for the new HR *(An effective HR function . . .)*	Possible follow-up measures
Knowing external business realities	1. Recognizes external business realities and adapts its practices and allocates resources accordingly	• Percentage of HR professionals who pass the business literacy tests (laid out in chapter 2).
Serving external stakeholders	2. Creates market value for investors by increasing intangibles	• P/E ratio compared to competitors over time. • Intangible value—total market value less tangible value (scores on intangibles audit in chapter 3).
	3. Increases customer share by connecting with target customers	• Share of targeted customers. • Extent to which customers participate in HR practices. • Satisfaction scores from target customers.
	4. Helps line managers deliver strategy by building organization capabilities	• Satisfaction scores from line managers on HR services. • Measure of key capabilities required for success (measures provided in chapter 4).
Serving internal stakeholders	5. Clarifies and establishes an employee value proposition and ensures that employees have abilities to do their work	• Employee commitment. • Target employee retention. • Employee productivity.

	6. Manages people processes in ways that add value	• For each HR practice, evaluate its:
		  – Cost
		  – Volume
		  – Timeliness
		  – Quality

	7. Manages performance management processes, and practices in ways that add value	– Human reaction • Perform a manager and employee assessment to see how they perceive HR practices delivering value to them.

continued

TABLE 12-2

Measures of HR investment impact *(continued)*

Elements of the HR value proposition	Criteria for the new HR *(An effective HR function . . .)*	Possible follow-up measures
	8. Manages information processes and practices in ways that add value	• Do research to evaluate how those affected by an HR practice differ from those who are not (for example, whether those who attend training perform better than those who do not).
	9. Manages work flow and organization processes in ways that add value	
Building HR resources	10. Has a clear strategic planning process for aligning HR investments with business goals	• Assess whether the HR planning process prioritizes HR investments. • Assess perceptions of the HR strategy planning process.
	11. Aligns its organization to the strategy of the business	• Evaluate the ratio of HR budget or head count to overall corporate budget or head count. • Survey perception of the HR organization.
Ensuring HR professionalism	12. Has staff who play clear and appropriate roles	• Evaluate the roles HR professionals play by a role assessment survey.
	13. Builds staff ability to demonstrate HR competencies	• Evaluate the competence of HR professionals using the HR competence survey. • Assess the perception of HR professionals by their clients.
	14. Invests in HR professionals through training and development experiences	• Assess behavior changes of those who participate in HR training events. • Evaluate development experiences on the extent to which participants learn and change behavior.

Follow-up can be a formal process of semiannual, annual, or biennial reviews designed to determine strengths and weaknesses of investments and which actions could lead to improved performance. These formal reviews are generally initiated and monitored by a senior executive who demands excellence from staff organizations like HR. They ensure that HR is accountable for figuring out what should be done and doing it.

Follow-up is also woven into daily routines, with data collected quickly and continually on how any one HR element is executed. Staff can collect surveys from workshop participants, administer employee attitude surveys quarterly, and conduct other pulse checks to monitor how well the HR organization is meeting stakeholders' expectations. At each HR staff meeting, participants should set aside time to review HR progress. HR should also take the opportunity to assess the outcomes of every significant HR event.

Ultimately, all follow-up is personal. When each HR professional takes personal responsibility for continual self-reflection and development, follow-up turns into performance improvement. Line managers expect such follow-up; senior HR executives encourage it by responding to it; and HR professionals benefit themselves and the organization when they engage in it.

Implications of HR Value Proposition

The picture of HR we present here may seem unfamiliar to some organizations, but it is, we believe, what is needed to meet the demands of the current and foreseeable business environment. It has implications across the board—for general managers, HR executives, professionals working in HR, and the profession of HR itself.

Implications for General Managers

General managers set expectations for HR departments, practices, and professionals. General managers demand value from HR investments by setting high standards. These standards communicate aspirations and shape how HR professionals act. General managers should continually follow up on standards to ensure that HR measures up. This follow-up engages general managers in HR issues and holds HR professionals accountable for them. When general managers are aware of the value that HR produces for them and for their organization, they encourage and advocate HR actions.

To have value-driven HR in your organization, your general manager must recognize HR's impact on investor, customer, business, and employee results. This awareness should be visible in talks and presentations both inside and outside the company. It means that HR issues should be part of every manager's performance scorecard. It means that general managers need to accept ownership for HR's efforts by personally referring to them as "my" work not "HR" work. It means that organization capabilities and individual abilities are not just rhetoric but action.

For HR to have maximum effectiveness, general managers must base their reputation and identity on their ability to deliver value through people. In private conversations with other business leaders, general managers need to discuss and hold them accountable for their HR actions. The general manager is a cheerleader for people and organizations, as well as a coach who helps design the HR processes and a player who helps implement them. When leaders make HR value a part of their personal agenda, HR value becomes part of the organization's leadership brand.

Implications for Senior HR Executives

Senior HR executives have many conversations that lead to action. With the HR value proposition as a foundation, these conversations focus on results relevant to each stakeholder.

- With *investors*, conversations focus on how intangibles become a determining factor in the creation of sustained market value. Actions focus on intangibles audits and how these audits can provide specific insights on how to improve shareholder value.

- With *customers*, conversations focus on customer needs and how HR practices can be aligned with customer expectations, with a view to increasing customer share. In addition to responding to customer feedback, action may involve ways to engage customers in designing and delivering HR practices.

- With *line managers*, conversations center on delivering business strategies through prioritizing and creating organization capabilities. Actions follow ideas as the concept of capabilities translates into investments of budget, time, focus, and energy.

- With *employees*, conversations provide insight into an employee value proposition that ensures that if and when employees deliver value, they will get value. Actions may then be specified to ensure that employees have both the ability and the attitude to do what is expected of them.

- With *HR professionals*, conversations help HR leaders fulfill their roles and demonstrate the competencies that are required to deliver value. Conversations are not only evaluative in nature but also focus on the developmental initiatives that will create more capable HR professionals and departments.

Each of these conversations is then sustained by creating HR strategies, organizations, and practices that endure. HR strategy that offers a clear line of sight from business realities to HR practices is designed by HR and owned by line managers to complement an existing business strategy. This strategy is supported by an HR organization that delivers HR transactions with efficiency and HR transformation with effectiveness. Consequently, investments in people, performance management, information, and work flow processes deliver sustained value. With strategies, organizations, and practices in place, conversations turn into commitments, and rhetoric into results.

Senior HR executives also need to develop more powerful HR agendas as laid out in the HR value proposition and then develop HR professionals who are able to deliver on the agendas. Individual HR professionals should avail themselves of job assignments and career moves as well as high-impact training experiences that cover the full range of the HR value proposition.

Implications for HR Professionals

Most HR professionals want to do good work and add greater value. When roles are clear, HR professionals can describe what they do in ways that clearly articulate expectations of themselves and others. When competencies are defined and demonstrated, HR professionals can ensure that they know how to deliver value.

To be competent in your role, you need a mental model of the value you create, and you should constantly be assessing yourself against that model—both formally and informally. Use the frameworks and tools described in chapters 9, 10, and 11, but also engage in daily and weekly personal reflections about what worked and what did not. Connect choices and consequences, then take corrective action and responsibility for improvement. With this kind of learning and accountability, you will become an HR professional who is respected not only for what you know and do but for the value you deliver.

Careers for HR professionals who fully grasp and deliver value vary widely. They may concentrate on one domain (people, performance management, information, or work flow practices) or in one organization structure (a center of expertise or a line of business). Or, more likely, they will move across domain and organizational boundaries. Increasingly, we envision top HR professionals moving into and out of formal HR assignments. We do not define the success or "arrival" of HR by the number of HR professionals who move into senior line management jobs (that actually belittles the importance of HR), but nonetheless HR professionals who fully deliver value will be able to work outside HR as well. Some companies—Unilever, Procter & Gamble, Motorola—regularly move HR professionals into and out of line management roles.

Implications for the HR Profession

Given the technological, economic and regulatory, and demographic realities of our global world, HR insights have been pushed to the forefront of business success. Leading thinkers, well-respected firms, and outstanding executives converge on issues central to HR. Good to great companies—firms with reputations as a best place to work—and leaders in management's hall of fame all exist because people and organization practices have come together at the right time in the right place to do the right thing.

Now more than ever, business success comes from HR. And the "DNA" for HR success is the HR Value Proposition. With this value proposition, the HR profession has a point of view about what can be and should be for all stakeholders, a set of standards directing HR investments in strategy, structure, and practices, and a template for ensuring that each HR professional contributes. The HR Value Proposition is the blueprint for the future of HR.

Notes

Chapter 1

1. Wayne Brockbank and Dave Ulrich, "Avoiding SPOTS: Creating Strategic Unity," in *Handbook of Business Strategy*, ed. Harold E. Glass (Boston: Warren, Gorham & Lamont, 1991).

2. One must keep in mind that in the oil field service business, the relationship between the vendor and the field customers is unusually close. Representatives can literally spend months together on drilling rigs and platforms in remote locations. However, boom and bust cycles in the oil business occur with great frequency. Thus the possibility of losing touch with current reality is very real.

3. See, for example, Anthony J. Rucci, Steven P. Kirn, and Richard T. Quinn, "The Employee-Customer-Profit Chain at Sears," *Harvard Business Review* 76, no. 1 (1998): 82.

Chapter 2

1. Brent Schlender, "Intel's $10 Billion Gamble," *Fortune*, November 11, 2002, 90.

2. Howard Rheingold, *Smart Mob: The Next Social Revolution* (Cambridge, MA: Perseus Books Group, 2002).

3. Ibid., 58.

4. Ibid., viii.

5. Robert D. Hof, "The eBay Economy," *BusinessWeek*, August 25, 2003, 124.

6. Gary Hufbauer, "World Economic Integration: The Long View," *Economic Insights*, (May/June)(1991):26.

7. Lynn A. Karoly and Constantijn W. A. Panis, *The 21st Century at Work: Forces Shaping the Future Workforce and Workplace in the United States* (Santa Monica, CA: The RAND Corporation, 2004).

8. Ibid., 113.

9. "America's Fortunes," *Atlantic Monthly*, January/February 2004, 110; see p. 102.

10. Nelson D. Schwartz, "Will 'Made in the USA' Fade Away?" *Fortune*, November 24, 2003, 98.

11. Anna Bernasek, "The $44 Trillion Abyss," *Fortune*, November 24, 2003, 113.

12, Karoly and Panis, *The 21st Century at Work*, 13.

13. Betty W. Su, "The U.S. Economy to 2010," *Monthly Labor Review* 124, no. 11 (2001): 3.

14. Karoly and Panis, *The 21st Century at Work*, 142.

15. Kathleen Newland, "Workers of the World, Now What?" *Foreign Policy* 114 (Spring 1999), 52.

16. World Bank, *Global Economic Prospects and the Developing Countries 2002* (Washington, DC: World Bank, 2001), 45.

17. Mitra Toossi, "A Century of Change: The U.S. Labor Force, 1950–2050," *Monthly Labor Review* 125, no. 5 (2002): 15.

18. Constantijn Panis, Michael Hurd, David Loughran, Julie Zissimopoulos, Steven Haider, and Patricia St. Clair, "The Effects of Changing Social Security Administration's Early Entitlement Age and the Normal Retirement Age," DRU-2903-SSA (Santa Monica, CA: The RAND Corporation, June 2002).

19. Kenneth Manton, Larry Corder, and Eric Stallard, "Chronic Disability Trends in the Elderly United States Populations: 1982–1994," *Proceedings of the National Academy of Sciences of the United States of America* 94, no. 6 (1997): 2593.

20. Howard N. Fullerton Jr. and Mitra Toossi, "Labor Force Projections to 2010: Steady Growth and Changing Composition," *Monthly Labor Review* 124, no. 11 (2001): 21.

21. Bureau of Labor Statistics, *Series Report ID: Lnu02300190* (Washington, DC: U.S. Department of Labor, 2003).

22. Rochelle Sharpe, "As Leaders, Women Rule," *BusinessWeek*, November 20, 2000, 74–81.

23. "Household data seasonally adjusted quarterly averages." *Employment and Earnings*. January 2004. 51:1, 172.

24. Linda Babcock and Sara Laschever, *Women Don't Ask: Negotiation and the Gender Divide* (Princeton, NJ: Princeton University Press, 2003).

25. Andrew Sum, Neeta Fogg, and Paul Harrington, "The Growing Gender Gaps in College Enrollment and Degree Attainment in the U.S. and Their Potential Economic and Social Consequences" (Washington, DC: Business Roundtable, May 2003).

26. Christina Hoff Sommers, "The War Against Boys," *Atlantic Monthly*, May 2000: 59.

27. Karoly and Panis, *The 21st Century at Work*.

28. Brian Grow, "Hispanic Nation," *BusinessWeek*, March 15, 2004, 58.

29. Tavia Simmons and Martin O'Connell, "Married-Couple and Unmarried Partner Households: 2000" (Washington, DC: U.S. Census Bureau, February 2003).

30. Elizabeth Warren and Amelia Warren Tyagi, *The Two-Income Trap: Why Middle-Class Mothers and Fathers Are Going Broke* (New York: Basic Books, 2003).

31. John C. McCarthy, "3.3 Million U.S. Services Jobs to Go Offshore," November 11, 2002, Forrester Research, http://www.forrester.com/ER/Research/Brief/Excerpt/0,1317,15900,FF.html.

32. National Institute for Literacy, "Literacy in the United States," August 2003, http://www.policyalmanac.org/education/archive/literacy.shtml.

33. Eric A. Hanushek, "The Long-Run Importance of School Quality," working paper 9071, National Bureau of Economic Research, Cambridge, MA, July 2002.

34. Jagdish N. Bhagwati, "Borders Beyond Control," *Foreign Affairs* 82, no. 1 (2003): 98.

Chapter 3

1. Baruch Lev, *Intangibles: Management, Measurement, and Reporting* (Washington, DC: Brookings Institution Press, 2001); Dave Ulrich and Norm Smallwood, *Why the Bottom Line Isn't: How to Build Value Through People and Organization* (New York: Wiley, 2003).

2. This architecture is drawn from Ulrich and Smallwood, *Why the Bottom Line Isn't.*

3. The focus on organization as capabilities has been prevalent since about 1990. See Dave Ulrich, "Organizational Capability: Competitive Advantage Through Human Resources," in *Handbook of Business Strategy 1989/1990 Yearbook*, ed. Harold Glass (Boston: Warren, Gorham, & Lamont, 1990), 15.1; George Stalk, Philip Evans, and Lawrence E. Shulman, "Competing on Capabilities: The New Rules of Corporate Strategy," *Harvard Business Review* 70, no. 2 (1992): 57; and Dave Ulrich and Norm Smallwood, "Capitalizing on Capabilities," *Harvard Business Review* 82, no. 6 (2004): 119.

4. Mark A. Huselid, Brian E. Becker, and Richard W. Beatty, *The Workforce Scorecard: Managing Human Capital to Execute Strategy* (Boston: Harvard Business School Press, 2005).

5. Adapted from Ulrich and Smallwood, "Capitalizing on Capabilities," 119.

6. Costs of attracting a new customer compared to keeping an old one vary by industry from 2:1 to 20:1. See John Goodman, "Basic Facts on Customer Complaint Behavior and the Impact of Service on the Bottom Line," June 1999, http://www.tarp.com/research.asp.

7. Ibid.

8. Some of the best customer service research is reported by Leonard Berry, *Discovering the Soul of Service: The Nine Drivers of Sustainable Business Success* (New York: Free Press, 1999).

Chapter 4

1. See work on learning in Arthur K. Yeung, David O. Ulrich, Stephen W. Nason, and Mary Ann Von Glinow, *Organizational Learning Capability* (New York: Oxford University Press, 1998).

2. See Peter Cappelli, "A Shifting Balance of Workers," Wharton@Work:eBuzz, January 2002, http://execed.wharton.upenn.edu/ebuzz/0201/knowledge.html.

3. This work comes from Richard Pinola, chairman and CEO of Right Management, "Thriving in a Changing Environment," http://www.amcham.hrcom.ru/files/122_RJP%20-%20Thriving%20in%20a%20Changing%20Environment%20part%202.ppt.

4. We summarize research on surveys from Theresa Welbourne. Her work comes from her experience as CEO of eePulse and has been published as "HR Metrics for HR Strategists," HR.com, August 2004, http://www.eepulse.com/documents/pdfs/are-you-being-strategic-updated-hrcom.pdf.

5. See Jón Erlendsson, "The Toyota Suggestion System," September 19, 2001, http://www.hi.is/~joner/eaps/ds_esug.htm.

6. For information on the use of town hall meetings at GE, see Dave Ulrich, Steve Kerr, and Ron Ashkenas, *The GE Work-Out: How to Implement GE's Revolutionary Method for Busting Bureaucracy and Attacking Organizational Problems* (New York: McGraw-Hill, 2002).

7. Information on the Maricopa County ombudsman system is available online at http://www.maricopa.gov/human_resources/ombudsman.asp.

Chapter 5

1. A few samples of HR practice lists: Gary Dessler, *Human Resource Management*, 9th ed. (New York: Prentice-Hall, 2002); Anne M. Bogardus, *PHR/SPHR: Professional in Human Resources Certification Study Guide* (New York: Sybex, 2003); Mark Effron, Robert Gandossy, and Marshall Goldsmith, eds., *Human Resources in the 21st Century* (New York: Wiley, 2003).

2. See Ed Michaels, Helen Handfield-Jones, and Beth Axelrod, *The War for Talent* (Boston: Harvard Business School Press, 2001); and Mike Johnson, *Winning the People Wars: Talent and the Battle for Human Capital*, 2nd ed. (London: Financial Times Prentice-Hall, 2001).

3. See Herbert G. Heneman III and Timothy A. Judge, *Staffing Organizations*, 4th ed. (New York: McGraw-Hill/Irwin, 2002); Thomas P. Bechet, *Strategic Staffing: A Practical Toolkit for Workforce Planning* (New York: AMACOM, 2002); and David Sears, *Successful Talent Strategies: Achieving Superior Business Results Through Market-Focused Staffing* (New York: AMACOM, 2003).

4. See Doris M. Sims, *Creative New Employee Orientation Programs: Best Practices, Creative Ideas, and Activities for Energizing Your Orientation Program* (New York: McGraw-Hill, 2001); and Jean Barbazette, *Successful New Employee Orientation: Assess, Plan, Conduct, and Evaluate Your Program*, 2nd ed. (San Francisco: Jossey-Bass/Pfeiffer, 2001).

5. See Dave Ulrich and Hope Greenfield, "The Transformation of Training and Development to Development and Learning," *American Journal of Management Development* 1, no. 2 (1995): 11; Robert L. Craig, ed., *The ASTD Training and Development Handbook: A Guide to Human Resource Development*, 4th ed. (New York: McGraw-Hill, 1996); and Dugan Laird, *Approaches to Training and Development*, 3rd ed., revised and updated by Sharon S. Naquin and Elwood F. Holton (New York: Basic Books, 2003).

6. Donald L. Kirkpatrick lays out four levels of measuring training impact: reaction (whether people liked it), learning (what participants learned), behavior (how participants behaved differently afterward), and results (what participants accomplished as a result of the training). See his *Evaluating Training Programs: The Four Levels*, 2nd ed. (San Francisco: Berrett-Koehler, 1998). Work on training for impact comes from David van Adelsberg and Edward A. Trolley, *Running Training Like a Business: Delivering Unmistakable Value* (San Francisco: Berrett-Koehler, 1999); Jill Casner-Lotto, ed., *Successful Training Strategies: Twenty-Six Innovative Corporate Models* (San Francisco: Jossey-Bass, 1988); and Albert A. Vicere, ed., *Executive Education: Process, Practice, and Evaluation* (Princeton, NJ: Peterson's Guides, 1989).

7. Michael M. Lombardo and Robert W. Eichinger, *The Leadership Machine: Architecture to Develop Leaders for Any Future* (Minneapolis, MN: Lominger, 2000).

8. Harry E. Chambers, *Finding, Hiring, and Keeping Peak Performers: Every Manager's Guide* (New York: Perseus, 2001).

9. Rodger W. Griffeth and Peter W. Hom, *Retaining Valued Employees* (Thousand Oaks, CA: Sage, 2001).

10. The concepts on measures and rewards are drawn from Edward E. Lawler III, *Strategic Pay: Aligning Organizational Strategies and Pay Systems* (San Francisco: Jossey-Bass, 1990); and Steven Kerr, "Some Characteristics and Consequences of Organizational Rewards," in *Facilitating Work Effectiveness*, eds. F. David Schoorman and Benjamin Schneider (Lexington, MA: Lexington Books, 1988). See also Geoffrey Colvin, "The Great CEO Pay Heist," *Fortune*, June 25, 2001, 64; and Alfred Rappaport, ed., *Harvard Business Review on Compensation* (Boston: Harvard Business School Press, 2002).

11. Steven Kerr, ed., *Ultimate Rewards: What Really Motivates People to Achieve* (Boston: Harvard Business School Press, 1997).

12. This framework is discussed in detail in Dave Ulrich and Norm Smallwood, *Why the Bottom Line Isn't: How to Build Value Through People and Organization* (New York: Wiley, 2003).

13. See Anthony J. Rucci, Steven P. Kirn, and Richard T. Quinn, "The Employee-Customer-Profit Chain at Sears," *Harvard Business Review* 76, no. 1 (1998): 82.

14. Bruce R. Ellig, *The Complete Guide to Executive Compensation* (New York: McGraw-Hill, 2001).

15. See Donna Deeprose, *How to Recognize and Reward Employees* (New York: AMACOM, 1994); and Bob Nelson, *1001 Ways to Reward Employees* (New York: Workman, 1994).

16. Marshall Goldsmith, "Try Feedforward Instead of Feedback," *Leader to Leader*, 2002 no. 25: 11.

Chapter 6

1. Jay R. Galbraith, *Designing Complex Organizations* (Boston: Addison-Wesley, 1973).

2. Ron Ashkenas, Dave Ulrich, Todd Jick, and Steve Kerr, *The Boundaryless Organization: Breaking the Chains of Organizational Structure*, rev. ed. (San Francisco: Jossey-Bass, 2002).

3. Deborah Bowker, "The Public Relations Perspective on Branding," in *Brands and Branding*, ed. Rita Clifton and John Simmons (Princeton, NJ: Bloomberg Press, 2004).

4. John Storck and Patricia A. Hill, "Knowledge Diffusion Through Strategic Communities," *Sloan Management Review* 41, no. 2 (2000): 63.

5. Chun Wei Choo and Nick Bontis, eds., *The Strategic Management of Intellectual Capital and Organizational Knowledge* (New York: Oxford University Press, 2002).

6. Henry Mintzberg, Bruce Ahlstrand, and Joseph Lampel, *Strategy Safari: A Guided Tour Through the Wilds of Strategic Management* (New York: Free Press, 1998).

7. Wayne Brockbank and Dave Ulrich, *Competencies for the New HR* (Washington, DC: University of Michigan Business School, Society for Human Resource Management, and Global Consulting Alliance, 2003).

8. George S. Day, "Creating a Market-Driven Organization," *Sloan Management Review* 41, no. 1 (1999): 11.

9. Ikujiro Nonaka and Hirotaka Takeuchi, *The Knowledge-Creating Company: How Japanese Companies Create the Dynamics of Innovation* (New York: Oxford University Press, 1995).

10. C. K. Prahalad and Venkat Ramaswamy, *The Future of Competition: Co-Creating Unique Value with Customers* (Boston: Harvard Business School Press, 2003).

11. Wayne Brockbank, Arthur Yeung, and Dave Ulrich, "Participation in Organizational Activities, Organizational Unity, Demography, and Performance Outcomes," paper presented at the National Meetings of the Academy of Management, Anaheim, CA, August 1988.

12. James Brian Quinn, "Outsourcing Innovation: The New Engine of Growth," *Sloan Management Review* 41, no. 4 (2000): 25.

13. Shaun Smith, "Brand Experience," in *Brands and Branding*, The Economist Series, ed. Rita Clifton, John Simmons, and Sameena Ahmad (Princeton, NJ: Bloomberg Press, 2004).

14. Julie Foehrenbach and Steve Goldfarb, "Employee Communications in the 90's: Greater Expectations," white paper published by International Association of Business Communicators and Towers, Perrin, Foster and Crosby, April 1990.

15. T. J. Larkin and Sandar Larkin, *Communicating Change: Winning Employee Support for New Business Goals* (New York: McGraw-Hill, 1994).

16. Roger D'Aprix, *Communicating for Change: Connecting the Workplace with the Marketplace* (San Francisco: Jossey-Bass, 1996).

17. Larkin and Larkin, *Communicating Change*, 98.

18. Michael Beer and Russell A. Eisenstat, "The Silent Killers of Strategy Implementation and Learning," *Sloan Management Review* 41, no. 4 (2000): 29.

19. Noel Tichy and Ram Charan, "The CEO as Coach: An interview with AlliedSignal's Lawrence A. Bossidy," *Harvard Business Review* 73, no. 2 (1995): 68.

20. Dave Ulrich, Steve Kerr, and Ron Ashkenas, *The GE Work-Out: How to Implement GE's Revolutionary Method for Busting Bureaucracy and Attacking Organizational Problems* (New York: McGraw-Hill, 2002).

21. Dave Packard, interview by Wayne Brockbank, Washington, DC, March 1982.

22. Jay R. Galbraith, *Designing Organizations: An Executive Guide to Strategy, Structure, and Process*, 2nd ed. (San Francisco: Jossey-Bass, 2001).

23. William F. Joyce, "Matrix Organizations: A Social Experiment," *Academy of Management Journal* 29, no. 3 (1986): 536.

24. C. K. Prahalad and Yves Doz, *The Multinational Mission: Balancing Local Demands and Global Vision* (New York: Free Press, 1987).

25. Henry Mintzberg, *Structure in Fives: Designing Effective Organizations* (Englewood Cliffs, NJ: Prentice-Hall, 1992).

26. Abraham Y. Nahm, Mark A. Vonderembse, and Xenophon A. Koufteros, "The Impact of Organizational Structure on Time-Based Manufacturing and Plant Performance," *Journal of Operations Management* 21, no. 3 (2003): 281.

27. Frank Ostroff, *The Horizontal Organization: What the Organization of the Future Actually Looks Like and How It Delivers Value to Customers* (New York: Oxford University Press, 1999).

28. Franklin Becker and William Sims, *Offices That Work: Balancing Cost, Flexibility, and Communication* (New York: Cornell University International Workplace Studies Program, 2000); Quarterman Lee, Arild Eng Amundsen, William Nelson, and Herbert Tuttle, *Facilities and Workplace Design: An Illustrated Guide*, Engineers in Business Series (Norcross, GA: Engineering & Management Press, 1997).

29. Alexi Marmot and Joanna Eley, *Office Space Planning: Designing for Tomorrow's Workplace* (New York: McGraw-Hill, 2000); Marily Zelinsky, *The Inspired Workspace: Interior Designs for Creativity and Productivity* (Gloucester, MA: Rockport, 2002).

30. Herman Miller, Inc., "Lighting in the Workplace," 2001, http://www.hmeurope.com/WhitePapers/wp_Lighting_in_Wkpl.pdf.

31. National Safety Council, *Accident Facts, 1992* (Chicago: National Safety Council, 1992). See also Herman Miller, Inc., "Body Support in the Office: Sitting, Seating, and Lower Back Pain," 2002, http://www.hermanmiller.com/hm/content/research_summaries/wp_Body_Support.pdf.

Chapter 7

1. See Wayne Brockbank, "If HR Were Really Strategically Proactive: Present and Future Directions of HR as Competitive Advantage," *Human Resource Management* 38, no. 4 (1999): 337.

2. Wayne Brockbank and Dave Ulrich, *Competencies for the New HR* (Washington, DC: University of Michigan Business School, Society for Human Resource Management, and Global Consulting Alliance, 2003).

3. From a theme suggested by Jim Collins, *Good to Great: Why Some Companies Make the Leap and Others Don't* (New York: HarperCollins, 2001).

Chapter 8

1. Herman Miller, Inc., "Where We've Been," About Us Page, http://www.hermanmiller.com/CDA/SSA/Category/0,1564,a10-c406,00.html.

2. Many consulting firms have built their business on HR shared services, designing and delivering an array of HR technologies. For example, see Mercer Human Resource Consulting (http://www.mercerhr.com/service/details.jhtml?idContent=1000310) and Deloitte (http://www.deloitte.com/dtt/section_node/0,2332,sid%253D26557,00.html).

3. Kathy McRae, "HR Shared Services—A Growing Trend," Human Resources, December 3, 2003, http://www.humanresourcesmagazine.com.au/articles/8c/0c01a08c. asp.

4. Debbie Burger, director, TotalAccess Center, Boeing, interview by the authors, March 2004.

5. See Edward E. Lawler III, Dave Ulrich, Jac Fitz-enz, and James C. Madden V, *Human Resources Business Process Outsourcing: Transforming How HR Gets Its Work Done* (San Francisco: Jossey-Bass, 2004).

Chapter 9

1. Edward E. Lawler III, "How to Make HR a Strategic Partner," paper presented at the 13th Annual Southeast Human Resource Conference, College Park, GA, October 21, 2003.

2. Gary S. Becker, "Human Capital," in *The Concise Encyclopedia of Economics*, ed. David R. Henderson (Indianapolis, IN: Liberty Fund, Inc., 2002), http://www.econlib. org/library/Enc/HumanCapital.html.

3. Watson Wyatt Worldwide, "Human Capital Index: Human Capital as a Lead Indicator of Shareholder Value," http://www.watsonwyatt.com/research/resrender. asp?id=W-488&page=1.

4. See Mark L. Lengnick-Hall and Cynthia A. Lengnick-Hall, *Human Resource Management in the Knowledge Economy: New Challenges, New Roles, New Capabilities* (San Francisco: Berrett-Koehler, 2003).

5. Warren R. Wilhelm, *Learning Architectures: Building Organization and Individual Learning* (Albuquerque, NM: GCA Press, 2003).

6. Lawler, "How to Make HR a Strategic Partner."

7. Jill Conner and Jeana Wirtenberg, "Managing the Transformation of Human Resources Work," *Human Resource Planning* 16, no. 2 (1993): 17.

8. Donna Blancero, John Boroski, and Lee Dyer, "Transforming Human Resource Organizations: A Field Study of Future Competency Requirements," working paper 95-28, Center for Advanced Human Resource Studies, Ithaca, NY, 1995.

9. The Walker Group, "In-Company Workshops for HR Leaders," http://www. walkergroup.com/HRBusinessSchool.html (accessed October 3, 2004).

10. Blancero, Boroski, and Dyer, "Transforming Human Resource Organizations."

11. See chapter 16, "Understanding the HR Profession," in Susan E. Jackson and Randall S. Schuler, eds., *Managing Human Resources Through Strategic Partnerships*, 8th ed. (Belmont, CA: South-Western College Publishing, 2003); and Blancero, Boroski, and Dyer, "Transforming Human Resource Organizations."

12. Lengnick-Hall and Lengnick-Hall, *Human Resource Management in the Knowledge Economy*.

13. See Arthur K. Yeung et al., *Organizational Learning Capability* (New York: Oxford University Press, 1998); and Dave Ulrich, Mary Ann Von Glinow, and Todd Jick, "High Impact Learning: Building and Diffusing Learning Capability," *Organizational Dynamics* 21, no. 2 (1993): 52.

14. Larry Bossidy and Ram Charan, with Charles Burck, *Execution: The Discipline of Getting Things Done* (New York: Crown Business, 2002).

15. Blancero, Boroski, and Dyer, "Transforming Human Resource Organizations."

16. Conner and Wirtenberg, "Managing the Transformation of Human Resources Work."

17. Dave Ulrich, Jack Zenger, and Norm Smallwood, *Results-Based Leadership: How Leaders Build the Business and Improve the Bottom Line* (Boston: Harvard Business School Press, 1999).

18. Dave Ulrich and Dick Beatty, "From Partners to Players: Extending the HR Playing Field," *Human Resource Management* 40, no. 4 (2001): 293.

19. Jackson and Schuler, "Understanding the Human Resources Profession."

20. Dave Ulrich and Norm Smallwood, *Why the Bottom Line Isn't: How to Build Value Through People and Organization* (New York: Wiley, 2003).

Chapter 10

1. David C. McClelland, "Business Drive and National Achievement," *Harvard Business Review* 40, no. 4 (1962): 99; David C. McClelland, "Testing for Competence Rather Than Intelligence," *American Psychologist* 28, no. 1 (1973): 1; and David C. McClelland, *A Guide to Job Competency Assessment* (Boston: McBer & Co., 1976).

2. Lyle M. Spencer and Signe M. Spencer, *Competence at Work: Models for Superior Performance* (New York: John Wiley & Sons, 1993).

3. Dave A. Kolb, *Experiential Learning: Experience as the Source of Learning and Development* (Upper Saddle River, NJ: Prentice-Hall, 1984).

4. Jim Intagliata, Dave Ulrich, and Norm Smallwood, "Leveraging Leadership Competencies to Produce Leadership Brand: Creating Distinctiveness by Focusing on Strategy and Results," *Human Resource Planning* 23, no. 12 (2000): 12.

5. Dave Ulrich, *Human Resource Champions: The Next Agenda for Adding Value and Delivering Results* (Boston: Harvard Business School Press, 1997); Steven C. Schoonover, *Human Resource Competencies for the Year 2000: The Wake-Up Call!* (Washington, DC: Society for Human Resource Management, 1998).

6. Our special thanks in this chapter to Dave Yakonich, who has managed the HR Competency Project for five years. During the four iterations of the Human Resource Competency Study, we have worked with a number of outstanding colleagues. In 1987 and 1992, Arthur Yeung and Dale Lake contributed heavily to the project. In 1997, Connie James played a central role. In 2002, David Yakonich capably managed the increasing complexity of the project. For details on the reports, see Dave Ulrich, Wayne Brockbank, and Arthur Yeung, "Beyond Belief: A Benchmark for Human Resources," *Human Resource Management* 28, no. 3 (1989); Dave Ulrich, Wayne Brockbank, Arthur Yeung, and Dale Lake, "Human Resource Competencies: An Empirical Assessment," *Human Resource Management*, 34, no. 4 (1995): 473; Wayne Brockbank, Alejandro Sioli, and Dave Ulrich, "So . . . We Are at the Table. Now What?" Working paper, University of Michigan, 2001; and Wayne Brockbank and Dave Ulrich, *Competencies for the New HR* (Ann Arbor: University of Michigan Business School, Society for Human Resource Management, and Global Consulting Alliance, 2002).

7. For an excellent overview, see Dana M. Muir, *A Manager's Guide to Employment Law: How to Protect Your Company and Yourself* (San Francisco: Jossey-Bass, 2003).

8. The criteria for effective measurements and rewards are based on the work of Steve Kerr, whose substantial influence on the HR field we gratefully acknowledge.

9. Steven Kerr, *Ultimate Rewards: What Really Motivates People to Achieve* (Boston: Harvard Business School Press, 1997), chapter 1.

10. We adopt the phrase "partners in the business" (as distinct from "business partners") from a presentation by Susan R. Meisinger, president and CEO of the Society for Human Resource Management, at the 2002 SHRM Leadership Conference. In a similar vein, Dick Beatty and Dave Ulrich have argued we should stop talking about being business partners and should start being "players" in the business.

11. An online self-assessment of the entire survey is available. For more information, send an e-mail request to hrcs@umich.edu.

Chapter 11

1. To explore adult learning, see Stephen D. Brookfield, *Understanding and Facilitating Adult Learning: A Comprehensive Analysis of Principles and Effective Practices* (San Francisco: Jossey-Bass, 1991); Malcolm S. Knowles, Elwood F. Holton, and Richard A. Swanson, *The Adult Learner: The Definitive Classic in Adult Education and Human Resource Development*, 5th ed. (Woburn, MA: Butterworth-Heinemann, 1998); and Michael W. Galbraith, ed., *Adult Learning Methods: A Guide for Effective Instruction*, 3rd ed. (Melbourne, FL: Krieger, 2004).

2. This list is drawn from Edward Prewitt, "What Managers Should Know About How Adults Learn," *Harvard Management Update* 2, no. 1, (1997).

3. Cynthia D. McCauley and Ellen Van Vestor, eds., *The Center for Creative Leadership Handbook for Leadership Development*, 2nd ed. (San Francisco: Jossey-Bass, 2003).

4. We have adapted this idea from Steven Covey and we appreciate his insights in sharing it with us.

5. Marshall Goldsmith, "Impact of Direct Report Feedback," http://www.marshallgoldsmith.com/html/articles/impact.html.

6. Michael M. Lombardo and Robert W. Eichinger, *Eighty-Eight Assignments for Development in Place: Enhancing the Developmental Challenge of Existing Jobs*, report no. 136 (Greensboro, NC: Center for Creative Leadership, 1989).

7. A complete listing of readings tied to each competence is available with the "HR Competency Toolkit"; for information, send e-mail to hrcs@umich.edu.

8. See Michael M. Lombardo and Robert W. Eichinger, *The Leadership Machine: Architecture to Develop Leaders for Any Future* (Minneapolis: Lominger, 2001), and *The LEADERSHIP ARCHITECT Norms and Validity Report* (Minneapolis: Lominger, 2003).

9. James J. Connolly and Chockalingam Viswesvaran, "Assessing the Construct Validity of a Measure of Learning Agility," paper presented at the Seventeenth Annual Conference of the Society for Industrial and Organizational Psychology, Toronto, Canada, April 2002. See also Michael M. Lombardo and Robert W. Eichinger, *Choices Architect Promotion Study Results* (Minneapolis: Lominger, 2003); Lombardo and Eichinger, *The LEADERSHIP ARCHITECT Norms and Validity Report*; and Robert J. Sternberg, *Successful Intelligence: How Practical and Creative Intelligence Determine Success in Life* (New York: Simon & Schuster, 1996).

Chapter 12

1. We have adapted this methodology from Bill Ouchi and are grateful for his insights.

Bibliography

"America's Fortunes." *Atlantic Monthly*. January/February 2004, 110.

Ashkenas, Ron, Dave Ulrich, Todd Jick, and Steve Kerr. *The Boundaryless Organization: Breaking the Chains of Organizational Structure*. Rev. ed. San Francisco: Jossey-Bass, 2002.

Babcock, Linda, and Sara Laschever. *Women Don't Ask: Negotiation and the Gender Divide*. Princeton, NJ: Princeton University Press, 2003.

Barbazette, Jean. *Successful New Employee Orientation: Assess, Plan, Conduct, and Evaluate Your Program*. 2nd ed. San Francisco: Jossey-Bass/Pfeiffer, 2001.

Bechet, Thomas P. *Strategic Staffing: A Practical Toolkit for Workforce Planning*. New York: AMACOM, 2002.

Becker, Franklin, and William Sims. *Offices That Work: Balancing Cost, Flexibility, and Communication*. New York: Cornell University International Workplace Studies Program, 2000.

Becker, Gary S. "Human Capital." In *The Concise Encyclopedia of Economics*, edited by David R. Henderson. Indianapolis, IN: Liberty Fund, Inc., 2002. http://www.econlib.org/library/Enc/HumanCapital.html.

Beer, Michael, and Russell A. Eisenstat. "The Silent Killers of Strategy Implementation and Learning." *Sloan Management Review* 41, no. 4 (2000): 29–40.

Bernasek, Anna. "The $44 Trillion Abyss." *Fortune*, November 24, 2003, 113.

Berry, Leonard. *Discovering the Soul of Service: The Nine Drivers of Sustainable Business Success*. New York: Free Press, 1999.

Bhagwati, Jagdish N. "Borders Beyond Control." Foreign Affairs 82, no. 1 (2003): 98–104.

Blancero, Donna, John Boroski, and Lee Dyer. "Transforming Human Resource Organizations: A Field Study of Future Competency Requirements." Working paper 95-28, Center for Advanced Human Resource Studies, Ithaca, NY, 1995.

Bogardus, Anne M. *PHR/SPHR: Professional in Human Resources Certification Study Guide*. New York: Sybex, 2003.

Bossidy, Larry, and Ram Charan, with Charles Burck. *Execution: The Discipline of Getting Things Done*. New York: Crown Business, 2002.

Bowker, Deborah. "The Public Relations Perspective on Branding." In *Brands and Branding*, edited by Rita Clifton and John Simmons. Princeton, NJ: Bloomberg Press, 2004.

Brill, Winston J. "What Is Creativity?" June 1, 2004. http://www.winstonbrill.com/bril001/html/comments/2001/prevcomments0601_body.html.

Brockbank, Wayne. "If HR Were Really Strategically Proactive: Present and Future Directions of HR as Competitive Advantage." *Human Resource Management* 38, no. 4 (1999): 337–352.

Brockbank, Wayne, Alejandro Sioli, and Dave Ulrich. "So . . . We Are at the Table! Now What?" Working paper, University of Michigan, 2001. http://webuser.bus. umich.edu/Programs/hrcs/res_NowWhat.htm.

Brockbank, Wayne, and Dave Ulrich. "Avoiding SPOTS: Creating Strategic Unity." In *Handbook of Business Strategy*, edited by Harold E. Glass. Boston: Warren, Gorham & Lamont, 1991.

———. *Competencies for the New HR*. Washington, DC: University of Michigan Business School, Society for Human Resource Management, and Global Consulting Alliance, 2003.

Brockbank, Wayne, Arthur Yeung, and Dave Ulrich. "Participation in Organizational Activities, Organizational Unity, Demography, and Performance Outcomes." Paper presented at the National Meetings of the Academy of Management, Anaheim, CA, August 1988.

Brookfield, Stephen D. *Understanding and Facilitating Adult Learning: A Comprehensive Analysis of Principles and Effective Practices*. San Francisco: Jossey-Bass, 1991.

Bureau of Labor Statistics. *Series Report ID: Lnu02300190*. Washington, DC: U.S. Department of Labor, 2003.

Burger, Debbie, director, TotalAccess Center, Boeing. Interview by the authors. March 2004.

Cappelli, Peter. "A Shifting Balance of Workers." Wharton@Work:eBuzz. January 2002. http://execed.wharton.upenn.edu/ebuzz/0201/knowledge.html.

Casner-Lotto, Jill, ed. *Successful Training Strategies: Twenty-Six Innovative Corporate Models*. San Francisco: Jossey-Bass, 1988.

Chambers, Harry E. *Finding, Hiring, and Keeping Peak Performers: Every Manager's Guide*. New York: Perseus, 2001.

Choo, Chun Wei, and Nick Bontis, eds. *The Strategic Management of Intellectual Capital and Organizational Knowledge*. New York: Oxford University Press, 2002.

Collins, Jim. *Good to Great: Why Some Companies Make the Leap and Others Don't*. New York: HarperCollins, 2001.

Colvin, Geoffrey. "The Great CEO Pay Heist." *Fortune*, June 25, 2001, 64.

Conner, Jill, and Jeana Wirtenberg. "Managing the Transformation of Human Resources Work." *Human Resource Planning* 16, no. 2 (1993): 17–34.

Connolly, James J., and Chockalingam Viswesveran. "Assessing the Construct Validity of a Measure of Learning Agility." Paper presented at the Seventeenth Annual Conference of the Society for Industrial and Organizational Psychology, Toronto, Canada, April 2002.

Craig, Robert L., ed. *The ASTD Training and Development Handbook: A Guide to Human Resource Development*. 4th ed. New York: McGraw-Hill, 1996.

D'Aprix, Roger. *Communicating for Change: Connecting the Workplace with the Marketplace*. San Francisco: Jossey-Bass, 1996.

Day, George S. "Creating a Market-Driven Organization." *Sloan Management Review* 41, no. 1 (1999): 11–22.

Deeprose, Donna. *How to Recognize and Reward Employees*. New York: AMACOM, 1994.

Deloitte Development LLC. "HR Operations & Technology." http://www.deloitte. com/dtt/section_node/0,2332,sid%253D26557,00.html.

Dessler, Gary. *Human Resource Management*. 9th ed. New York: Prentice-Hall, 2002.

Effron, Mark, Robert Gandossy, and Marshall Goldsmith, eds. *Human Resources in the 21st Century*. New York: Wiley, 2003.

Ellig, Bruce R. *The Complete Guide to Executive Compensation*. New York: McGraw-Hill, 2001.

Erlendsson, Jón. "The Toyota Suggestion System." September 19, 2001. http://www.hi.is/~joner/eaps/ds_esug.htm.

Foehrenbach, Julie, and Steve Goldfarb. "Employee Communications in the 90's: Greater Expectations." White paper published by International Association of Business Communicators and Towers, Perrin, Foster and Crosby, April 1990.

Fullerton, Howard N., Jr., and Mitra Toossi. "Labor Force Projections to 2010: Steady Growth and Changing Composition." *Monthly Labor Review* 124, no. 11 (2001): 21–38.

Galbraith, Jay R. *Designing Complex Organizations.* Boston: Addison-Wesley, 1973.

———. *Designing Organizations: An Executive Guide to Strategy, Structure, and Process.* 2nd ed. San Francisco: Jossey-Bass, 2001.

Galbraith, Michael, ed. *Adult Learning Methods: A Guide for Effective Instruction.* 3rd ed. Melbourne, FL: Krieger, 2004.

Goldsmith, Marshall. "Impact of Direct Report Feedback." http://www.marshallgoldsmith.com/html/articles/impact.html.

———. "Try Feedforward Instead of Feedback." *Leader to Leader* 2002, no. 25: 11–14.

Goodman, John. "Basic Facts on Customer Complaint Behavior and the Impact of Service on the Bottom Line." June 1999. http://www.tarp.com/research.asp.

Griffeth, Rodger W., and Peter W. Hom. *Retaining Valued Employees.* Thousand Oaks, CA: Sage, 2001.

Grow, Brian. "Hispanic Nation." *BusinessWeek*, March 15, 2004, 58.

Hanushek, Eric A. "The Long-Run Importance of School Quality." Working paper 9071, National Bureau of Economic Research, Cambridge, MA, July 2002.

Heneman, Herbert G., III, and Timothy A. Judge. *Staffing Organizations.* 4th ed. New York: McGraw-Hill/Irwin, 2002.

Herman Miller, Inc. "Lighting in the Workplace." 2001. http://www.hmeurope.com/WhitePapers/wp_Lighting_in_Wkpl.pdf.

———. "Body Support in the Office: Sitting, Seating, and Lower Back Pain." 2002. http://www.hermanmiller.com/hm/content/research_summaries/wp_Body_Support.pdf.

———. "Where We've Been," About Us Page. http://www.hermanmiller.com/CDA/SSA/Category/0,1564,a10-c406,00.html.

Hof, Robert D. "The eBay Economy." *BusinessWeek*, August 25, 2003, 124.

"Household data seasonally adjusted quarterly averages." *Employment and Earnings.* January 2004. 51:1, 172.

Hufbauer, Gary. "World Economic Integration: The Long View." *Economic Insights* (May/June)(1991):26.

Huselid, Mark A., Brian E. Becker, and Richard W. Beatty. *The Workforce Scorecard: Managing Human Capital to Execute Strategy.* Boston: Harvard Business School Press, 2005.

Intagliata, Jim, Dave Ulrich, and Norm Smallwood. "Leveraging Leadership Competencies to Produce Leadership Brand: Creating Distinctiveness by Focusing on Strategy and Results." *Human Resource Planning* 23, no. 12 (2000): 12–22.

Jackson, Susan E., and Randall S. Schuler, eds. *Managing Human Resources Through Strategic Partnerships.* 8th ed. Belmont, CA: South-Western College Publishing, 2003.

Johnson, Mike. *Winning the People Wars: Talent and the Battle for Human Capital.* 2nd ed. London: Financial Times Prentice-Hall, 2001.

Joyce, William F. "Matrix Organizations: A Social Experiment." *Academy of Management Journal* 29, no. 3 (1986): 536–561.

Karoly, Lynn A., and Constantijn W. A. Panis. *The 21st Century at Work: Forces Shaping the Future Workforce and Workplace in the United States.* Santa Monica, CA: The RAND Corporation, 2004.

Kerr, Steven. "Some Characteristics and Consequences of Organizational Rewards." In *Facilitating Work Effectiveness,* edited by F. David Schoorman and Benjamin Schneider. Lexington, MA: Lexington Books, 1988.

Kerr, Steven, ed. *Ultimate Rewards: What Really Motivates People to Achieve.* Boston: Harvard Business School Press, 1997.

Kirkpatrick, Donald L. *Evaluating Training Programs: The Four Levels.* 2nd ed. San Francisco: Berrett-Koehler, 1998.

Knowles, Malcolm S., Elwood F. Holton, and Richard A. Swanson. *The Adult Learner: The Definitive Classic in Adult Education and Human Resource Development.* 5th ed. Woburn, MA: Butterworth-Heinemann, 1998.

Kolb, David A. *Experiential Learning: Experience as the Source of Learning and Development.* Upper Saddle River, NJ: Prentice-Hall, 1984.

Laird, Dugan. *Approaches to Training and Development.* 3rd ed., revised and updated by Sharon S. Naquin and Elwood F. Holton. New York: Basic Books, 2003.

Larkin, T. J., and Sandar Larkin. *Communicating Change: Winning Employee Support for New Business Goals.* New York: McGraw-Hill, 1994.

Lawler, Edward E. III. *Strategic Pay: Aligning Organizational Strategies and Pay Systems.* San Francisco: Jossey-Bass, 1990.

———. "How to Make HR a Strategic Partner." Paper presented at the 13th Annual Southeast Human Resource Conference, College Park, GA, October 21, 2003.

Lawler, Edward E. III, Dave Ulrich, Jac Fitz-enz, and James C. Madden V. *Human Resource Business Process Outsourcing: Transforming How HR Gets Its Work Done.* San Francisco: Jossey-Bass, 2004.

Lee, Quarterman, Arild Eng Amundsen, William Nelson, and Herbert Tuttle. *Facilities and Workplace Design: An Illustrated Guide.* Engineers in Business Series. Norcross, GA: Engineering & Management Press, 1997.

Lengnick-Hall, Mark L., and Cynthia A. Lengnick-Hall. *Human Resource Management in the Knowledge Economy: New Challenges, New Roles, New Capabilities.* San Francisco: Berrett-Koehler, 2003.

Lev, Baruch. *Intangibles: Management, Measurement, and Reporting.* Washington, DC: Brookings Institution Press, 2001.

Lombardo, Michael M., and Robert W. Eichinger. *Eighty-Eight Assignments for Development in Place: Enhancing the Developmental Challenge of Existing Jobs.* Report no. 136. Greensboro, NC: Center for Creative Leadership, 1989.

———. *The Leadership Machine: Architecture to Develop Leaders for Any Future.* Minneapolis: Lominger, 2001.

———. *The LEADERSHIP ARCHITECT Norms and Validity Report.* Minneapolis: Lominger, 2003.

———. *Choices Architect Promotion Study Results.* Minneapolis: Lominger, 2003.

Manton, Kenneth, Larry Corder, and Eric Stallard. "Chronic Disability Trends in the Elderly United States Populations: 1982–1994." *Proceedings of the National Academy of Sciences of the United States of America* 94, no. 6 (1997): 2593–2598.

Maricopa County Ombudsman Page. http://www.maricopa.gov/human_resources/ombudsman.asp.

Marmot, Alexi, and Joanna Eley. *Office Space Planning: Designing for Tomorrow's Workplace.* New York: McGraw-Hill, 2000.

McCarthy, John C. "3.3 Million U.S. Services Jobs to Go Offshore." November 11, 2002. Forrester Research. http://www.forrester.com/ER/Research/Brief/Excerpt/ 0,1317,15900,FF.html.

McCauley, Cynthia D., and Ellen Van Vestor, eds. *The Center for Creative Leadership Handbook for Leadership Development.* 2nd ed. San Francisco: Jossey-Bass, 2003.

McClelland, David C. "Business Drive and National Achievement." *Harvard Business Review* 40, no. 4 (1962): 99–112.

———. "Testing for Competence Rather Than Intelligence." *American Psychologist* 28, no. 1 (1973): 1–14.

———. *A Guide to Job Competency Assessment.* Boston: McBer & Co., 1976.

McRae, Kathy. "HR Shared Services—A Growing Trend." *Human Resources,* December 3, 2003. http://www.humanresourcesmagazine.com.au/articles/8c/0c01a08c.asp.

Mercer Human Resource Consulting. "Employee Service Center Design & Implementation." http://www.mercerhr.com/service/details.jhtml?idContent=1000310.

Michaels, Ed, Helen Handfield-Jones, and Beth Axelrod. *The War for Talent.* Boston: Harvard Business School Press, 2001.

Mintzberg, Henry. *Structure in Fives: Designing Effective Organizations.* Englewood Cliffs, NJ: Prentice-Hall, 1992.

Mintzberg, Henry, Bruce Ahlstrand, and Joseph Lampel. *Strategy Safari: A Guided Tour Through the Wilds of Strategic Management.* New York: Free Press, 1998.

Muir, Dana M. *A Manager's Guide to Employment Law: How to Protect Your Company and Yourself.* San Francisco: Jossey-Bass, 2003.

Nahm, Abraham Y., Mark A. Vonderembse, and Xenophon A. Koufteros. "The Impact of Organizational Structure on Time-Based Manufacturing and Plant Performance." *Journal of Operations Management* 21, no. 3 (2003): 281–306.

National Institute for Literacy. "Literacy in the United States." August 2003. http://www.policyalmanac.org/education/archive/literacy.shtml.

National Safety Council. *Accident Facts, 1992.* Chicago: National Safety Council, 1992.

Nelson, Bob. *1001 Ways to Reward Employees.* New York: Workman, 1994.

Newland, Kathleen. "Workers of the World, Now What?" *Foreign Policy* no. 114, (Spring 1999), 52–65.

Nonaka, Ikujiro, and Hirotaka Takeuchi. *The Knowledge-Creating Company: How Japanese Companies Create the Dynamics of Innovation.* New York: Oxford University Press, 1995.

Ostroff, Frank. *The Horizontal Organization: What the Organization of the Future Actually Looks Like and How It Delivers Value to Customers.* New York: Oxford University Press, 1999.

Packard, Dave. Interview by Wayne Brockbank. Washington, DC, March 1982.

Panis, Constantijn, Michael Hurd, David Loughran, Julie Zissimopoulos, Steven Haider, and Patricia St. Clair. "The Effects of Changing Social Security Administration's Early Entitlement Age and the Normal Retirement Age." DRU-2903-SSA. Santa Monica, CA: The RAND Corporation, 2002.

Pinola, Richard. "Aligning HR Strategies for the Business: A CEO Perspective (Part 2)." PowerPoint presentation at the AmCham HR Forum 2003, Thriving in a Changing Environment, Moscow, Russia, June 2003. http://www.amcham.hrcom. ru/files/122_RJP%20-%20Thriving%20in%20a%20Changing%20Environment %20part%202.ppt.

Prahalad, C. K., and Yves Doz. *The Multinational Mission: Balancing Local Demands and Global Vision.* New York: Free Press, 1987.

Prahalad, C. K., and Venkat Ramaswamy. *The Future of Competition: Co-Creating Unique Value with Customers*. Boston: Harvard Business School Press, 2003.

Prewitt, Edward. "What Managers Should Know About How Adults Learn." *Harvard Management Update* 2, no. 1 (1997).

Quinn, James Brian. "Outsourcing Innovation: The New Engine of Growth." *Sloan Management Review* 41, no. 4 (2000): 25–36.

Rappaport, Alfred, ed. *Harvard Business Review on Compensation*. Boston: Harvard Business School Press, 2002.

Rheingold, Howard. *Smart Mobs: The Next Social Revolution*. Cambridge, MA: Basic Books, 2003.

Rucci, Anthony J., Steven P. Kirn, and Richard T. Quinn. "The Employee-Customer-Profit Chain at Sears." *Harvard Business Review* 76, no. 1 (1998): 82–99.

Schlender, Brent. "Intel's $10 Billion Gamble." *Fortune*, November 11, 2002, 90.

Schoonover, Steven C. *Human Resource Competencies for the Year 2000: The Wake-Up Call!* Washington, DC: Society for Human Resource Management, 1998.

Schwartz, Nelson D. "Will 'Made in the USA' Fade Away?" *Fortune*, November 24, 2003, 98.

Sears, David. *Successful Talent Strategies: Achieving Superior Business Results Through Market-Focused Staffing*. New York: AMACOM, 2003.

Sharpe, Rochelle. "As Leaders, Women Rule." *BusinessWeek*, November 20, 2000, 74-81.

Simmons, Tavia, and Martin O'Connell. "Married-Couple and Unmarried Partner Households: 2000." Washington, DC: U.S. Census Bureau, February 2003. http://www.census.gov/prod/2003pubs/censr-5.pdf .

Sims, Doris M. *Creative New Employee Orientation Programs: Best Practices, Creative Ideas, and Activities for Energizing Your Orientation Program*. New York: McGraw-Hill, 2001.

Smith, Shaun. "Brand Experience." In *Brands and Branding*, The Economist Series, edited by Rita Clifton and John Simmons. Princeton, NJ: Bloomberg Press, 2004.

Sommers, Christina Hoff. "The War Against Boys." *Atlantic Monthly*, May 2000, 59.

Spencer, Lyle M., and Signe M. Spencer. *Competence at Work: Models for Superior Performance*. New York: John Wiley & Sons, 1993.

Stalk, George, Philip Evans, and Lawrence E. Shulman. "Competing on Capabilities: The New Rules of Corporate Strategy." *Harvard Business Review* 70, no. 2 (1992): 57–69.

Sternberg, Robert J. *Successful Intelligence: How Practical and Creative Intelligence Determine Success in Life*. New York: Simon & Schuster, 1996.

Storck, John, and Patricia A. Hill. "Knowledge Diffusion Through Strategic Communities." *Sloan Management Review* 41, no. 2 (2000): 63–74.

Su, Betty W. "The U.S. Economy to 2010." *Monthly Labor Review* 124, no. 11 (2001): 3–20.

Sum, Andrew, Neeta Fogg, and Paul Harrington. "The Growing Gender Gaps in College Enrollment and Degree Attainment in the U.S. and Their Potential Economic and Social Consequences." Washington, DC: Business Roundtable, 2003. http://www.businessroundtable.org/pdf/943.pdf.

Tichy, Noel, and Ram Charan. "The CEO as Coach: An interview with AlliedSignal's Lawrence A. Bossidy." *Harvard Business Review* 73, no. 2 (1995): 68–78.

Toossi, Mitra. "A Century of Change: The U.S. Labor Force, 1950–2050." *Monthly Labor Review* 125, no. 5 (2002): 15–28.

Ulrich, Dave. *Human Resource Champions: The Next Agenda for Adding Value and Delivering Results*. Boston: Harvard Business School Press, 1997.

———. "Organizational Capability: Competitive Advantage Through Human Resources." In *Handbook of Business Strategy 1989/1990 Yearbook*, edited by Harold Glass, 15.1–15.15. Boston: Warren, Gorham, & Lamont, 1990.

Ulrich, Dave, and Dick Beatty. "From Partners to Players: Extending the HR Playing Field." *Human Resource Management* 40, no. 4 (2001): 293–308.

Ulrich, Dave, Wayne Brockbank, and Arthur Yeung. "Beyond Belief: A Benchmark for Human Resources." *Human Resource Management* 28, no. 3 (1989): 311–335.

Ulrich, Dave, Wayne Brockbank, Arthur Yeung, and Dale Lake. "Human Resource Competencies: An Empirical Assessment." *Human Resource Management* 34, no. 4 (1995): 473–495.

Ulrich, Dave, and Hope Greenfield. "The Transformation of Training and Development to Development and Learning." *American Journal of Management Development* 1, no. 2 (1995): 11–22.

Ulrich, Dave, Steve Kerr, and Ron Ashkenas. *The GE Work-Out: How to Implement GE's Revolutionary Method for Busting Bureaucracy and Attacking Organizational Problems*. New York: McGraw-Hill, 2002.

Ulrich, Dave, and Norm Smallwood. *Why the Bottom Line Isn't: How to Build Value Through People and Organization*. New York: Wiley, 2003.

———. "Capitalizing on Capabilities." *Harvard Business Review* 82, no. 6 (2004): 119.

Ulrich, Dave, Mary Ann Von Glinow, and Todd Jick. "High Impact Learning: Building and Diffusing Learning Capability." *Organizational Dynamics* 21, no. 2 (1993): 52–66.

Ulrich, Dave, Jack Zenger, and Norm Smallwood. *Results-Based Leadership: How Leaders Build the Business and Improve the Bottom Line*. Boston: Harvard Business School Press, 1999.

Van Adelsberg, David, and Edward A. Trolley. *Running Training Like a Business: Delivering Unmistakable Value*. San Francisco: Berrett-Koehler, 1999.

Vicere, Albert A., ed. *Executive Education: Process, Practice, and Evaluation*. Princeton, NJ: Peterson's Guides, 1989.

The Walker Group. "In-Company Workshops for HR Leaders." http://www.walkergroup.com/HRBusinessSchool.html.

Warren, Elizabeth, and Amelia Warren Tyagi. *The Two-Income Trap: Why Middle-Class Mothers and Fathers Are Going Broke*. New York: Basic Books, 2003.

Watson Wyatt Worldwide. "Human Capital Index: Human Capital as a Lead Indicator of Shareholder Value. http://www.watsonwyatt.com/research/resrender.asp?id=W-488&page=1.

Welbourne, Theresa M. "HR Metrics for HR Strategists." August 2004. http://www.eepulse.com/documents/pdfs/HRMetricsForHRStrategists.pdf.

Wilhelm, Warren R. *Learning Architectures: Building Organization and Individual Learning*. Albuquerque, NM: GCA Press, 2003.

World Bank. *Global Economic Prospects and the Developing Countries 2002*. Washington, DC: World Bank, 2001, 45.

Yeung, Arthur K., David O. Ulrich, Stephen W. Nason, and Mary Ann Von Glinow. *Organizational Learning Capability*. New York: Oxford University Press, 1998.

Zelinsky, Marily. *The Inspired Workspace: Interior Designs for Creativity and Productivity*. Gloucester, MA: Rockport, 2002.

Index

301

About the Authors

Dave Ulrich is on a three-year sabbatical (until July 2005) from the University of Michigan, where he is a professor of business, to serve as president of the Canada Montreal Mission for the Church of Jesus Christ of Latter-day Saints. Professionally, he studies how organizations use human resources to build capabilities of speed, learning, collaboration, accountability, talent, and leadership. He has helped generate multiple award-winning databases that assess alignment between business strategies, HR practices, and HR competencies, and he has consulted and done research with more than half the *Fortune* 200.

He has published more than one hundred articles and book chapters and twelve books, including *Why the Bottom Line Isn't: How to Build Value Through People and Organization* (with Norm Smallwood), *Results-Based Leadership: How Leaders Build the Business and Improve the Bottom Line* (with Norm Smallwood and Jack Zenger), and *Human Resource Champions: The Next Agenda for Adding Value and Delivering Results.*

He was editor of *Human Resource Management Journal* (1990–1999) and has served on the editorial boards of four other journals. At present, he is on the Herman Miller Board of Directors and is a Fellow in the National Academy of Human Resources. In 2001, he was ranked by *BusinessWeek* as number one management educator and guru, and in 2000, he was listed in *Forbes* as one of the "world's top five" business coaches.

E-mail: dou@umich.edu

Wayne Brockbank is clinical professor of business at the University of Michigan Business School, as well as faculty director and core instructor of the Strategic Human Resource Planning Program, the Human Resource Executive Program, and the Advanced Human Resource Executive Program at the university's Executive Education Center, programs that have been consistently rated over the last twelve years as the best HR executive programs in the United States and Europe by the *Wall Street Journal* and *BusinessWeek.*

He is director of the Michigan Human Resource Executive Programs in Hong Kong, Singapore, and India as well as the Michigan Global Program in Management Development in India. He is also a distinguished visiting professor of business administration at Instituto De Altos Estudios Empresariales (Argentina) and teaches at Mt. Eliza University (Australia).

His research focuses on linkages between HR practices and business strategy, high-value-added HR strategies, and implementing business strategy through people. He has published on these topics in the *Human Resource Management Journal, Human Resource Planning,* and *Personnel Administrator* and has contributed numerous book chapters. In 2000 the editorial board of the *Human Resource Management Journal*